Rachel Deletto

ERWIN CHEMERINSKY is the dean of UC Berkeley School of Law. His writings have appeared in *The New York Times*, *Los Angeles Times*, *The Washington Post*, and *The Boston Globe*, among other publications. His books include *The Conservative Assault on the Constitution* and *The Case Against the Supreme Court*, among many others. In January 2017, *National Jurist* magazine again named him the most influential person in legal education in the United States.

ALSO BY ERWIN CHEMERINSKY

Free Speech on Campus (with Howard Gillman)

Closing the Courthouse Door: How Your Constitutional Rights Became Unenforceable

Criminal Procedure (with Laurie Levenson)

Federal Jurisdiction

Constitutional Law

The Case Against the Supreme Court

Constitutional Law: Principles and Policies

The Conservative Assault on the Constitution

Enhancing Government: Federalism for the 21st Century

Interpreting the Constitution

We the People

We the People

A PROGRESSIVE READING *of the* CONSTITUTION *for the* TWENTY-FIRST CENTURY

Erwin Chemerinsky

DEAN AND JESSE H. CHOPER
DISTINGUISHED PROFESSOR OF LAW
UNIVERSITY OF CALIFORNIA,
BERKELEY SCHOOL OF LAW

PICADOR

New York

picadorusa.com • instagram.com/picador
twitter.com/picadorusa • facebook.com/picadorusa

For book club information, please visit facebook.com/picadorbookclub or email marketing@picadorusa.com.

Designed by Nicola Ferguson

Library of Congress Cataloging-in-Publication Data

Names: Chemerinsky, Erwin, author.
Title: We the people : a progressive reading of the constitution for the twenty-first century / Erwin Chemerinsky, Dean and Jesse H. Choper Distinguished Professor of Law, University of California, Berkeley School of Law.
Description: New York : Picador, 2018. | Includes bibliographical references.
Identifiers: LCCN 2018022702 | ISBN 9781250166005 (trade paperback) | ISBN 9781250165992 (ebook)
Subjects: LCSH: Constitutional law—United States—Interpretation and construction. | United States. Constitution. | Constitutional law—Philosophy. | Judicial review—United States. | Judicial power—United States.
Classification: LCC KF4552.C54 2018 | DDC 342.73—dc23
LC record available at https://lccn.loc.gov/2018022702

Our books may be purchased in bulk for promotional, educational, or business use. Please contact your local bookseller or the Macmillan Corporate and Premium Sales Department at 1-800-221-7945, extension 5442, or by email at MacmillanSpecialMarkets@macmillan.com.

First Edition: November 2018

10 9 8 7 6 5 4 3 2 1

For my grandchildren,
Andrew and Sarah:
May you live in a world where there truly is
liberty and justice for all.

CONTENTS

We the People of the United States, in Order to form a more perfect Union, establish Justice, insure domestic Tranquility, provide for the common defence, promote the general Welfare, and secure the Blessings of Liberty to ourselves and our Posterity, do ordain and establish this Constitution for the United States of America.

PREFACE

Like most liberals, I found the outcome of the 2016 presidential election to be devastating. I never have been so afraid for the country or the things that I believe in. I worry what the Trump administration's environmental policies will mean for the future of the planet. I fear that his xenophobic policies on immigration will be calamitous for so many people's lives. I am concerned that his ugly rhetoric has legitimized the expression of racism in a way that has not been seen for decades. Until the white supremacist demonstration in Charlottesville in August 2017, I never had seen someone in public carrying a sign saying, KIKES BELONG IN THE OVEN. President Trump did not even condemn this, though every prior president since the 1930s has found it easy to denounce Nazism and white supremacy.

As someone who has spent his professional career teaching, writing about, and litigating about constitutional law, I am worried what the election of Donald Trump will mean for the future of the Supreme Court and the Constitution. Republican voters understood the importance of this election for the Supreme Court much more than Democrats did. Of those who voted for Trump, 56 percent said that the Supreme Court was the most important factor in their choice for president, as compared to only 41 percent of those who voted for Hillary Clinton.[1]

For the first time since the end of the Warren Court in 1969, there will be a conservative majority on the Court for years, possibly decades, to come. The Court will become even more conservative with President Trump replacing Anthony Kennedy. Given this new reality, I feel it is imperative that liberals articulate an alternative vision of the Constitution to that being put forward by Donald Trump and the conservatives on the Supreme Court.

Conservative justices, advocates, and professors have clearly expressed their vision of the Constitution for decades. It is strongly pro–law enforcement, favoring the government and police over the constitutional rights of criminal defendants. It is powerfully pro-business, favoring the interests of corporations over those of employees and consumers. It regards race discrimination as a thing of the past and staunchly opposes race-conscious actions to remedy the legacy of discrimination and achieve diversity. It rejects the notion of separation of church and state. It strongly opposes constitutional protection of reproductive freedom for women and approves any and all restrictions on abortion rights.

We must develop and defend an alternative progressive vision for the Constitution: that is my goal in this book. I write it not in the belief that my vision will come to be the law soon but in the hope and conviction that it will someday. As Dr. Martin Luther King, Jr., often proclaimed, "The arc of the moral universe is long, but it bends towards justice." Over the course of American history, there have been great gains in individual freedom and enormous advances in equality for racial minorities, women, and gays and lesbians, though obviously much remains to be done. Now we are at a moment with a president who is not committed to these values and face the reality of a Supreme Court that will likely be more hostile to them for the foreseeable future.

But this will change. Someday there will be a majority on the Court committed to using the Constitution to advance liberty and equality. For now, we must provide the foundation for their work. At the very least, we must provide an intellectual framework for opposing the regressive policies of the Trump administration and the conservatives on the Supreme Court.

Actually, focusing on the Supreme Court alone is a huge mistake. The Constitution belongs to all of us—to "We the People." Every elected official, at every level of government, takes an oath to uphold the Constitution: they each need to have an understanding of what that should mean. Constitutional issues constantly arise and affect all of us, often in the most important and intimate aspects of our lives, so we, too, should have informed views about the meaning of the Constitution. Each of us needs to interpret the document for ourselves in evaluating government actions, as well as court decisions.

Even though there is a Republican president and a conservative majority on the Supreme Court appointed by Republican presidents, progressives must not yield the Constitution to them. We must develop and defend and fight for a progressive vision of constitutional law. We need to fight for that vision in Congress and in state legislatures, in state courts and in federal courts, including the Supreme Court. There are sure to be losses along the way, but with careful planning and strategizing we can succeed in the long term. Most of all, we need a progressive vision of the Constitution.

This book is my attempt at articulating this progressive vision.

PART I

CONSERVATIVES AND THE CONSTITUTION

1

THE FUTURE OF THE SUPREME COURT AND THE CONSTITUTION

WHAT MIGHT HAVE BEEN

Everything changed in the Supreme Court on Saturday, February 13, 2016, when Justice Antonin Scalia died. From 1971, when President Nixon had his third and fourth nominees confirmed for the Court, until February 13, 2016, there were always at least five justices, and at times as many as eight justices, who had been appointed by a Republican president. For forty-five years, whenever the Court was ideologically divided, more often than not there were five votes for a conservative result.

But with the death of Antonin Scalia, there were suddenly only four justices appointed by Republican presidents: Chief Justice John Roberts and Justices Anthony Kennedy, Clarence Thomas, and Samuel Alito. And there were an equal number appointed by Democratic presidents: Justices Ruth Bader Ginsburg, Stephen Breyer, Sonia Sotomayor, and Elena Kagan. Although there have been times in American history where justices' ideology did not correspond to the political party of the appointing president, that is not true today.

Roberts, Thomas, and Alito are very conservative. Many have a misleading impression of Roberts because he joined the liberal justices to uphold the Affordable Care Act (2010).[1] But overall Roberts virtually always votes with his conservative colleagues, especially in the high-profile areas such as abortion rights, affirmative action, rights for criminal defendants, gay and lesbian rights, gun rights, voting rights, and religious freedom. At the same time, Ginsburg, Breyer, Sotomayor, and Kagan consistently vote in a liberal direction.

Kennedy has been the swing justice, by far the justice who votes most often in the majority. In 2016–2017, officially known as October Term 2016, he was in the majority in 97 percent of all the decisions. The year before, he was in the majority in 98 percent of the cases. He has been the fifth vote with the four liberal justices to strike down laws prohibiting same-sex marriage,[2] restricting access to abortion,[3] and challenging affirmative action programs.[4] But overall, he votes with the conservatives about 75 percent of the time in ideologically divided 5–4 rulings. For example, he was the key fifth vote to strike down gun control laws for the first time in American history,[5] to reject constitutional challenges to the death penalty,[6] to allow corporations to spend unlimited amounts of money in election campaigns,[7] and to allow business owners to refuse to provide contraceptive coverage for their employees based on the owners' religious beliefs.[8]

In the past, there have been ideological surprises on the Supreme Court. Justices John Paul Stevens and David Souter were appointed by Republican presidents (Gerald Ford and George H. W. Bush, respectively), but by the end of their tenure on the Court they were consistently with the liberal bloc. Justice Byron White was appointed by President John F. Kennedy, but he voted much more often with the conservative justices, for example, rejecting a constitutional right to abortion and dissenting in cases expanding rights for criminal defendants.[9] Earlier, Justice Felix Frankfurter was appointed by President Franklin Roosevelt and expected to be liberal, but he turned out to be a very conservative justice.

Such ideological surprises are much less likely today. Some of that is because the country is more divided along ideological lines than at many earlier times, and this is reflected in the justices who are picked. For instance, President Dwight Eisenhower was a Republican, but he was not particularly ideologically defined; there was uncertainty as to whether he was going to run for president as a Democrat or a Republican. He appointed two liberals to the Court: Earl Warren and William Brennan, a Democrat. It is impossible to imagine a president today appointing someone from the other political party.

There is also far more vetting today to make sure of a nominee's ideology. Republicans want to be sure that there are no more David Souters. Souter, a former justice on the New Hampshire Supreme Court and briefly a federal court of appeals judge, was picked for the Court by President George H. W. Bush in 1990. Presidential adviser John Sununu and Senator Warren Rudman assured President Bush that Souter would be a "home run" in his conservatism. Once on the Court, however, he more often voted with the liberal justices: he was the fifth vote to reaffirm *Roe v. Wade* (1973)[10] and limit prayer in public schools.[11] Both Republican and Democratic presidents have learned from this and now do a much more thorough vetting of the ideology of prospective nominees. The last picks for the Supreme Court—Roberts, Alito, Sotomayor, Kagan, and Gorsuch—have all been exactly what the party of their nominating president have wanted.

The death of Justice Scalia and the resulting 4–4 split on the Court offered the possibility of a majority of justices appointed by a Democratic president for the first time since 1971. This is important because major ideological shifts on the Supreme Court are rare. The Court became very conservative by the 1880s and remained that way until 1936, striking down over two hundred progressive laws, such as those limiting child labor and imposing minimum wages and maximum hours in the workplace.

This changed in 1937, and soon after, President Franklin Roosevelt was able to fill the Court with Democrats committed to upholding New Deal programs. From the late 1930s through 1971, the majority of the justices had been appointed by Democratic presidents. Especially under the leadership of Chief Justice Earl Warren, the Court was famously liberal, striking down laws requiring racial segregation, applying the Bill of Rights to state and local governments, significantly increasing the rights of criminal defendants, and greatly expanding voting rights.

President Richard Nixon was able to select four Supreme Court justices between 1969 and 1971: Warren Burger, Harry Blackmun, Lewis Powell, and William Rehnquist. There has been a solid Republican-appointed majority on the Court ever since. Replacing Justice Scalia with a Democrat would have dramatically shifted the Court's ideological balance for the first time since then. That is why Senate Republicans refused to hold hearings or a vote on President Barack Obama's nomination of Chief Judge Merrick Garland for the Supreme Court. Unquestionably, Garland was superbly qualified. He had the perfect résumé for the position: a graduate of Harvard College and Harvard Law School, he clerked on the Supreme Court, was a federal prosecutor and a partner at a law firm before becoming a federal court of appeals judge. He served longer as a federal appellate judge than any Supreme Court nominee in history. By all accounts, he is a moderate, which is perhaps why President Obama picked him, hoping that would get him confirmed even in a presidential election year.

But from the day of Justice Scalia's death, Mitch McConnell, the Senate majority leader, made clear that the Senate Republicans would not consider Garland's nomination because it was the last year of Obama's presidency. This was unprecedented. Supreme Court vacancies had occurred twenty-four times before during the last year of a president's term. The Senate had confirmed in twenty-one of those cases and refused to approve in the other three. But this time, the Senate did absolutely nothing, and there wasn't a thing that President Obama or Senate Democrats could do about it.

If Hillary Clinton had been elected president, she might have renominated Garland or perhaps picked someone younger and more liberal, but with the election of Donald Trump, the Republican strategy of blocking Garland paid off. President Trump replaced Scalia with a staunch conservative: Neil Gorsuch. In his first months on the Court, Gorsuch voted together with Clarence Thomas—as conservative as any justice in recent memory—100 percent of the time. In his first full year on the Court, he was with the conservative justices in virtually every case. Gorsuch was a very conservative federal court of appeals judge and was known for his conservative views when serving in the Department of Justice during the George W. Bush administration. No one, liberal or conservative, has any doubts that Neil Gorsuch will be exactly what the Republicans hoped for: a justice who will be at least as conservative as the jurist he replaced, Antonin Scalia.

WHAT IT MEANS

The ideological balance on the Court remains the same as before Justice Scalia's death. The major progressive shift that would have occurred with Clinton's election obviously did not happen and will not happen for a long time, with President Trump replacing Anthony Kennedy. Keeping this ideological balance has real consequences. Consider these examples.

Guns

Few issues so closely correspond to ideology and political party affiliation as the meaning of the Second Amendment. From 1791 until 2008, the Supreme Court had never invalidated any law as violating the Second Amendment. The Court always ruled that the Second Amendment was about a right to have guns for the purpose of militia service. But in *District of Columbia v. Heller* (2008), the Court, 5–4, struck down a thirty-two-year-old District of Columbia ordinance that prohibited private ownership or possession of handguns.[12] Justice Scalia wrote for the Court, joined by Chief Justice Roberts and Justices Kennedy, Thomas, and Alito. Two years later, in *McDonald v. City of Chicago*, the same five justices were the majority in a 5–4 decision holding that the Second Amendment is a fundamental right that applies to state and local governments.[13] These are the only cases in all of American history to invalidate laws as violating the Second Amendment.

Without Scalia, the Court was split 4–4 on the meaning of the Second Amendment. Merrick Garland or a Clinton nominee would have meant a Court that was unlikely to extend gun rights and very well might have overruled *Heller* and *McDonald*. Replacing Scalia with a conservative, Gorsuch, means a Court likely to strike down many other laws regulating firearms.

Unions

In June 2018, the Supreme Court dealt a severe blow to unions by holding that nonunion members cannot be required to pay the share of the union dues that support the collective bargaining activities of the union. In 1977, in *Abood v. Detroit Board of Education*, the Supreme Court reaffirmed that no one can be forced to join a public employees union. The Court, though, held that nonunion members can be required to pay the share of the union dues that go to support the collective bargaining activities of the union.[14] The Court explained that nonunion members benefit from collective bargaining in their wages, their hours, and their working conditions. They should not be able to be free riders. The Court said, though, that nonunion members cannot be required to pay the share of the union dues that go to support the political activities of the unions; that would be impermissible compelled speech in violation of the First Amendment.

In two recent cases, in 2011 and 2014, the five conservative justices then on the Court—Roberts, Scalia, Kennedy, Thomas, and Alito—strongly indicated a desire to overrule *Abood* and prevent public employees from being required to pay their "fair share" of the union dues that go to support collective bargaining.[15]

A case, *Friedrichs v. California Teachers Association* (2016), was filed to provide that vehicle. Rebecca Friedrichs, an elementary-school teacher at a charter school in Orange County, California, objected to having to pay the share of the union dues that go to support collective bargaining. Hers was to be the test case to give the Court the vehicle to overrule *Abood*.

The case was argued on Monday, January 11, 2016, and there seemed little doubt that the Court was poised to overrule *Abood*. Not one of the five conservative justices asked a single question or made a single comment that left doubt about how he was going to vote. This would be devastating in California and twenty-one other states that do not have so-called right-to-work laws; there would be a substantial decrease in union revenues, union membership, and union political influence.

Justice Scalia died before the Court issued its decision on *Friedrichs*, so the justices announced that they were deadlocked 4–4, which means that the case was dismissed without decision by the Supreme Court.[16] *Abood* remains the law. But with the appointment of Justice Gorsuch, the overruling of *Abood* seemed a certainty. Indeed, on June 27, 2018, in *Janus v. American Federation*, the Court did the expected and overruled *Abood*.[17] This will be a very significant blow to unions and their political influence.

Separation of church and state

Views on the establishment clause of the First Amendment, which prohibits Congress from enacting any law "respecting an establishment of religion," very much track political party ideology. Conservatives interpret this provision narrowly as only prohibiting the government from establishing a church or coercing religious participation. Liberals see the establishment clause as, in the words of Thomas Jefferson, creating a wall separating church and state. Prior to Justice Scalia's death, the Court was split 5–4 between these two views, with the conservative position having the majority to allow much more government support for religion and much more religious involvement in government activities.

Replacing Scalia with Garland or a Clinton nominee would have meant five justices in favor of enforcing the separation of church and state. But with Trump's appointment of Gorsuch, there again is a majority to allow much more in the way of prayer in public schools and other government events, religious symbols on government property, and government aid to parochial schools for religious instruction.[18]

Access to the courts

In a series of ideologically divided 5–4 decisions, with Justice Scalia in the majority, the Supreme Court in recent years has greatly protected businesses at the expense of injured consumers and employees. This has occurred especially in interpreting federal statutes and rules of procedure. The Court, for example, has ruled that clauses requiring arbitration in form contracts must be enforced and can be used to keep those with valid claims from suing in court.[19] Similarly, the Court has significantly restricted the ability of those hurt to sue in class action suits.[20] Especially when a large number of people each suffer a small injury, the only remedy is often a class action or nothing.

Replacing Scalia with a Democratic appointee would have shifted this balance. The Roberts Court has been the most pro-business Court since the mid-1930s, virtually always in 5–4 rulings, with the majority composed of Roberts, Scalia, Kennedy, Thomas, and Alito. Gorsuch replacing Scalia means that this will continue, and new limits on access to the courts, especially to sue businesses, will likely be imposed.

Campaign finance

For forty years, the Supreme Court has held that people have a First Amendment right to spend unlimited amounts of money in election campaigns.[21] *Citizens United v. Federal Election Commission*, in 2010, extended this to hold that corporations can spend unlimited sums from their corporate treasuries to get candidates elected or defeated.[22] Large expenditures by rich individuals and corporations on behalf of candidates always raise the appearance of government officials beholden to those who spent the money to get them elected. Political races sometimes are decided by the money given, especially those of lower visibility where large expenditures can make a real difference. A progressive Court could have not only overruled *Citizens United* but also reconsidered the earlier holdings that equate money with speech and allow unlimited expenditures by the rich in election campaigns. In her campaign, Hillary Clinton said that she wanted to appoint justices who would overrule *Citizens United*, and it is very likely that she would have done so.

THE FUTURE

Since 1960, seventy-eight years old is the average age at which a Supreme Court justice has left the bench. At the time of Donald Trump's inauguration on January 20, 2017, Ruth Bader Ginsburg was eighty-three, Anthony Kennedy was eighty, and Stephen Breyer was seventy-eight. No one should have been surprised when Anthony Kennedy announced his resignation on June 27, 2018.

This will create the most conservative Supreme Court since at least the mid-1930s. I have no doubt whatsoever that it will mean five votes to overrule *Roe v. Wade* and eliminate all constitutional protection for abortion rights, five votes to eliminate all forms of affirmative action, five votes to eliminate the rule that requires the exclusion of illegally obtained evidence in criminal cases. No one doubts that there will be cases brought to the Court to achieve these results as soon as there is a majority on the Court to come to these results. These have been the conservative targets for decades, but there have never been more than four votes for these results. Replacing Kennedy or Breyer will mean a majority for all of these conservative outcomes.

And if President Trump gets such a pick, that likely would create a solid conservative majority for years to come. In 2018, when Justice Kennedy retired, John Roberts was sixty-three, Samuel Alito was sixty-eight, and Clarence Thomas was seventy. Neil Gorsuch was forty-nine when he was sworn in as a justice on April 10, 2017. It is easy to imagine these four justices remaining on the Court ten or fifteen years, or even longer. With the new justice, it means a very conservative Court for years to come.

HOW SHOULD PROGRESSIVES RESPOND?

How progressives react to this reality will have enormous long-term consequences. Conservatives responded to the liberal decisions of the Supreme Court, such as to the rulings of the Warren Court era and to cases like *Roe v. Wade*, by developing and honing a clear vision of constitutional interpretation. Think tanks like the Heritage Foundation and groups like the Federalist Society led this effort. Conservative scholars, such as Robert Bork, wrote books articulating an intellectual framework to guide conservative justices, politicians, lawyers, and academics.

Progressives must fight back by offering an alternative vision of constitutional interpretation and constitutional law based on fulfilling the Constitution's promise of liberty and justice for all. The conservative approach to constitutional law is an emperor with no clothes; it is conservative justices imposing their conservative values while professing not to do so. Constitutional law inherently and always is about value choices by those in the robes on the high court, whether the justices are conservative or liberal. Progressives need to expose how conservatives are using the Constitution to advance their own agenda, which favors business over consumers and employees and government power over individual rights.

But it is not enough to reveal the conservatives' false promise of judicial neutrality. Progressives must offer their own vision for what the Constitution should be understood to mean and how this view far better achieves the goals of our nation, as stated in the Preamble, of ensuring democratic rule, effective government, justice, liberty, and equality.

A new vision is long overdue. Progressives have spent too much of the last forty-five years trying to preserve the legacy of the Warren Court's most important rulings and looking for areas of occasional advance. We have reacted to Republican-dominated Supreme Courts by criticizing erosions of rights in particular areas but not by developing a progressive vision for the Constitution. Now more than ever, it is urgent to do this. An alternative vision will provide the basis for opposing conservative changes in constitutional law in the years ahead and ultimately guide judges and justices to forge an inspiring direction in the future.

The stakes are huge. Because of the election of Donald Trump and the shift on the Supreme Court, constitutional issues are likely to dominate the public discourse much more than at any time in recent American history. Basic questions about the meaning of the Constitution are going to arise in countless areas, ranging from immigration policy to reproductive freedom to the environment. How these are answered will do much to determine the country and the world we live in for decades to come.

That is my goal in this book: to articulate a progressive vision of constitutional law. My focus is not on what the Supreme Court is likely to do in the foreseeable future. If Hillary Clinton had won, this would have been a very different book, one focused on what a Court with a majority of justices appointed by Democratic presidents should be doing. But Donald Trump's election means a conservative Court now and perhaps for the rest of my life.

SHOULD WE TURN AWAY FROM THE CONSTITUTION AND THE COURT?

In light of the ideological composition of the Supreme Court for the foreseeable future, it is reasonable to ask whether progressives should direct their attention away from the Constitution and the judiciary. The odds are low for the Court to be a vehicle for progressive results in my lifetime. I predict that many liberals in the years ahead will argue against the power of the Supreme Court to declare laws unconstitutional and advocate for a very minimal role for the judiciary and the Constitution.

The Constitution does not expressly give to the courts the power to review the constitutionality of laws and executive actions. No court had this power in England and it might be expected that the Constitution would have said so if it meant to change government in such an important way. The power of judicial review was created in *Marbury v. Madison*, in 1803, which held that the courts may declare unconstitutional both federal laws and executive actions. Chief Justice John Marshall explained that the Constitution exists to impose limits on government and those limits are rendered meaningless if not enforced. He famously declared that "it is emphatically the province and duty of the judicial department to say what the law is."[23]

Judicial review has existed for almost all of American

history, but it is not an inevitable aspect of having a constitution. The Netherlands, for example, has a written constitution, but that document explicitly states that it does not empower the courts to strike down government actions. The Netherlands has functioned as a democracy and without tyranny even though its courts do not have the power of judicial review.

In recent years, some prominent scholars have made a strong case for eliminating judicial review in the United States. Harvard law professor Mark Tushnet wrote a book titled, *Taking the Constitution Away from the Courts.*[24] In a chapter titled "Against Judicial Review," he asks what would happen if the Court overruled *Marbury v. Madison* and said, "We will no longer invalidate statutes, state or federal, on the ground that they violate the Constitution." He says that over time "the effects of doing away with judicial review, considered from a standard liberal or conservative perspective, would probably be rather small, taking all issues into account."

Professor Tushnet says that a nation without judicial review need not look like Stalinist Russia: "The examples of Great Britain and the Netherlands show that it is possible to develop systems in which the government has limited powers and individual rights are guaranteed, without having U.S.-style judicial review." Professor Tushnet argues that a "popular constitutionalism" would develop where the people and their elected officials would feel more need to comply with the Constitution once they knew that the courts were not engaged in judicial review. Professor Tushnet believes that the results of popular constitutionalism would be more progressive than the constitutional law that results from Supreme Court decisions. And he wrote this long before the Trump presidency and the Supreme Court that may emerge from it.

Professor Tushnet is not alone among prominent constitutional scholars in making this argument. For example, Larry Kramer, former dean of the Stanford Law School, wrote a well-received book espousing what he also terms popular constitutionalism.[25] Although Professor Kramer does not define popular constitutionalism with any precision and he does not go so far as to call for the elimination of judicial review, he does call for an end to "judicial supremacy" and a return of constitutional interpretation to the people. Professor Kramer, for example, argues that the people can be trusted, and he defends the deliberative processes of Congress as at least equal to those of the judiciary. He rightly points out that if Congress makes a mistake, it can be changed by that or the next or a future Congress. The change can be based on public pressure or election returns. But if the Court makes a mistake, the only way to overturn it is a constitutional amendment or to wait until the Supreme Court changes its mind.

Influential political scientists, too, have advocated for the elimination of judicial review. Pulitzer Prize winner James MacGregor Burns, a professor of government at Williams College, urges the elimination of judicial review, "based on the fact that the Constitution never granted the judiciary a supremacy over the government, nor had the Framers ever conceived it. It would remind Americans that the court's vetoes of acts of Congress are founded in a ploy by John Marshall that was exploited and expanded by later conservatives until the court today stands supreme and unaccountable, effectively immune to the checks and balances that otherwise fragment and disperse power throughout the constitutional system."[26]

Professor Burns argues, like Professors Tushnet and Kramer, that without judicial review elected government officials would be more vigilant about their duties to uphold the Constitution.

Voices such as Mark Tushnet, Larry Kramer, and James MacGregor Burns must be taken seriously. And they are not alone among contemporary academics who have called for an elimination, or at least substantial curtailment, of judicial review. I predict that this will be the rallying cry among many progressives in the years ahead. I am tempted to join them, especially as I contemplate the composition of the Court for years to come.

But I think that this effort is misguided and focusing attention on it will gain little. The Supreme Court and the lower federal courts will continue to engage in judicial review, regardless of what progressives say. Conservative justices will continue to strike down laws as they have in recent years, such as campaign finance restrictions and gun control statutes and key provisions of the Voting Rights Act. Calls to eliminate this power are not going to matter in the least, so why divert our attention? I believe our focus should remain on the desired meaning of the Constitution and its contents.

The Constitution, to be sure, is a flawed document. As written, it institutionalized and protected slavery. It prohibited Congress from restricting the importing of slaves for twenty years, counted slaves as only three-fifths of a person in drawing congressional districts, and mandated the return of escaped slaves to their owners. The Constitution, as written, gave no rights to women. It was written in the late eighteenth century for an agrarian slave society and it seems absurd to use it to answer twenty-first-century questions, such as whether the government ought to limit minors' access to violent videogames or whether the police need a warrant to use cell tower information to track a person's movements.

Yet we should also admire the Constitution for providing for democratic rule with orderly transitions of power since it was ratified in 1787. The separation of powers, and the checks and balances it creates, have prevented tyrannical rule. Overall, there has been a tremendous expansion of liberty and equality under it over the course of American history. Besides, if we turn our backs on the Constitution, what is the alternative and why believe that it would be any better?

Once I accept that the Constitution is worth keeping, then I also think it follows that it needs to be enforced. The classic argument for judicial review—put forth in *Marbury v. Madison*—is that the Constitution exists to limit the government, and those limits often will be meaningless unless there are courts to enforce them.

Especially for progressives, it is crucial to remember that those without political power have nowhere to turn for protection except the Constitution and the judiciary. In a telling passage, Professor Tushnet admits "my wife is Director of the National Prison Project of the American Civil Liberties Union. She disagrees with almost everything I have written in this chapter." The reality is that the political process has no incentive to be responsive to the constitutional rights of prisoners. Admittedly, the Rehnquist and Roberts Courts have an overall less than stellar record of protecting prisoners' rights, but I do not think that one could deny that judicial review has dramatically improved prison conditions for countless inmates who would otherwise be abandoned by the political process.[27] When is the last time a legislature adopted a law to expand the rights of prisoners or criminal defendants? Moreover, how much worse might it be if politicians and prison officials knew that the constitutionality of their actions could not be reviewed by the courts?

More generally, there is little incentive for the political process to protect unpopular minorities, such as racial or political minorities. How long would it have been before southern state legislatures declared segregation of public facilities unconstitutional if not for *Brown v. Board of Education* (1954) and the decisions that followed it? How long would it have taken Congress, dominated by Southerners in key committee chairs, to have acted in this regard?

Sometimes the political process will even fail the majority. Reapportionment is the classic example here. By the 1960s, many state legislatures were badly malapportioned, with legislative districts of vastly different sizes. The migration of population from rural to urban areas was not accompanied by a redrawing of election districts. The result was that urban districts were much more populous than rural districts but had less representation. Malapportioned state legislatures were not about to reapportion themselves so as to decrease the political power of those in office. Every incentive led those who benefited from malapportionment to retain the existing system. Only judicial review could institute one person, one vote.

These, of course, are just some of the examples where the political process cannot be relied on to comply voluntarily with the Constitution. In all of these areas, it is likely the courts or nothing for enforcing and upholding the Constitution.

Judicial review also is essential to ensure that state and local governments comply with the Constitution. The nature of the federalist structure of American government is that there are fifty states and tens of thousands of local governments that can violate the Constitution. These include not only every town, city, and county but every school board and zoning commission. Scholars like Tushnet, Kramer, and Burns focus especially on Congress and the president in discussing the incentives for voluntary compliance with the Constitution. Kramer, for example, compares favorably the deliberative proves in Congress to that of the Supreme Court.

This focus ignores, however, the likelihood of constitutional infringements by all the other levels of government and the corresponding benefits of judicial review. A few examples illustrate this point. Without judicial review, the Bill of Rights would not be applied to the states. It was not until well into the twentieth century that the Supreme Court held that the Bill of Rights applies to state and local governments. Although most states might voluntarily comply with most of the Bill of Rights, some states certainly would not follow all of its provisions, especially where it is expensive or politically unpopular to do so. For instance, many states did not provide free attorneys to criminal defendants in felony cases until *Gideon v. Wainwright* in 1963.[28] In this respect, those who advocate for the elimination of judicial review ignore its benefits in securing state and local compliance with the Constitution. How many local governments would advance religion in all sorts of ways if not for courts enforcing the First Amendment's prohibition of laws respecting the establishment of religion?

As I have become increasingly disillusioned with the Supreme Court, and as I look to what the Court will be like in the years ahead, I have become more sympathetic to those who call for the elimination or substantial curtailment of judicial review. Yet, on reflection, I believe this would be a huge mistake. The danger lies in overestimating the likelihood of voluntary compliance by the other branches of government and underestimating the likely benefits of judicial review. I have spent the last thirty-five years arguing appeals on behalf of prisoners and those whose civil liberties have been violated. The first Supreme Court case I argued was on behalf of a man who was sentenced to life in prison with no possibility of parole for fifty years for stealing $153 worth of videotapes from Kmart. (I lost 5–4, with the Court rejecting my argument that the sentence was cruel and unusual punishment.) The second Supreme Court case I argued was on behalf of a homeless man who was challenging a six-foot-high, three-foot-wide monument of the Ten Commandments that sits exactly at the corner between the Texas State Legislature and the Texas Supreme Court. (I lost 5–4, with the Court rejecting my argument that this violated the establishment clause of the First Amendment.) I argued the first case on behalf of Guantanamo detainees, in federal district court and in the U.S. Court of Appeals for the Ninth Circuit, in 2002.

As one who often argues cases on behalf of prisoners or those whose civil liberties have been violated, I have the sense that popular constitutionalism is the product of an academic detachment that fails to recognize that, for clients like mine, it is often the courts or nothing. Prisoners and civil rights litigants may very well lose in the courts, but often the judicial process is their only recourse.

WHAT NOW?

If the answer for progressives is not to turn their back on the Constitution and the courts, it must be to argue for an alternative vision to the one put forward by conservatives.

The first step—and this is the focus of chapter 2—must be to refute the conservatives' legal notion of "originalism," whereby all constitutional issues, including such controversial questions as the death penalty or affirmative action, can be resolved based solely on the original text of the Constitution and its meaning at the time it was written. Conservatives maintain that this allows justices to decide cases without imposing their own values. That is nonsense. There is no such thing as "value-neutral judging." It is a myth that conservatives have advanced for decades and continue to espouse for their own purposes.

It is simply wrong to think that Supreme Court justices—liberal or conservative—can decide constitutional cases without making value judgments or that decisions in controversial areas are about anything other than the ideology of the justices. This is a smokescreen to make Americans think conservatives are basing their decisions on the "true" meaning of the Constitution, when actually their rulings are a product of their own conservative views. In 2008, for the first time in U.S. history, the five conservative justices on the Roberts Court declared a local gun control ordinance to be unconstitutional—a violation of the Second Amendment. In 2010, these same justices found that corporations have the right to spend unlimited amounts of money in election campaigns. In 2013, they invalidated a federal civil rights law in the area of race—a key provision of the Voting Rights Act of 1965—for the first time since the nineteenth century.

By any measure, all these cases were conservative judicial activism: each overruled precedent invalidated a law that was enacted with overwhelming support, broadly decided a matter when a narrow ruling was possible, and did so to advance conservative political values. Every one of these decisions was based on the ideology and values of the conservative Republican justices, not the text or the original meaning of the Constitution. It is laughable to say that the framers of the First Amendment intended that corporations should be able to spend unrestricted sums from their campaign treasuries to get candidates elected or defeated. Those who wrote the First Amendment did not envision campaign spending as it exists today, let alone modern corporations.

If the conservatives' approach is empty and misleading, how do progressives replace it? The document should be interpreted to fulfill its central values. Therefore, it is essential to begin by identifying the core underlying values that the Constitution is meant to achieve. This is the focus of chapter 3. The place to start is at the very beginning, with the Preamble, which articulates the purposes for the document. The Preamble states: "We the People of the United States, in Order to form a more perfect Union, establish Justice, insure domestic Tranquility, provide for the common defence, promote the general Welfare, and secure the Blessings of Liberty to ourselves and our Posterity, do ordain and establish this Constitution for the United States of America."

The Preamble exists to do much more than tell us that the document is to be called the "Constitution" and that it is meant to establish a government. The Preamble describes the core values that the Constitution seeks to achieve: democratic government, effective governance, justice, and liberty.

Unfortunately, the Preamble has been largely ignored in Supreme Court decisions and scholarly writings. It has been treated as a mere rhetorical flourish to the Constitution. But, on the contrary, it is much more: it provides a lens through which the Constitution can be examined, articulating the basic values of the document that follows.

Finally, the bulk of this book, chapters 4 to 8, details how the Constitution should be interpreted to achieve the ideals announced in the Preamble: democratic government, effective governance, justice, freedom, and (implicitly) equality for all Americans. Each of these chapters describes a progressive vision for one of these core values.

I, of course, am not making an argument that I know the intent of the framers of the Constitution in these areas. Their intent cannot be known and should not limit contemporary constitutional law. The Constitution must be adapted to the problems of each generation; we are not living in the world of 1787 and should not pretend that the choices for that time can guide ours today. Chief Justice John Marshall expressed this realization almost two hundred years ago when he said that "we must never forget that it is a Constitution we are expounding," a Constitution "meant to be adapted and endure for ages to come."

My goal is to show how the values stated in the Preamble provide guidance in understanding the meaning of the Constitution and how they should help in deciding today's most important and controversial issues.

Given Donald Trump's election, it is not likely that my vision will be adopted in the immediate future. But that's not the point. Conservatives, in their think tanks and Federalist Society cliques, have spent years articulating and elaborating a conservative vision of constitutional law and the role of the Supreme Court. They did this even during years when conservatives were out of power. Liberals may have thought it futile to create a different and progressive vision with conservative justices in the majority on the Supreme Court for the last forty-five years. Perhaps, too, progressives have been wedded for too long to the Warren Court's vision and not thought enough beyond it. Now is the time to provide and defend and fight for an alternative, grander, and more inclusive interpretation of the Constitution.

Looking at the Constitution in a progressive way would produce a very different approach, one that would do much more to provide liberty and justice for all. In most areas, it would not take more than the shift of a single justice to create decisions pointing constitutional law in a fairer direction that does much more to realize the promise of the Preamble and the Constitution. Maybe the unexpected will happen and there will be a progressive majority on the Court sooner than I or anyone expects. Some of what I propose can be accomplished through legislative action at the federal or state levels; much can be done under state constitutional law when the Supreme Court and federal courts do not act.

But I am confident that someday the things that I propose will happen and what is said today will powerfully influence what can be done then. Also, if we fight for a progressive interpretation of the Constitution, we might sometimes have surprising successes.

It is so tempting to look at the composition of the Supreme Court as a historic inevitability. But in reality it is a product of coincidences between the timing of vacancies and who is in the White House. If Hubert Humphrey rather than Richard Nixon won in 1968, and it was a very close election, then a Democratic president would have picked four new justices between 1969 and 1971 and that would have continued a liberal majority on the Court for decades more. If Al Gore or John Kerry had been president in 2005 when William Rehnquist and Sandra Day O'Connor left the Court, there would be five justices appointed by Democratic presidents on the Court today, notwithstanding the election of Donald Trump, the appointment of Neil Gorsuch, and the resignation of Anthony Kennedy. If Hillary Clinton had been elected president—and she did win the popular vote by three million votes—and had replaced Antonin Scalia, the next years and perhaps decades of constitutional law would be vastly different.

So I think it is important to step away from the current composition of the Supreme Court and focus instead on what should be the meaning of the Constitution itself. How should progressives interpret this majestic but flawed document? The Constitution, and how it is interpreted, affects all of us, often in the most intimate and important aspects of our lives. How should it be interpreted to create a nation where there truly is liberty and justice for all? That is the question I seek to answer in this book.

2

THE CONSERVATIVES' FALSE CLAIM OF VALUE-NEUTRAL JUDGING

In 2010, the Supreme Court heard oral arguments in a case that concerned the constitutionality of a California law that prohibited the sale or rental of violent video games to minors without parental consent.[1] Many states had adopted similar statutes. Legislators were shocked by the graphic violence and were concerned by the studies that showed a correlation between playing such video games and violent behavior. The concern was that the participatory aspect of video games makes them different from comic books or television programs or movies, all of which also can have violent content.

As was his practice, Justice Scalia was very active in the oral argument and was pressing the attorney defending the California law about whether the state's law could be reconciled with the original understanding of the First Amendment. Finally, Justice Alito interjected and said, "Well, I think what Justice Scalia wants to know is what James Madison thought about video games." Putting it that way shows the absurdity of trying to answer today's constitutional questions by looking at the world of 1787 when the Constitution was drafted or 1791 when the First Amendment was ratified or 1868 when the Fourteenth Amendment was approved.

The Court, in a 7–2 decision, found that video games are a form of speech and that the California law is unconstitutional. Justice Scalia wrote the opinion for the Court. I do not question the wisdom of the decision, but rather whether it can be squared with Justice Scalia's often stated view—referred to as "originalism"—that the meaning of a constitutional provision is fixed at the time it was adopted and can be changed only through the constitutional amendment process. Justice Scalia, in countless speeches, proclaimed that the Constitution is "not a living document" and is "dead, dead, dead."[2] Not long before he died, Justice Scalia remarked in an interview in *California Lawyer* that discrimination against women never violates equal protection because the framers of the Fourteenth Amendment never meant to protect them.[3] The comment attracted national media attention, with the reaction being mostly of the "there he goes again, saying something provocative." But the response should be that this shows why Scalia's originalist philosophy is unacceptable.

Nor is this an isolated example of the difficulty of answering contemporary issues from the perspective of a society that could not have imagined them. Social attitudes—about race, gender, and sexual orientation, for instance—are so different today that it makes no sense to find answers to constitutional questions about them in the original understanding of constitutional provisions written and adopted long ago.

Technology, too, shows the absurdity of looking for answers to modern questions in eighteenth-century understandings. In *United States v. Jones* (2012), the Court had before it a case where the police put a GPS device on the undercarriage of Antoine Jones's car without a valid warrant and tracked his movements for twenty-eight days.[4] The Court unanimously held that this violated the Fourth Amendment. Justice Antonin Scalia wrote the opinion for the Court and held that putting the GPS device on the car was a trespass. He relied on an English law precedent from 1765. But what if the police had tracked Jones's movements, not through a GPS device physically placed on the car but rather through cellular or satellite technology? That is precisely decided by the Supreme Court in *Carpenter v. United States.*[5] The Court held 5–4, with Chief Justice Roberts joining the four liberal justices, that police must get a warrant before obtaining cellular location information. It is silly to think that the case could be resolved by looking at the text or intention of the Fourth Amendment as it was written in 1791. I am confident that even if he were alive, not even Justice Scalia could find an eighteenth-century English law precedent about whether use of cellular technology is a search within the meaning of the Fourth Amendment.

Yet conservative justices and professors repeatedly tell us that the Constitution must be interpreted solely on the basis of its original understanding. Justice Neil Gorsuch, declared: "Judges should instead strive (if humanly and so imperfectly) to apply the law as it is, focusing backward, not forward, and looking to text, structure, and history to decide what a reasonable reader at the time of the events in question would have understood the law to be."[6]

Despite decades of powerful criticism, originalism seems to be growing in acceptance. A recent Marist Poll, sponsored by the Knights of Columbus, found that "a majority of Americans (52 percent versus 40 percent) want the Supreme Court to interpret the Constitution 'as it was originally written' and not on what they think the 'Constitution means now.'"[7]

Why? Conservatives repeatedly emphasize that they want a method of interpretation that avoids forcing justices and judges to make value choices. In one of the initial and most influential arguments in favor of originalism, Judge Robert Bork (who was later nominated for the Supreme Court and rejected by the Senate) said that "a Court that makes rather than implements value choices cannot be squared with the presuppositions of a democratic society."[8]

In a particularly famous defense of originalism, Edwin Meese, the then attorney general, advocated for the "text of the document and the original intention of those who framed it . . . [as] the judicial standard in giving effect to the Constitution."[9] Accusing the Supreme Court of "roam[ing] at large in a veritable constitutional forest," he concluded that a "jurisprudence seriously aimed at the explication of original intention would produce defensible principles of government that would not be tainted by ideological predilection."[10]

Antonin Scalia is the justice most associated with originalism. He often explained that the alternative to his approach had judges making value choices, and that was inconsistent with democratic rule. For instance, in one opinion he defended originalism by declaring: "Although assuredly having the virtue (if it be that) of leaving judges free to decide as they think best when the unanticipated occurs, a rule of law that binds neither by text nor by any particular, identifiable tradition is no rule of law at all."[11]

When John Roberts went before the Senate Judiciary Committee for his confirmation hearings in 2005, in his opening statement he famously declared: "Judges are like umpires. Umpires don't make the rules; they apply them. The role of an umpire and a judge is critical. They make sure everybody plays by the rules. But it is a limited role. Nobody ever went to a ball game to see the umpire."[12] In this way, Roberts was conveying that he believes that the views of justices are irrelevant; judges are not to make value choices in interpreting the Constitution. No one expects or wants baseball umpires to be making calls based on their views or values.

After the death of Justice Antonin Scalia on February 13, 2016, Republicans repeatedly touted the idea that Supreme Court justices should just "apply the law" and decide cases without ideology playing any role. Senator Chuck Grassley, the chair of the Senate Judiciary Committee, issued a statement rejecting the idea that a justice's views or life experiences should affect his or her decisions.[13] Every Republican candidate in the 2016 presidential primaries espoused this position and the conviction that Supreme Court justices should follow the original meaning of the Constitution. They did this as a basis for blocking the Democratic appointee, Chief Judge Merrick Garland, and as a way of presenting themselves as defenders of judicial restraint. Donald Trump also expressed this view during the presidential debates with Hillary Clinton.[14]

The centerpiece of the conservative approach to the Constitution for the last several decades has been the premise that judges should decide cases without making value choices and that they have an approach to constitutional interpretation—originalism—that achieves that. This has understandable rhetorical appeal. There is discomfort in thinking of unelected justices imposing their own views on society or constitutional law being nothing more than the preferences of those on the Court at a particular moment.

THE FALSE CLAIM OF JUDICIAL RESTRAINT

But it is simply wrong to think that Supreme Court justices—liberal or conservative—can decide constitutional cases without making value choices or that decisions in controversial areas are about anything other than the ideology of the justices. The claim of value-neutral judging is a smokescreen to make Americans think conservatives are basing their decisions on the "true" meaning of the Constitution, when actually their rulings are a product of their own conservative views.

Beginning at least with Richard Nixon's campaign for president in 1968, conservatives have championed judicial restraint and lamented judicial activism. But looking at the behavior of conservatives on the Supreme Court shows that they, as much as or more than any liberal justices, impose their own values in deciding constitutional cases. Consider a few examples.

In 2008, in *District of Columbia v. Heller*, the Roberts Court declared a local ordinance prohibiting private ownership and possession of handguns to be unconstitutional—a violation of the Second Amendment.[15] Since its adoption in 1791, the Supreme Court had always interpreted the Second Amendment literally, as being about a right to have guns for militia service.[16] It had never before declared any law regulating firearms unconstitutional. This was a first. The ruling was 5–4, with Justice Scalia writing for the Court, joined by Chief Justice Roberts and Justices Kennedy, Thomas, and Alito.

In 2010, in *Citizens United v. Federal Election Commission*, these same five justices found that corporations have the right to spend unlimited amounts of money in election campaigns.[17] The Court declared unconstitutional a provision of a federal law—the McCain-Feingold Bipartisan Campaign Finance Reform Act of 2002—which limited expenditures by corporations and unions in federal elections. The bill had been overwhelmingly passed by Congress, with strong bipartisan support, and signed into law by President George W. Bush. The Court explicitly overruled a precedent from just eight years earlier that had upheld the very provisions the Court declared unconstitutional in *Citizens United*.

In 2013, in *Shelby County v. Holder*, these same five justices invalidated a federal civil rights law in the area of race—a key provision of the Voting Rights Act of 1965—for the first time since the nineteenth century.[18] The

Court held that it was unconstitutional for Congress to require that jurisdictions with a history of race discrimination get preapproval from the Justice Department before changing their election systems. The Court said that this violated the constitutional principle that Congress is required to treat all states the same. The basis for this constitutional principle was then, and is now, unknown.

There is nothing in the Constitution that says that Congress must treat all states the same. In fact, the very same Congress that ratified the Fourteenth Amendment also passed the Reconstruction Act of 1867 that imposed military rule on the South, likely the most extreme example in history of Congress treating some states differently from others.

Each of these examples of conservative judicial activism will have enormous consequences. Striking down laws restricting handguns means more deaths and serious bodily injuries. Corporations and unions spending unlimited amounts of money in election campaigns have changed who runs for office and who gets elected, as well as the confidence people have in the electoral system. Invalidating key provisions of the Voting Rights Act of 1965 makes it easier for state and local governments with a history of race discrimination in voting to continue to do so. There is no way to understand any of these 5–4 decisions other than as a reflection of the values of the five conservative justices on the Court.

The simple reality is that liberals and conservatives both sometimes want to defer to government and sometimes to declare government action unconstitutional; both sometimes want to follow precedent and sometimes to overrule it. They differ as to when, and it is all based on their ideology and preferences. Two consecutive days in June 2013 powerfully illustrate this.

On Tuesday, June 25, 2013, the Court, in a 5–4 decision, in *Shelby County v. Holder*, declared unconstitutional key provisions of the federal Voting Rights Act. The conservative justices were in the majority and Justice Ginsburg wrote for the dissent, urging judicial restraint and deference to Congress.[19] The next day, Wednesday, June 26, 2013, the Court, in a 5–4 decision, in *United States v. Windsor*, declared unconstitutional a key provision of the federal Defense of Marriage Act (1996), which provided that for the purpose of federal benefits a marriage had to be between a man and a woman.[20] Justice Kennedy, joined by the four liberal justices, were the majority; the conservatives dissented, urging judicial restraint and deference to Congress. Only Justice Kennedy was in the majority in both decisions.

Conservatives and liberals both want courts to strike down actions that they perceive as unconstitutional; they just disagree as to when.

THE INEVITABILITY OF VALUE CHOICES IN CONSTITUTIONAL DECISION-MAKING

To be clear, I am not saying that conservatives engage in judicial activism, while liberals practice judicial restraint. I actually find those labels meaningless and long have thought that "judicial activism" is just the label people use for the decisions they dislike. My point is that all justices—liberals and conservatives alike—inevitably must make value choices. No method of constitutional interpretation, including originalism, can avoid that. The only difference is that conservatives pretend that they are doing something different.

There are many reasons why value choices are inevitable in interpreting the Constitution.[21] First, the Constitution was intentionally written in broad, open-ended language that rarely provides guidance for issues that must be resolved by the Supreme Court. Justices are obligated to give meaning to ambiguous words written almost 230 years ago. What is "speech"? For example, should spending money in an election campaign be regarded as speech? This, of course, is the key issue in terms of whether laws regulating campaign spending violate the First Amendment.[22] The text of the Constitution cannot answer this question of whether spending money is speech. Nor was there any thinking about that when the First Amendment was drafted; campaign spending did not exist as it does today.

What is "cruel and unusual punishment," which is forbidden by the Eighth Amendment? For over a half century, the Supreme Court has said that this is to be interpreted based on "evolving standards of decency."[23] But there is no way to determine that apart from the views and values of the justices.

For example, in recent years, the Court has had to decide whether it is cruel and unusual punishment to impose the death penalty on the intellectually disabled or for crimes committed by juveniles or through the use of particular drugs in lethal injections.[24] Whether these penalties are inconsistent with "evolving standards of decency" cannot be determined based on what those who drafted and ratified the Eighth Amendment thought in 1791. Whether such punishments are consistent with evolving standards of decency cannot be answered except through the values of today; the text and the framers' intent are useless.

The meaning of the Eighth Amendment and "cruel and unusual punishment" was the issue in the first case I argued in the Supreme Court, *Lockyer v. Andrade*, in 2003.[25] The question was whether it was cruel and unusual punishment to impose, under California's three-strikes law, a sentence of life in prison with no possibility of parole for fifty years for a man who shoplifted $153 worth of videotapes. The Court, in a 5–4 decision split along ideological lines, upheld the sentence even though my client had never committed a violent crime and even though no one in the history of the country had received a life sentence for shoplifting before. The five conservative justices made a value choice to allow state governments to impose draconian punishments for minor crimes. My client would not have been eligible for parole until 2046, when he would have been eighty-seven years old; thankfully, California voters in 2012 amended the law to say that a third strike had to be a serious or violent crime and he was subsequently released from prison.

One of the most controversial parts of the Constitution, the Second Amendment, reads: "A well regulated Militia, being necessary to the security of a free State, the right of the people to keep and bear Arms, shall not be infringed." Is this a right to have guns only for militia service or does this create a more general right of people to possess firearms? Conservatives tend to favor gun rights, while liberals support gun control. It was not surprising, then, that the Court split 5–4 exactly along ideological lines in *District of Columbia v. Heller.*

The conservative justices in the majority chose to read the Second Amendment as a right of individuals to possess handguns in their homes for the sake of security, while the liberals argued that the Second Amendment is a right to have guns solely for the purpose of militia service. Either is a plausible reading of the text of the Second Amendment and either can be supported by its history. Inescapably, how a justice reads the Second Amendment and decides cases about it are a reflection of that individual's views. There is nothing value-neutral about it—or about the five conservative justices, for the first time in history, adopting the NRA's view of the Second Amendment. Justice Scalia's majority opinion said that the first half of the Second Amendment is "prefatory" language, while the second half is "operative." But that is pure sophistry; why isn't all of the language of the Second Amendment to be deemed operative language?

Even parts of the Constitution that are seemingly clear require interpretation. The Constitution says that the president must be a "natural born Citizen." But does that mean a citizen as of birth or that the person was born within the United States? Ted Cruz came up against this controversy in his run for the presidency because he was born outside the United States, but he was an American citizen at birth. There is still no answer as to what it means to be a natural-born citizen and whether it would have been constitutional for Ted Cruz to have been elected president. The words of the Constitution and the intent of the framers provide no resolution.

Nor is looking back to history to discover the framers' intent or the original understanding behind a constitutional provision likely to be helpful. So many people were involved in drafting and ratifying the Constitution that it is not tenable to think that there was a single understanding waiting to be discovered. In teaching constitutional law, I point out to my students the many instances where James Madison and Alexander Hamilton—the most frequently quoted architects of the Constitution because of their *Federalist Papers* essays—disagreed. These involved major issues, with enormous contemporary significance, such as whether there are inherent presidential powers[26] and the scope of Congress's power to tax and spend.[27] Nor is Justice Scalia's approach to discovering original meaning—looking to practices at the time of a constitutional provision's ratification—likely to be useful; there were probably great variations, and besides, adopting a constitutional provision could have been more about changing ongoing practices than ratifying them. Former constitutional law professor Barack

Obama explained: "Anyone like Justice Scalia, looking to resolve our modern constitutional dispute through strict construction, has one big problem: The founders themselves disagreed profoundly, vehemently, on the meaning of their masterpiece. Before the ink on the constitutional parchment was dry, arguments had erupted not just about minor provisions, but about first principles; not just between peripheral figures, but within the revolution's very core."[28]

Historians long have reminded us that "what [history] yields is heavily dependent upon the premises of its users."[29] The famous historian R. G. Collingwood succinctly expressed this when he said: "History means interpretation. . . . We can view the past, and achieve our understanding of the past, only through the eyes of the present."[30] It is hardly surprising, then, that when Justice Scalia and Justice Stevens each looked exhaustively at history in deciding whether the Second Amendment protects a right to own and possess handguns, they came to opposite conclusions that exactly mirrored their ideology. More generally, Justice Scalia, the Court's most ardent originalist, interpreted the Constitution to allow unlimited government aid to parochial schools, to permit prayers in public schools, to protect a right of people to have guns in their homes, to permit the death penalty, to allow states to prohibit same-sex marriage, to permit states to completely prohibit all abortions. It is hardly coincidence that Antonin Scalia, a conservative, found in the original meaning of the Constitution the choices expressed in the 2016 Republican platform.

Second, value choices are inevitable in interpreting the Constitution because following just the text and the original understanding would lead to absurd and undesirable results. The world of today is so radically different from that of 1787, when the Constitution was drafted, or 1791, when the Bill of Rights was ratified, or 1868, when the Fourteenth Amendment was adopted. For example, Article II refers to the president and vice president with the pronoun "he." The framers undoubtedly intended that those holding these offices would be men. From an originalist philosophy, it would be unconstitutional to elect a woman as president or vice president until the document is amended.

The same Congress that ratified the Fourteenth Amendment also voted to segregate the District of Columbia public schools. Under an originalist philosophy, *Brown v. Board of Education of Topeka, Kansas* (1954) was wrongly decided and laws mandating segregation were constitutional.

As Justice Scalia said, and Robert Bork before him, from an originalist perspective, sex discrimination does not violate the Constitution because the original understanding of the Fourteenth Amendment did not mean to stop this. But few would accept a view of the Constitution that would make *Brown v. Board of Education* an illegitimate decision or see no constitutional limit on sex discrimination.

This is why the Constitution is and always has been regarded as a living document. Even the power of judicial review—the authority of courts to review the constitutionality of executive and legislative acts—is nowhere mentioned in the text of the Constitution. It is at best unclear whether it was intended by the Constitution's drafters.

There would be a radical change in constitutional law if a majority of the Court were ever to adopt an originalist philosophy. No longer would the Bill of Rights apply to state and local governments. No longer would there be the protection of rights not mentioned in the text of the Constitution, such as the right to travel, freedom of association, and the right to privacy. This would mean the end of constitutional protection for liberties such as the right to marry, the right to procreate, the right to custody of one's children, the right to keep the family together, the right of parents to control the upbringing of their children, the right to purchase and use contraceptives, the right to abortion, the right to refuse medical care, the right to engage in private consensual homosexual activity. No longer would women or gays and lesbians be protected from discrimination under the equal protection clause. In fact, no longer would equal protection apply to the federal government; the equal protection clause of the Fourteenth Amendment, by its terms and intent, applies only to state and local governments.

Of course, originalists can try to avoid these problems by foregoing constraint and developing a theory that allows the justices discretion to avoid the unacceptable results. Some who call themselves originalists—like Will Baude, Randy Barnett, Jack Balkin—look at the more abstract goals of a constitutional provision, rather than the specific understanding of those who drafted and ratified it.[31] Baude, for example, defends the Supreme Court's decision in *Obergefell v. Hodges* (2015),[32] which struck down state laws prohibiting same-sex marriage, under his theory of originalism. But then, as Eric Segall powerfully shows in a new book, *Originalism as Faith*, originalism and nonoriginalism become indistinguishable. If the meaning of a constitutional provision is stated at an abstract enough level, almost any result can be justified. The goals of the Constitution included equality and liberty; stated at that level of abstraction, there is no result that cannot be justified. Scholars can call it originalism if they want, but the constraint on judging that inspired originalism is gone.

This illustrates an even greater problem with the conservative claim that originalism constrains judges: the original meaning of a constitutional provision can be stated at many different levels of abstraction and the choice of the level of abstraction is arbitrary and all about the results the interpreter wants to achieve.

Consider, for example, the Fourteenth Amendment's assurance that no state can deny any person equal protection of the laws. Should the purpose of this provision be seen just as protecting former slaves who were deemed to desperately need its assistance when the Fourteenth Amendment was ratified? Or should the equal protection clause be regarded as protecting those of African descent? Or should be it be seen as protecting all racial minorities? Or should its purpose be regarded as protecting all who have historically suffered discrimination? Or should the focus be on its language, which says that the government shall not deny "to any person" equal protection of the laws? All are reasonable ways to understand the equal protection clause; there is no principled way to choose one level of abstraction over another. Yet, under some of these approaches discrimination against gays and lesbians is unconstitutional; under other views the equal protection clause provides them no protection whatsoever.

The reality is that even conservatives abandon originalism when it does not serve their purpose. For example, the Congress that ratified the Fourteenth Amendment also adopted numerous race-based programs, like the Freedmen's Bureau, to benefit racial minorities.[33] Following the original meaning of the Fourteenth Amendment should lead originalists, such as Justices Scalia and Thomas, to favor affirmative action. Not surprisingly, they never mention this original understanding when they express their strong hostility to affirmative action programs.

There is nothing whatsoever to indicate that those who drafted and ratified the First Amendment meant to protect the right of corporations to spend unlimited amounts of money in election campaigns. But that, of course, did not keep the five conservative justices from finding such a right in *Citizens United v. Federal Election Commission*.

Finally, and perhaps most importantly, the desire for value-neutral judging in constitutional cases is an impossible quest because the balancing of competing interests is inescapable, and a justice's own ideology and life experiences inevitably determine how he or she—or anyone interpreting the Constitution—strikes the balance. This is a crucial flaw in the claims of originalists and others who claim to have a way to interpret the Constitution that is not about the values of the justices.

No constitutional right is absolute, and constitutional cases constantly involve balancing the government's interest against the claim of a right. To pick an easy example, the Fourth Amendment prohibits "unreasonable" searches and arrests. But what is reasonable or unreasonable cannot be answered from the text of the Constitution or any original understanding. Whether it is unreasonable for police to access cell tower location information without a warrant, the issue in *Carpenter v. United States* requires that the Court make a choice that balances privacy interests with law enforcement needs. When the Court considered whether the police can take a DNA sample from a person arrested for a serious crime to see if it matches DNA from an unsolved crime in the police data base, the Court explicitly balanced the law enforcement benefits of obtaining the information against the intrusion to privacy and ruled, 5–4, in favor of the government.[34]

Over the last half century, the Supreme Court has articulated principles for how balancing generally is to be done in most constitutional cases. If the government infringes a fundamental right, such as freedom of speech, or discriminates based on race or national origin, it must meet "strict scrutiny": its action must be shown to be necessary to achieve a compelling government interest. This is a heavy burden, which the government rarely meets. By contrast, if the government discriminates based on sex or against nonmarital children, its action must meet "intermediate scrutiny" and be shown to be substantially related to achieve an important government interest. All other government actions that discriminate, say, on the basis of age or disability, or that interfere with rights that are not deemed fundamental, only have to meet "rational basis review." This means that they will be upheld so long as they are rationally related to a legitimate government purpose. The government almost always prevails under rational basis review.

These tests are about how the weights should be arranged on the scales for the balancing of competing interests. If the government is discriminating based on race or interfering with a fundamental right, the scale is weighted to favor the challenger and the government has a significant burden to meet to justify its action. But if it is a type of discrimination that does not raise suspicion (say, a fourteen-year-old challenging not being able to get a driver's license until age sixteen), the scale is weighted to favor the government and the challenger who must meet a heavy burden.

But what is a "compelling" or "important" or "legitimate" government interest inevitably requires a value choice. It never can be answered by the text of the Constitution or its original understanding. For example, in cases involving whether colleges and universities can engage in affirmative action, the central question is whether diversity in the classroom is a compelling government interest.[35] The justices all agreed that the use of race in admissions must meet strict scrutiny. The disagreement was entirely over whether achieving diversity is a compelling interest and what must be shown for a college or university to demonstrate that its affirmative action program is necessary.[36] But that requires a value choice by the justices. Not surprisingly, the liberal and more moderate justices have found that achieving diversity is a compelling interest, while the most conservative justices reject this as a sufficient basis to allow affirmative action programs.

Take another example: laws prohibiting same-sex marriage. No one denied that this was discrimination based on sexual orientation; the issue was whether the discrimination was justified. At the very least, treating same-sex couples differently from opposite-sex couples still has to meet rational basis review, which requires that the government interest has to be rationally related to a legitimate government purpose. Every justice on the Court therefore had to face the question of whether there is any "legitimate" reason to keep gays and lesbians from marrying. Originalism can provide no answer.

The conclusion is thus inescapable that anyone interpreting the Constitution—the Supreme Court, lower federal court judges, members of a legislature, you or me—is inevitably engaged in the process of making value choices. Does society's interest in protecting children justify the laws restricting speech by prohibiting child pornography? Does the need for public safety justify laws keeping ex-felons from having firearms? Does protecting girls from pregnancy justify statutory rape laws that make it a crime to have sex with a girl under age eighteen but not a boy under age eighteen? The examples are endless.

As I wrote over a quarter of a century ago, "constitutional law is now, will be, and always has been about, largely a product of the views of the Justices."[37] The conservatives' quest for value-neutral judging is a futile one; their claim that they have achieved it through originalism is, to be blunt, nonsense.

The ideology and values of each justice on the Court make all the difference. Republicans, of course, know this as much as Democrats. That is why there was such an intense fight over who would replace Justice Scalia and why Merrick Garland never got a hearing from the Republicans. We need to stop pretending that there is such a thing as value-free judging and get rid of ridiculous and untrue slogans like "justices apply the law, they don't make the law." Everything the Supreme Court does makes the law.

The fact that justices' values and views determine the outcome of cases does not mean that justices are the same as politicians. Those holding elected office must be responsive to the voters if they want to remain in their seats. Supreme Court justices serve for life and are expected to be independent of electoral politics. Lobbying of elected government officials is accepted; lobbying of Supreme Court justices is never permissible and never occurs. Legislators sometimes trade votes; so far as we know, Supreme Court justices never do.

But justices are like politicians in one crucial way: they constantly make choices that come down to their views and values. Justices Scalia and Ginsburg disagreed in almost every major case, not because one is smarter or understands constitutional law better or avoids decisions based on value choices. Rather, their disagreements reflect their differing ideologies, life experiences, and worldviews.

One of the consequences of the 2016 presidential election is that originalism lives on as an important approach to constitutional interpretation. If Hillary Clinton had won the presidency, there would have been a majority of justices appointed by Democratic presidents and originalism would have been relegated to dissents, especially by Justice Clarence Thomas. Neither Chief Justice John Roberts nor Justice Samuel Alito tend to write their opinions in originalist terms. None of the Democratic appointees to the Court embrace originalism. Conservative law professors would have continued to champion originalism and would have used it to criticize liberal decisions. The academic debate over originalism would have continued, but as a method of constitutional interpretation invoked by the Court, it would have faded into obscurity.

Everything, though, is different because Donald Trump won the presidency. Neil Gorsuch, a self-avowed originalist, and not Merrick Garland, replaced Antonin Scalia. It is President Trump who is replacing Kennedy and who will fill any other vacancies in the next three years. Trump's list is filled with conservatives with strong Federalist Society ties who espouse a belief in originalism. Even though the flaws of originalism have been revealed for decades, conservatives espouse it and pretend that it provides answers to decide constitutional cases. Do they not see the problems with originalism? Of course, they do. But the rhetoric of originalism allows them to portray themselves as untainted by value choices and adherents of the "true" meaning of the Constitution. It is important that progressives point out over and over again that this is truly an emperor with no clothes.

BUT IF NOT ORIGINALISM, THEN WHAT?

Never in American history has a majority of the Supreme Court embraced originalism (though that could still come depending on when vacancies occur and who fills them). On many occasions, the Supreme Court has expressly and forcefully rejected originalism. In *McCulloch v. Maryland*, in 1819, Chief Justice John Marshall famously reminded us that "we must never forget that it is a Constitution we are expounding," a Constitution "meant to be adapted and endure for ages to come."[38]

In 1934, during the Depression, the Court upheld a Minnesota law that prevented foreclosure on farm mortgages.[39] This law violated the text of Article I, Section 9, of the Constitution that prevents states from impairing the obligation of contracts. Also, it was undisputed that the original intent of the provision was to keep states from adopting exactly this kind of debtors' relief laws. But the Court, recognizing the necessity of such legislative actions at the time, rejected the relevance of the original understanding and declared:

> It is no answer to say that this public need was not apprehended a century ago, or to insist that what the provision of the Constitution meant to the vision of that day it must mean to the vision of our time. If by the statement that what the Constitution meant at the time of its adoption it means today, it is intended to say that the great clauses of the Constitution must be confined to the interpretation which the framers, with the conditions and outlook of their time, would have placed upon them, the statement carries its own refutation. It was to guard against such a narrow conception that Chief Justice Marshall uttered the memorable warning: "We must never forget, that it is a constitution we are expounding" . . . "a constitution intended to endure for ages to come, and, consequently, to be adapted to the various crises of human affairs."

It is hard to imagine a clearer rejection of originalism.

Similarly, in *Brown v. Board of Education*, the Court explicitly rejected as irrelevant the fact that the original understanding of the equal protection clause allowed states to impose segregation based on race.[40] Chief Justice Earl Warren, writing for a unanimous Court, declared: "In approaching this problem, we cannot turn the clock back to 1868 when the Amendment was adopted, or even to 1896 when *Plessy v. Ferguson* was written. We must consider public education in the light of its full development and its present place in American life throughout the

Nation. Only in this way can it be determined if segregation in public schools deprives these plaintiffs of the equal protection of the laws."

The Court again explicitly rejected originalism as a method of interpreting the Constitution in *Harper v. Virginia Board of Elections* (1966), which declared poll taxes—the requirement that people pay a fee in order to vote—to be unconstitutional.[41] Justice William Douglas wrote for the Court: "Likewise, the Equal Protection Clause is not shackled to the political theory of a particular era. In determining what lines are unconstitutionally discriminatory, we have never been confined to historic notions of equality, any more than we have restricted due process to a fixed catalogue of what was at a given time deemed to be the limits of fundamental rights. Notions of what constitutes equal treatment for purposes of the Equal Protection Clause do change."[42]

More recently, in *Obergefell v. Hodges*, in declaring unconstitutional state laws prohibiting same-sex marriage, Justice Anthony Kennedy wrote for the Court and explained how the Constitution must be regarded as a living, not a dead, document: "The nature of injustice is that we may not always see it in our own times. The generations that wrote and ratified the Bill of Rights and the Fourteenth Amendment did not presume to know the extent of freedom in all of its dimensions, and so they entrusted to future generations a charter protecting the right of all persons to enjoy liberty as we learn its meaning. When new insight reveals discord between the Constitution's central protections and a received legal stricture, a claim to liberty must be addressed."[43]

But if constitutional law is not, never has been, and should not be about divining the original meaning of a constitutional provision, what is the proper basis for decisions? After all, one of Justice Scalia's constant refrains in defending originalism was that he had a theory of constitutional interpretation but his opponents don't.

As I have explained above, no method of constitutional interpretation—not Justice Scalia's or any other—obviates the need for the justices or whoever is interpreting the Constitution to make value choices. The process of interpreting the Constitution always involves beginning with the document's text. Sometimes it is clear. Article I, for example, says that members of the House of Representatives serve for two years and senators have a six-year term. Article II says that the president must be thirty-five years old. Article III is explicit that there will be a Supreme Court. But virtually always the cases coming to the Supreme Court, or that raise legal or public controversies, involve textual provisions that aren't clear as to their meaning.

Certainly interpretation can include any insights to be gained from looking at the original understanding, if any can be determined, though with the understanding that it is not determinative. History and tradition as to how the Constitution has been interpreted, including prior precedent, matter, and current social needs are also very relevant. Justice Kennedy expressed this well in his majority opinion in *Obergefell v. Hodges*:

> The identification and protection of fundamental rights is an enduring part of the judicial duty to interpret the Constitution. That responsibility, however, "has not been reduced to any formula." Rather, it requires courts to exercise reasoned judgment in identifying interests of the person so fundamental that the State must accord them its respect. That process is guided by many of the same considerations relevant to analysis of other constitutional provisions that set forth broad principles rather than specific

> requirements. History and tradition guide and discipline this inquiry but do not set its outer boundaries. That method respects our history and learns from it without allowing the past alone to rule the present.[44]

Most of all, though, the Constitution should be interpreted to achieve its underlying values. The world of the early twenty-first century is vastly different from that of the late eighteenth century when the Constitution was drafted. It is silly to think that we can be governed by the specific views of those who knew nothing about the issues we face today. But their values, the goals animating the document and its provisions, are enduring.

But what are these values? That is the focus of the next chapter.

PART II

A PROGRESSIVE READING OF THE CONSTITUTION

3

THE VALUES OF THE CONSTITUTION

REDISCOVERING THE PREAMBLE

BEGINNING AT THE BEGINNING

If constitutional interpretation should be based on achieving the underlying values of the Constitution, where are these values to be found? The place to start is at the very beginning, with the Preamble, which articulates the purposes for the document: "We the People of the United States, in Order to form a more perfect Union, establish Justice, insure domestic Tranquility, provide for the common defence, promote the general Welfare, and secure the Blessings of Liberty to ourselves and our Posterity, do ordain and establish this Constitution for the United States of America."

The Preamble is much more than the opening statement of a constitution establishing a government. It describes the core values that the Constitution, and the government it creates, seeks to achieve democratic government, effective governance, justice, and liberty. It begins by proclaiming that the Constitution is created by "We the People." The people are sovereign. This phrase makes clear that the United States is to be a democracy, not a monarchy or a theocracy or a totalitarian government, the dominant forms of government throughout the world in 1787 and before. It tells us that the Constitution exists to ensure that the national government has the authority to do everything that is part of creating a "more perfect Union" and providing for "the general Welfare." It states that the Constitution is meant to ensure justice and to protect liberty.

Seeing the Preamble as the articulation of the underlying values of the Constitution is not new. Joseph Story, who served for decades on the Supreme Court in the nineteenth century, wrote in 1833 that a "preamble of a statute is a key to open the mind of the makers, as to the mischiefs, which are to be remedied, and the objects, which are to be accomplished by the provisions of the statute. . . . [and] it is properly resorted to, where doubts or ambiguities arise upon the words of the enacting part."[1] As Eric Axler expressed much more recently, "To discover the spirit of the Constitution, it is of the first importance to attend to the principal ends and designs it has in view. These are expressed in the [Preamble.]"[2] Former congressman Peter Rodino, Jr., similarly said that the Preamble is the "heart, soul, and spirit of the Constitution."[3] Thus, he and coauthor Gilbert Carrasco said that the "Preamble should be the focal point in constitutional interpretation. It declares the framers 'constitutional aspiration' and gives the document as a whole its direction."[4]

This, of course, is not unique to the United States Constitution but common to constitutions all over the world that begin with preambles. The Supreme Court of India, for example, declared: "It seems to me that the Preamble of our Constitution is of extreme importance and the Constitution should be read and interpreted in the light of the grand and noble vision expressed in the Preamble."[5] The preamble of a constitution is thus not idle words; it is the distillation and articulation of the central purpose of the document. Preambles to constitutions "are not just the hortatory language that introduces a series of operative provisions, they are not just the 'ornately designed cover' of a book called 'the Constitution.' If a preamble has been written the words it contains have a reason."[6]

The preamble is thus the obvious place to begin in discerning the values of the Constitution. Unfortunately, though, it has been largely ignored in Supreme Court decisions and in scholarly writings. As has been widely noted, "While almost every other provision has been subjected to exhaustive analysis and a rich and often long history of judicial construction, the preamble has been surprisingly ignored by the overwhelming majority of commentators and relegated to sheer irrelevance by the courts."[7] It has been treated as a mere rhetorical flourish to the Constitution.

The Supreme Court set the tone of dismissing the Preamble in 1905, in *Jacobson v. Massachusetts,* a case about the constitutionality of compulsory vaccination laws, when the Court ruled that laws cannot be challenged or declared unconstitutional based on the Preamble. The Court declared: "Although that Preamble indicates the general purposes for which the people ordained and established the Constitution, it has never been regarded as the source of any substantive power conferred on the Government of the United States or on any of its Departments."[8] Since then, the Court has taken this to mean that the Preamble is essentially to be ignored. Courts "have rejected, repeatedly, the argument that constitutional rights or limitations can be inferred directly from the preamble."[9] Over a half century ago, William Crosskey remarked that the Preamble's words "are now universally regarded as empty verbal flourish."[10]

In the few occasions over the last century in which the Preamble has been mentioned, the Supreme Court has summarily rejected its relevance to constitutional interpretation and decisions. The result is that it plays no role in constitutional arguments and analysis. Textbooks on constitutional law, including mine, never discuss it.[11] I have taught constitutional law for thirty-eight years, but until recently—as a result of my work on this book—I almost totally ignored the Preamble in my classes. As one commentator noted, "the preamble remains a neglected subject in the study of American constitutional theory and receives scant attention in the literature."[12]

But this has been a mistake because the Preamble states the ideals for the Constitution and for the republic. It also is a mistake to ignore any words of the Constitution in interpreting the document. In the foundational case of *Marbury v. Madison*, the Court declared "it cannot be presumed that any clause in the constitution is intended to be without effect; and therefore such construction is inadmissible, unless the words require it." Yet, for over a century, the Court has treated the Preamble as being entirely without effect.

Early in American history, it was different; the justices used the Preamble as part of constitutional interpretation. In *Martin v. Hunter's Lessee* (1816), the Court established its authority to review state court decisions and invoked the Preamble: "The constitution of the United States was ordained and established, not by the states in their sovereign capacities, but emphatically, as the preamble of the constitution declares, by 'the people of the United States.' There can be no doubt that it was competent to the people to invest the general government with all the powers which they might deem proper and necessary; to extend or restrain these powers according to their own good pleasure, and to give them a paramount and supreme authority."[13]

In another foundational case for American government, *McCulloch v. Maryland*, Chief Justice John Marshall invoked the Preamble and stressed the importance of its language—that the government was created by the people.[14] Maryland had claimed that it was the state governments who formed the United States and that therefore it is the states who are sovereign. Maryland argued on this basis that it was constitutional for it to tax the Bank of the United States. The Court rejected Maryland's argument, quoting the Preamble and declaring: "The government proceeds directly from the people; is 'ordained and established,' in the name of the people."

Yet in the two centuries since *McCulloch*, the Court has stopped looking to the Preamble in interpreting the Constitution. The Preamble is regarded as just rhetoric at the beginning of the document, often to be memorized in junior high school civics classes, but with no legal or interpretive significance. By ignoring the Preamble, we forget the idealistic vision that inspired the Constitution and what it was meant to achieve.

WHAT ARE THE VALUES STATED IN THE PREAMBLE?

If the Preamble is read carefully and taken seriously, basic constitutional values can be found within it that should guide the interpretation of the Constitution. The Preamble states that "We the People" have created a Constitution "to form a more perfect Union, establish Justice, insure domestic Tranquility, provide for the common defence, [and] promote the general Welfare." I find in this four crucial values.

First, there is the commitment to a democratic form of government, as expressed in the first three words: "We the People." Or as Abraham Lincoln famously declared in the Gettysburg Address, it is a "government of the people, by the people, for the people."

Second, there is the desire of creating an effective government. The Constitution followed the failed Articles of Confederation, which were the initial effort to govern after the new nation was formed. Under the Articles of

Confederation, there was a very weak federal government. Congress had no authority to tax or to regulate individuals' conduct. The president had little power. There was no federal judiciary. Those who met in Philadelphia in 1787 recognized this and chose not to revise the Articles of Confederation, but rather to draft a new document: the Constitution. An effective government must do many things: create a peaceful society ("ensure domestic Tranquility"), ensure protection from external threats ("provide for the common defence"), and act to benefit its citizens ("promote the general Welfare").

Third, there is the desire to "establish Justice." The goal is a government that is fair in its treatment of its citizens. There must be both fair processes of government and just outcomes from government actions. So many of the complaints in the Declaration of Independence were about the unfairness and lack of justice under English rule. The Declaration of Independence lamented the absence of trial by jury in the American colonies. It spoke of judges who lacked independence and were beholden to the king, meaning a lack of fair proceedings for those before them. It strongly objected to the absence of voting rights and therefore taxation without representation.

Finally, the Preamble says that it exists to provide freedom: to "secure the Blessings of Liberty to ourselves and our posterity." The Constitution is founded to protect individual freedom, to ensure a society where personal liberty, not a duty to the state, is central. In part, of course, this was about structuring government to prevent tyrannical rule. But it was more than that: it was about ensuring government in a manner that would protect basic aspects of liberty for its citizens. Alexander Hamilton even stated that the Bill of Rights was not necessary because the Preamble was able to function as one.[15]

It is notable that there is another key value that is omitted: equality. Equality is never mentioned in the

Preamble or for that matter in the seven articles of the Constitution that were drafted in 1787 or the ten amendments that were ratified in 1791. This is not surprising for a Constitution that explicitly protected the institution of slavery and gave women no rights. The Declaration of Independence proclaimed that "all men are created equal," but the Constitution does not say or imply this. It was not until 1868, when the Fourteenth Amendment was adopted, that the Constitution came to include a guarantee of equal protection of the laws.

But as the Supreme Court has decided since at least the mid-1950s, equality is an implicit and inherent part of liberty.[16] The Fourteenth Amendment applies only to state and local governments, which leads to the embarrassment that there is no constitutional provision that keeps the federal government from denying equal protection. But it can't be right that the federal government can discriminate, including based on race or sex, with impunity and without constitutional constraints. So the Supreme Court sensibly ruled that the due process clause of the Fifth Amendment—which provides that the federal government cannot deny a person life, liberty, or equality—includes an assurance of equal protection as well.

I believe, then, that these five values, four explicitly stated in the Preamble and one that should be seen as implied, should guide interpretion of the Constitution: democratic governance, effective governance, justice, liberty, and equality. In fact, I would go further and argue that virtually every provision in the Constitution can be seen as embodying and implementing one or more of these five values.

Before considering this for each of these five values, I want to be clear as to what I am not doing. I am not making an originalist argument that the meaning of these concepts should be derived from what the drafters of the

Constitution intended. Instead, I am arguing that looking at the structure of the Constitution confirms that these are the five values that should be seen as most important. Nor am I saying or implying that these values will yield determinate, clear answers to constitutional issues. As I explained in chapter 2, there is no method of constitutional interpretation that can do that.

Rather, my hope is to show that it is reasonable, indeed persuasive, to see these as the core values of the Constitution. They are found not just in the Preamble, but confirmed by looking at the structure of the document and what it contains. As the late Yale law professor Charles Black, Jr., persuasively argued over a half century ago, a great deal can be understood by looking at the structure of the Constitution.[17] My goal, then, is to show that the structure of the Constitution confirms that these are the central values that should guide constitutional interpretation.

Democratic Governance

It is profoundly significant that the Constitution begins with the words "We the People." Many countries, in the preambles to their constitutions, invoke God as the basis for government authority. As Liav Orgard explains: "Some preambles emphasize God's supremacy, such as the preambles to the Canadian Charter ('the supremacy of God') or the Swiss Constitution ('in the Name of Almighty God'). Other preambles refer to a specific religion: the Greek preamble refers to the Holy Trinity; in the Irish preamble, the Holy Trinity is mentioned as 'our final end' and a source of authority toward which all actions of 'men and states must be referred.'"[18]

The absence of invocation of religion, or any mention of God in the Constitution, reflects a desire to create a secular government. This should not be surprising because those who drafted the Constitution saw themselves as children of the Enlightenment, where reason had replaced religion as a basis for decisions.

The greatest significance of beginning the document with the words "We the People" was to convey that indeed it was the people who were creating the Constitution and therefore the people who hold ultimate sovereignty. This was in stark contrast to England, and most countries in the world at the time, where sovereignty was thought to reside in a monarchy.

The original version of the Preamble stated: "We the people of the States of New-Hampshire, Massachusetts, Rhode-Island and Providence Plantations, Connecticut, New-York, New-Jersey, Pennsylvania, Delaware, Maryland, Virginia, North-Carolina, South-Carolina, and Georgia, do ordain, declare, and establish the following Constitution for the Government of Ourselves and our Posterity."[19] The text was changed by the Committee of Style, whose members were William Samuel Johnson, Alexander Hamilton, Gouverneur Morris, James Madison, and Rufus King. However, there is no historical record of the drafting process of the Preamble or the reasons for the changes made by the Committee of Style.

Both the initial version and the one adopted begin with the key words "We the People." But the initial version identifies them as people of the states that then existed, while the final version says, "We the People of the United States." In one sense, these phrasings mean exactly the same thing: the people of the United States, by definition, were the people of these states that existed at the time. The difference, though, seems important. In the enacted version, the people saw themselves and declared themselves to be United States citizens; their regional identity as citizens of particular states was subordinate. There also is an important enduring quality in that "We the People of the United States" can include all who will come to be part of this at any future time and not just those who are in the enumerated states. It is also notable, in light of current controversies, that it does not say, "We the citizens of the United States," although there are constitutional provisions limited to citizens.[20] The Constitution should be interpreted to protect *all* of the people within it—citizen and non-citizen, documented or undocumented.

Making it clear that the Constitution was created by the people, and not by the state governments, has had great significance. At various points in American history there have been claims that state governments created the United States government and therefore possess ultimate sovereignty. This was Maryland's argument as to why it had the power to tax the Bank of the United States. In the early nineteenth century, John Calhoun argued that states are sovereign and could interpose their sovereignty between the federal government and the states to prevent abolition of slavery. This argument was tried again during the 1950s and 1960s by southern states trying to avoid desegregation.

There is a textual basis for this claim of state sovereignty. Article VII of the Constitution provides that "the ratification of the conventions of nine states, shall be sufficient for the establishment of this Constitution between the states so ratifying the same." The Constitution was ratified by the states, not by a national referendum. But as explained above, early in American history, the Supreme Court, in *McCulloch v. Maryland*, emphatically rejected this argument. Chief Justice John Marshall wrote: "The government proceeds directly from the people; is 'ordained and established' in the name of the people. . . . The assent of the States, in their sovereign capacity, is implied, in calling a convention, and thus submitting that instrument to the people. But the people were at perfect liberty to accept or reject it; and their act was final. It required not the affirmance, and could not be negatived, by the state governments."[21]

Marshall's argument is rhetorically powerful; it concludes that "the government of the Union . . . is, emphatically, and truly, a government of the people."[22] The Court rejected the view that the Constitution should be regarded as a compact of the states and that the states retain ultimate sovereignty under the Constitution. Ever since, Chief Justice Marshall's view has been the law of the Constitution.

Most important, though, the phrase "We the People" conveys that the United States shall be a democracy. There are many forms of government, and democracy was hardly the most common in the late eighteenth century. Although defining democracy is a difficult task and one beyond my scope here, at the very least it includes officials being chosen by election and serving for fixed terms in office. That is exactly what the Constitution provides. Article I specifies that members of the House of Representatives serve for two-year terms and are elected by the voters, while senators serve six-year terms and, until the adoption of the Seventeenth Amendment in 1913, were chosen by state legislatures. Under Article II, the president is chosen by the Electoral College and serves for a four-year term.[23] These provisions are not incidental to the Constitution: they ensure that those exercising power will serve for a limited number of years and face regular electoral review. The First Amendment, too, is crucial for democracy. Open discussion of candidates is essential for voters to make informed selections in elections: it is through speech that people can influence their government's choice of policies; public officials are held accountable through criticisms that can pave the way for their replacement.

It is notable that many of the amendments adopted

since the Bill of Rights are about perfecting the democratic process and especially expanding who can participate in elections. The Fifteenth Amendment assures that the right to vote cannot be infringed based on race or previous conditions of servitude. The Seventeenth Amendment, mentioned above, provides that the people will directly choose their senators. The Nineteenth Amendment guarantees women the right to vote, declaring: "The right of citizens of the United States to vote shall not be denied or abridged by the United States or by any State on account of sex." The Twenty-third Amendment provides for the District of Columbia to participate in the Electoral College. The Twenty-fourth Amendment outlaws the poll tax—a requirement that people pay a fee in order to vote—in federal elections. The Twenty-sixth Amendment guarantees the right to vote for those eighteen or older.

All of this reflects how much creating democratic rule is truly at the heart of the Constitution and must be regarded as a central value of the Constitution.

Effective Governance

In parsing the words of the Preamble, it is striking how much of it is about creating an effective federal government. Core characteristics of any effective government are stated in the Preamble: the Constitution exists to "insure domestic Tranquility, provide for the common defence, promote the general Welfare." This focus on effective government should not be a surprise and was not accidental. Those who drafted the Constitution were acutely aware of the failure of the Articles of Confederation. Indeed, at the Constitutional Convention, Edmund Randolph explained that a key purpose of the Preamble was to recognize the past failure in governance and to create a successful government: "The object of our preamble ought to be briefly to declare, that the present federal government is insufficient to the general happiness [and] that the conviction of this fact gave birth to this convention."[24]

The challenge for the framers was to create a government that had sufficient powers to be able to govern effectively and deal with problems that were sure to emerge, but one that was sufficiently constrained by checks and balances so as to avoid tyranny and the type of abuses that occurred under British rule (and elsewhere through world history). To achieve the goals of a federal government that could "insure domestic Tranquility, provide for the common defence, promote the general Welfare," they gave Congress many specific powers, including the power to raise taxes, to pay debts, to provide for the common defense and the general welfare, to borrow money, to "regulate Commerce with foreign Nations, and among the several States, and with the Indian Tribes," to coin money, to establish post offices and roads, to issue copyrights and patents, to create courts, to raise an army and a navy, and many other powers. They amplified all of this by saying that Congress could "make all laws which shall be necessary and proper for carrying into Execution the foregoing Powers, and all other Powers vested by this Constitution in the Government of the United States, or in any Department or Officer thereof."

But the framers also were distrustful of congressional power. They limited Congress to the powers "herein granted." They required that it take the action of both houses of Congress, with each quite differently constituted, to enact a law. They gave the president the power to veto a bill passed by Congress, though with Congress possessing the ability to override the veto.

Unlike the Articles of Confederation, the president was given significant powers and there was a federal judiciary, in the form of a Supreme Court and whatever other federal courts Congress would choose to create. All of this was meant to establish a government with the necessary powers to effectively govern and achieve the goals of the Preamble, but without a significant risk of abuses of power.

Far more than the framers could have imagined, the Constitution has succeeded in this. The government they designed has lasted for almost two and a half centuries. It has fought many wars, most successfully. It has grown from being a small nation largely protected by the Atlantic Ocean in the eighteenth-century world to one that stretches across the continent and beyond and into the greatest power the world ever has seen. It has endured a great depression and many serious recessions and become a very wealthy nation, albeit with many still impoverished and with great and growing wealth inequalities. And it has done this all with constant orderly changes of power and without what would be regarded as tyrannical rule, though with decades of slavery and times of serious denials of liberty and freedom.

Focusing on the Constitution's mission of creating an effective government is important in analyzing some of the most important issues that have arisen and likely will continue to arise: the scope of Congress's power to deal with serious social and economic issues. Throughout American history there have been battles over the authority of the federal government to take actions that aid citizens who are less powerful: eliminating slavery, banning child labor, prohibiting race discrimination, protecting the environment. All too often the Supreme Court has limited federal power in these areas, such as in striking down the first federal statute limiting the use of child labor,[25] declaring unconstitutional key provisions of the Voting Rights Act,[26] and invalidating important federal environmental laws.[27] The guidance of the Preamble has been overlooked: the Constitution exists to ensure that the national government has the authority to do all of these things that are part of a "more perfect Union" and provide for "the general Welfare." As William Crosskey declared: "Unless the Preamble is supposed to have been a delusion and a snare, the government established by the Constitution was one with power adequate to the objects the Preamble covers."[28]

Establishing Justice

The Preamble, of course, explicitly states its goal to "establish Justice" and no one would deny that this is among the most important purposes of the Constitution. The concept of justice is critical for civilized governance. In 1215, the Magna Carta declared that the government must provide justice and that justice requires *both* a fair process and fair results. This concept long predates even the Magna Carta. The Bible, Deuteronomy 16:20, says, "Justice, justice shalt thou pursue." Commentators have suggested that the word "justice" is repeated twice in the Bible to convey the importance of both procedural and substantive fairness. In American constitutional law, this means a requirement for both procedural due process (the government must follow adequate procedures when depriving a person of life, liberty, or property) and substantive due process (the government must have adequate reasons when taking away a person's life, liberty, or property).

This, too, is reflected in the structure of the Constitution, though it was made far more explicit in the Bill of Rights that were added soon after its ratification. Article III of the Constitution, which creates the Supreme Court and the authority for Congress to establish lower federal courts, provides that judges "shall hold their

Offices during good Behaviour." The Constitution thus bestows life tenure on federal judges. That is, they hold their positions until they die, retire, or are impeached and removed from office. This job security is to help ensure that judges decide cases based on their best understanding of the facts and law of the matters before them, not to please the voters at a coming election. Many studies have shown that judges who are elected, rather than appointed for life, are much less likely to issue unpopular rulings, such as in favor of those who are on death row. It is impossible to imagine elected judges in southern states striking down the laws that mandated segregation or enforcing the Supreme Court's desegregation orders. Judicial independence is seen as key to the assurance of justice.

Article III, Section 2, guarantees trial by jury, thought to be a crucial check on government power. It provides that "The trial of all Crimes, except in Cases of Impeachment, shall be by jury; and such Trial shall be held in the State where the said Crimes shall have been committed." Article III also seeks to assure justice in some of the most important cases that could arise: accusations of treason. The Constitution provides that "Treason against the United States, shall consist only in levying War against them, or in adhering to their Enemies, giving them Aid and Comfort. No person shall be convicted of Treason unless on the Testimony of two Witnesses to the same overt act, or on Confession in open Court."

But it is the Bill of Rights, with its much greater focus on individual rights than the text of the Constitution, that contains many provisions that are about ensuring justice. The Fifth Amendment, for example, says that no person can be deprived of life, liberty, or property without due process of law. It is remarkable how many of the provisions of the Bill of Rights are about securing justice for those accused of crimes. The Fourth Amendment protects people from arbitrary searches or arrests by the police, declaring: "The right of the people to be secure in their persons, houses, papers, and effects, against unreasonable searches and seizures, shall not be violated, and no Warrants shall issue, but upon probable cause, supported by Oath or affirmation, and particularly describing the place to be searched, and the persons or things to be seized."

The Fifth Amendment prohibits double jeopardy, meaning that a person cannot be tried twice for the same crime, requires a grand jury indictment for a person to be tried for a federal crime, and says that no person can be compelled to be a witness against himself. The Sixth Amendment focuses on "criminal prosecutions" and assures the "right to a speedy and public trial, by an impartial jury," to be confronted with the witnesses against him, and "to have the Assistance of Counsel for his defence." The Eighth Amendment forbids excessive bail and says, "nor shall cruel and unusual punishment be imposed."

There is a logical structure to these amendments: the Fourth Amendment limits what police can do in investigating crimes. The Fifth Amendment restricts prosecutors in bringing criminal prosecutions, such as in preventing double jeopardy and in requiring a grand jury indictment. The Sixth Amendment then governs how criminal trials are to be conducted. And the Eighth Amendment, among other things, says that people cannot be subjected to excessive fines or cruel and unusual punishment. All of this is about fulfilling the Preamble's goal of establishing justice. The provisions are a reaction to the abuses under English rule, where government had the power to search through colonists' possessions, prosecute them for suspected violations of law on weak evidence, and transport them across the seas to trial in England by a judge appointed by the king. A person could be held in prison indefinitely awaiting trial. A trial could occur without a defendant being able to confront his accuser or having assistance of counsel. Harsh punishments, far disproportionate to the crime committed, could be imposed. Many of the Constitution's provisions, and especially those in the Bill of Rights, reflect the desire to prevent these abuses and overall, the central importance of justice.

Securing Liberty

The Preamble states the goal that the Constitution exists to "secure the Blessings of Liberty to ourselves and our Posterity." Interestingly, despite this commitment, the framers of the Constitution saw no need to provide a detailed statement of rights in the Constitution they drafted. Although protecting individual liberties is now regarded by most people as the Constitution's most significant goal, there are few parts of the Constitution, apart from the Bill of Rights, that pertain to individual rights. Article I, Sections 9 and 10, respectively, say that neither the federal nor state governments can enact an ex post facto law or a bill of attainder. An ex post facto law is one that criminally punishes conduct that was lawful when it was done or that increases the punishment for a crime after it was committed. A bill of attainder is a law that orders the punishment of a person without a trial. Article I, Section 9, says that Congress cannot suspend the writ of habeas corpus, except in instances of rebellion or invasion. This was to ensure that those who claim to be illegally held by the government can get a remedy from the courts. Article I, Section 10, also provides that no state shall impair the obligations of contracts.

Article IV provides that the "Citizens of each State shall be entitled to all Privileges and Immunities of Citizens in the several States." This provision limits the ability of a state to discriminate against out-of-state residents with regard to what are called "privileges and immunities."

The only other provisions of the Constitution, apart from the Bill of Rights, that deal with individual liberties focus on protecting the rights of slave owners. Article I, Section 9, prohibited Congress from banning the importation of slaves until 1808, and Article V, which concerns constitutional amendments, provides that this provision cannot be amended. Article IV, Section 2, contains the fugitive slave clause, which required that a slave escaping from one state, even to a nonslave state, be returned to his or her owner. Slavery was very much a part of the fabric of the Constitution, and it was not abolished until the Thirteenth Amendment was adopted in 1865 after the conclusion of the Civil War.

There are many explanations for the absence of a more elaborate statement of individual rights in the Constitution. Some believe that the framers thought it unnecessary because rights were adequately protected by the limitations on the power of the national government and the checks and balances created by the Constitution. Also, the framers might have been fearful that enumerating some rights could be taken as implicitly denying the existence of other liberties. Thus, the Ninth Amendment to the Constitution declares: "The enumeration in the Constitution, of certain rights, shall not be construed to deny or disparage others retained by the people."

Several states ratified the Constitution, but with the insistence that a Bill of Rights be added.[29] Almost immediately after Congress began its first session, James Madison started drafting amendments to the Constitution. Seventeen amendments passed the House of Representatives and were sent to the Senate.[30] The Senate approved twelve of them. Interestingly, one that the Senate did not approve would have prohibited state infringement of freedom of conscience, speech, press, and jury trial; Madison referred to this as "the most valuable amendment in the whole lot."

Many of the constitutional amendments that were ratified were about protecting liberties. In addition to the many criminal procedure protections described above, the First Amendment protects religious freedom by preventing Congress from enacting any law "respecting an establishment of religion or prohibiting the free exercise thereof," or "abridging the freedom of speech, or of the press; or the right of the people peaceably to assemble, and to petition the government for a redress of grievances." As discussed in the earlier chapters, the Second Amendment protects a right of people to "keep and bear arms," though its language is an enigma in its declaration: "A well regulated Militia, being necessary to the security of a free State, the right of the people to keep and bear Arms, shall not be infringed." The Third Amendment prevents the government from requiring that people house soldiers, a practice of the British government that was objected to in the Declaration of Independence. The Fifth Amendment provides that the government can take private property for public use, but only if it pays just compensation, and also ensures that the government must provide due process when it deprives a person of life, liberty, or property. The Seventh Amendment protects a right to trial by jury in civil cases.

Many of the freedoms protected by the Supreme Court are not enumerated but come instead from its interpreting the word "liberty" in the due process clauses. For example, over the course of the last century, the Court has protected rights that are not mentioned in the Constitution's text, such as freedom of association, the right to marry, the right to procreate, the right to custody of one's children, the right to keep the family together, the right of parents to control the upbringing of their children, the right to purchase and use contraceptives, the right to abortion, the right of competent adults to refuse medical care, and the right of adults to engage in private consensual homosexual activity. All of this reflects the importance of "securing liberty" as a central value of the Constitution, as stated in its Preamble, reflected in its provisions, and embodied in decades of Supreme Court jurisprudence.

Two characteristics about the protection of individual rights in the Constitution should be noted. First, the Constitution's protections of individual liberties apply only to the government; private conduct generally does not have to comply with the Constitution. Only the Thirteenth Amendment, which prohibits slavery and involuntary servitude, directly protects individuals from private conduct.

Second, the Bill of Rights provisions protecting individual liberties initially were deemed to apply only to the federal government and not to state or local governments. Not until the twentieth century did the Supreme Court decide that almost all of the Bill of Rights provisions apply to state and local governments through the due process clause of the Fourteenth Amendment.

Achieving Equality

My goal through this chapter has been to identify the values of the Preamble and to show that they are reflected throughout the text of the Constitution. My hope is that those of all ideologies can agree that these are core values of the Constitution. But unlike the other values I have identified—democratic government, effective governance, establishing justice, securing liberty—equality is never mentioned in the Preamble. Nor is it mentioned in the text of the Constitution or any of the Bill of Rights provisions. Unlike the other values, it is not plausible to argue that equality was a central value of the Constitution when it was drafted in 1787. As I have explained, the Constitution protected the rights of slave owners and accorded women no rights; it was really about protecting the rights of white male property owners.

My argument for treating equality as a central value of the Constitution must go beyond the Preamble. I would think that few today would deny the importance of this value, even though there will be enormous disagreement about what it should mean. I, of course, can argue—as the Supreme Court has concluded—that equality is implicit in a guarantee of liberty. That is how the Court has found a constitutional requirement for equal protection that applies to the federal government.[31] But there is also something inherently unsatisfying about this argument because equality is not simply an aspect of liberty; equality is a crucial value in itself. Indeed, there is a constant tension between liberty and equality. Any law that prohibits discrimination limits a freedom to discriminate.

I think it is stronger to argue that the Fourteenth Amendment reflects and embodies the importance of equal protection as a central value of the Constitution. It is a huge mistake—often made by originalists—to focus on the Constitution as originally written and ignore how it was subsequently changed. The post–Civil War amendments—the Thirteenth, Fourteenth, and Fifteenth Amendments—profoundly changed the relationship between the federal government and the states. The Thirteenth Amendment denied the ability of states to allow slavery. The Fourteenth Amendment says that *state* governments cannot deprive their citizens of the privileges or immunities of citizenship, or deprive any person of life, liberty, or property without due process of law, or deny any person equal protection of the laws.

Although the Fourteenth Amendment made equal

protection for all persons a core constitutional value, it took a long time for this to be recognized. In its initial decisions concerning equal protection, the Court took a very narrow approach. The first Supreme Court case to interpret the Thirteen and Fourteenth Amendments came soon after they were ratified, in 1873, in the *Slaughterhouse Cases.*[32] Seeing a huge surplus of cattle in Texas, the Louisiana legislature gave a monopoly in the livestock landing and the slaughterhouse business for the city of New Orleans to the Crescent City Live-Stock Landing and Slaughter-House Company. The law required that the company allow any person to slaughter animals in the slaughterhouse for a fixed fee. The monopoly was created to give enormous profits to a small group of people in Louisiana. They could cheaply buy Texas cattle and then sell it for monopoly profits.

Several butchers brought suit challenging the grant of the monopoly. They argued that the state law impermissibly violated their right to practice their trade. The butchers invoked many of the provisions of the recently adopted constitutional amendments. They argued that the restriction created involuntary servitude, deprived them of their property without due process of law, denied them equal protection of the laws, and abridged their privileges and immunities as citizens.

The Supreme Court narrowly construed all of these provisions and rejected the plaintiffs' challenge to the legislature's grant of a monopoly. As for equal protection, the Court said that the equal protection clause only was meant to protect blacks and offered the prediction that "we doubt very much whether any action of a State not directed by way of discrimination against the negroes as a class, or on account of their race, will ever be held to come within the purview of this provision."[33] That, of course, is not what the Constitution says. The Fourteenth Amendment could have been written so that it was limited to guaranteeing equal protection to former slaves or to those of African descent. But instead it says that "*no* person" shall be denied equal protection of the laws.

For almost a century after the *Slaughterhouse Cases*, the Court followed this narrow reading of the equal protection clause and refused to use it to stop other types of discrimination. For example, two years after the *Slaughterhouse Cases*, in 1875, the Supreme Court held that it was constitutional to deny women the right to vote.[34] Virginia Minor, a leader of the women's suffrage movement in Missouri, attempted to register to vote on October 15, 1872, in St. Louis County, Missouri. Missouri refused to allow this because she was a woman. Her husband, Francis Minor, who was a lawyer, filed a lawsuit against Reese Happersett, the registrar who had rejected her application to register to vote. Minor argued that the denial of the right to vote to women violated equal protection and infringed the "privileges or immunities" of citizenship guaranteed by the Fourteenth Amendment. In *Minor v. Happersett*, in 1875, the Court flatly rejected these contentions and held it constitutional for a state to deny women the right to vote.

It took another forty-five years, until the Nineteenth Amendment was adopted in 1920, for women to be granted the right to vote. It was not for another ninety-six years, until 1971, that the Supreme Court for the first time found that sex discrimination violated equal protection. The Court's prophecy in the *Slaughterhouse Cases* that equal protection would never be used except to stop race discrimination turned out to be wrong, but it took a century for the Court to abandon that view which so ignores the Fourteenth Amendment's assurance that no person may be denied equal protection of the laws.

At the same time that the Court was limiting equal protection to racial discrimination, it was also refusing to find racist government actions to be unconstitutional.

An institution that exists especially to protect minorities did exactly the opposite, consistently upholding laws that harmed minority races. The Court did not create the racist attitudes that led to the laws that required segregation of the races. The Court did not adopt those laws. But the Court could have declared them unconstitutional and held that laws mandating segregation are based on the assumption of the superiority of one race and the inferiority of another and that is inconsistent with a guarantee of equal protection of the laws. Or the Court could have ruled narrowly by finding that the facilities were not equal and that separate and unequal facilities violate the Constitution. Either way, the Court could have prevented and ended the apartheid that lasted for decades.

The most important case was *Plessy v. Ferguson,* in 1896.[35] It, too, is widely regarded as one of the Supreme Court's worst decisions in history. In *Plessy v. Ferguson,* the Court upheld laws that mandated that blacks and whites use "separate but equal" facilities.

A Louisiana law adopted in 1890 required railroad companies to provide separate but equal accommodations for whites and blacks; the law required there to be separate coaches, divided by a partition, for each race. In 1892, Louisiana prosecuted Homer Adolph Plessy, a man who was seven-eighths Caucasian, for refusing to leave the railroad car assigned to whites. This was a test case deliberately brought by those who opposed government-mandated segregation. Plessy—an octoroon, so-called because one of his eight great-grandparents was of African descent—was regarded as the ideal plaintiff to challenge laws like Louisiana's that had become so common in the South after the end of Reconstruction.

In a 7–1 decision, the Supreme Court ruled against Plessy and upheld the Louisiana law. The opinion was written by Justice Henry Billings Brown, who had been appointed to the Court in 1890 by President Benjamin

Harrison. Justice Brown, a Northerner who had grown up in Massachusetts and practiced law in Detroit before becoming a federal judge, concluded that laws requiring "separate but equal" facilities are constitutional and declared: "We cannot say that a law which authorizes or even requires the separation of the two races in public conveyances is unreasonable, or more obnoxious to the Fourteenth Amendment than the acts of Congress requiring separate schools for colored children in the District of Columbia, the constitutionality of which does not seem to have been questioned, or the corresponding acts of state legislatures." The same Congress that ratified the Fourteenth Amendment had also voted to segregate the District of Columbia public schools, indicating that it did not see government-mandated segregation as a denial of equal protection.

Plessy argued to the Supreme Court that laws requiring segregation are based on an assumption of the inferiority of blacks and thus stigmatize them with a second-class status. Such actions by a state government, deeming one race superior and the other inferior, should be regarded as inimical to the Constitution's guarantee of equal protection of the laws. The Supreme Court rejected this argument: "We consider the underlying fallacy of the plaintiff's argument to consist in the assumption that the enforced separation of the two races stamps the colored race with a badge of inferiority. If this be so, it is not by reason of anything found in the act, but solely because the colored race chooses to put that construction upon it."[36] Stunningly, then, the Court said that it was the fault of the "colored race" that it saw laws segregating the races as being based on a belief in white superiority, even though that was often expressed in legislatures and by elected officials, especially in southern states.

Justice Harlan was the sole dissenter and wrote that "everyone knows that the statute in question had its origin in the purpose, not so much to exclude white persons from railroad cars occupied by blacks, as to exclude colored people from coaches occupied by or assigned to white persons."[37] Of course, he is right: laws requiring segregation were all about proclaiming the superiority of one race and the inferiority of the other. Justice Harlan concluded eloquently: "In view of the Constitution, in the eye of the law, there is in this country no superior, dominant, ruling class of citizens. There is no caste here. Our Constitution is color-blind, and neither knows nor tolerates classes among citizens. In respect of civil rights, all citizens are equal before the law. The humblest is the peer of the most powerful."

Justice Harlan, of course, was correct: *Plessy v. Ferguson* is remembered as among the most tragically misguided Supreme Court decisions in American history. But it took over half a century before the Supreme Court repudiated its racist holding. After *Plessy*, "separate but equal" became the law of the land, even though separate was anything but equal. Southern states, border states, and even parts of some northern states had laws that segregated the races in every aspect of life. Whites and blacks were born in separate hospitals, played in separate parks and on separate beaches, drank from separate water fountains and used separate bathrooms, attended separate schools, ate at separate restaurants and stayed at separate hotels, served in separate army units, and were buried in separate cemeteries. By every measure and standard, separate was never equal, as the facilities for blacks were never nearly the same as those for whites.

It is often forgotten today that *Plessy v. Ferguson* was not an isolated Supreme Court decision. In case after case, the Court reaffirmed and upheld the ability of states to enforce apartheid.

For example, "separate but equal" was expressly approved in the realm of education. In *Cumming v. Board of*

Education, in 1899, the Court upheld the government's operation of a high school open only for white students while none was available for blacks.[38] The Court emphasized that local authorities were to be allowed great discretion in allocating funds between blacks and whites and that "any interference on the part of Federal authority with the management of such schools cannot be justified except in the case of a clear and unmistakable disregard of rights secured by the supreme law of the land."

In *Berea College v. Kentucky,* in 1908, the Supreme Court affirmed the conviction of a private college that had violated a Kentucky law that required the separation of the races in education.[39] In *Gong Lum v. Rice,* in 1927, the Supreme Court concluded that Mississippi could exclude a child of Chinese ancestry from attending schools reserved for whites.[40] The Court said that the law was settled that racial segregation was permissible and that it did not "think that the question is any different, or that any different result can be reached . . . where the issue is as between white pupils and the pupils of the yellow races."[41]

All of this did not begin to change until *Brown v. Board of Education.*[42] Of course, all of this is a powerful argument against originalism. Few today would accept a method of interpretation that provides no protection from discrimination under equal protection to women or that finds segregation to be constitutional. It is also why the values of the Constitution should not be identified or defended in term of the original understanding. Equal protection should be deemed a core value of the Constitution even if it has been viewed as such only for the last half century.

The recognition of the importance of equality as a basic constitutional value, in part, is about fundamental fairness. It is wrong to treat a person differently from others similarly situated—especially if it is on the basis of immutable characteristics like race, sex, or sexual orientation—without a sufficient reason. Also, the history of racism, sexism, and homophobia should cause us to be suspicious when the government uses these characteristics as a basis for a decision and insists that there is an adequate justification for the government's action.

These are the core values of the Constitution: democratic government, effective governance, establishing justice, securing liberty, providing equality. In the next chapters, I will offer a progressive vision of the meaning of the Constitution, one that, I believe, will allow for each of these values to be more fully realized.

4

ENSURING DEMOCRATIC GOVERNMENT

In chapter 3, I explained how the Preamble and the structure of the Constitution create a commitment to democratic government. But there are crucial aspects of contemporary American government that are inconsistent with this commitment. I focus on three of these—the Electoral College, partisan gerrymandering, and racial discrimination in voting—and what should be done to change them.

THE ELECTORAL COLLEGE

The only number that matters in a presidential election is 270. That is the number of electoral votes it takes to be elected president of the United States. There are 538 electors and victory requires getting a majority in the Electoral College. If no candidate receives a majority, then the House of Representatives chooses the president, with each state getting one vote.

Each state has the number of electors equal to the sum of its senators and representatives. Additionally, the Twenty-third Amendment allocates three electors to the District of Columbia. The six states with the most electors are California (55), Texas (38), New York (29), Florida (29), Illinois (20), and Pennsylvania (20). The seven smallest states in population—Alaska, Delaware, Montana, North Dakota, South Dakota, Vermont, and Wyoming—each have 3 electors.

Each state determines its own method for choosing electors. Today, all the states select electors based on who wins the popular vote. But in the nineteenth century, in about half the states, electors were chosen by the state legislatures.

In principle, the electors are to vote in accord with the popular vote in their state. Occasionally, there has been an elector who fails to do so, but this so-called faithless elector has never decided the outcome of a presidential election.

The Electoral College does not actually meet. Rather, the electors in each state gather on the Monday after the second Tuesday in December and determine how the state will allocate its electoral votes. "People frequently speak of this group as the 'electoral college,' but, in reality, that term is something of a misnomer," explains Matthew Hoffman. "In fact, it is hard to imagine any body less collegial. Strictly speaking, the 'electoral college' is not a single body at all, but rather an aggregation of fifty-one different bodies, each of which meets and votes separately. This configuration is not a historical accident, but a well-considered constitutional requirement. Both Article II and the Twelfth Amendment specifically mandate that the electors meet to cast their ballots 'in their respective states.'"[1] Although this likely reflected concerns about travel at a time when it was far more difficult, it also was to prevent the group from deliberating and functioning as a collegial body where votes could be changed by discussion and compromise.

The Electoral College emerged as the way of choosing the president late in the deliberations at the Constitutional Convention of 1787. Many different methods of selecting the president were debated, such as by direct popular election, selection by the governors of the states, and election by Congress as in a parliamentary system.[2] The Electoral College, once proposed, attracted widespread support at the convention.

In large part, this reflected the framers' distrust of majority rule. They had the Senate chosen by state legislatures, Supreme Court justices and lower-court federal judges selected by the president with Senate approval, and the president determined by the Electoral College. There is no doubt that the Electoral College was created because of a distrust of the people and democracy. Alexander Hamilton, in *Federalist* No. 68, explained that the "immediate election [of the president] should be made by men most capable of analyzing the qualities adapted to the station. . . . A small number of persons, selected by their fellow-citizens from the general mass, will be most likely to possess the information and discernment requisite to such complicated investigations."[3] "If the manner of it [presidential election] be not perfect," said Hamilton, "it is at least excellent. It unites in an eminent degree all the advantages the union of which was to be desired."[4] This anti-democratic feature of the Electoral College was enthusiastically embraced.

Also, small states strongly favored the Electoral College because it gave them much greater influence than they would have had in the direct election of the president. In fact, it is possible today that states with only 22 percent of the country's population can choose the president.

The Electoral College was also very much a product of the compromises concerning slavery that were at the core of the Constitution's drafting and ratification. In Article I, the Constitutional Convention had agreed to the three-fifths clause—whereby slaves were counted as three-fifths of a person for purposes of determining population size, which was the basis for allocating seats in the House of Representatives. The southern states had small nonslave populations relative to the northern states; the three-fifths clause helped to equalize the balance of power in the House. But if the president were elected by direct vote, that advantage would disappear: actual voters in the North would outnumber voters in the South because slaves could not vote. The Electoral College was proposed as a way of dealing with this: state electors would be allocated according to the number of seats in Congress and the three-fifths clause meant that the South's half-million slaves counted toward that.

This was explicitly understood and expressed at the Constitutional Convention. Oliver Ellsworth of Connecticut proposed "electors," appointed by the state legislatures. But according to his plan, these electors would be apportioned based on population, so small states would have no special advantage.[5] In response, James Madison, a slaveholder from Virginia, said that "one difficulty . . . of a serious nature" made election by the people impossible, noting that the "right of suffrage was much more diffusive in the Northern than the Southern States; and the latter could have no influence in the election on the score of the Negroes."[6] As Paul Finkelman states, "In order to guarantee that the nonvoting slaves could nevertheless influence the presidential election, Madison favored the creation of the electoral college."[7]

Hugh Williamson, a delegate to the Constitutional Convention from North Carolina, was even more explicit about this. He noted that under a direct election of the president, Virginia would be at a disadvantage because "her slaves will have no suffrage."[8] The same would be true for all of the South.

As Yale law professor Akhil Reed Amar has repeatedly pointed out, the Electoral College "was originally much more about slavery than about a big-state, small-state balance."[9] This, in itself, should make us deeply uncomfortable with the Electoral College.

Most fundamentally, the Electoral College is inconsistent with the core constitutional value of democratic governance. Five times in American history, including twice in the early part of the twenty-first century—in 1824, 1876, 1888, 2000, and 2016—the candidate who lost the popular vote became president of the United States. On November 6, 2012, Donald Trump tweeted, "The electoral college is a disaster for a democracy." For once, I can say that Donald Trump was right. The United States is the only country in the world that chooses its head of state in this way and the only nation where a person who loses the popular vote can be chosen as its chief executive.

The Electoral College is undesirable, yes—but I want to go further: I believe that it is unconstitutional and should be declared so.

Before I explain why, it is worth thinking about whether a provision of the Constitution can itself be unconstitutional. The answer is clearly yes if it violates one of the subsequent amendments to the Constitution. Article I authorizes Congress to regulate interstate commerce and this would allow federal licensing of the press; but the First Amendment unquestionably makes that unconstitutional. Article III permits a federal court to hear a suit against a state by citizens of other states; but the Eleventh Amendment was adopted to preclude such litigation and has been interpreted broadly by the Supreme Court to prevent states from being sued. The amendments to the Constitution modify its text.

The Supreme Court has long held that the Fifth Amendment assurance of due process of law includes a requirement that the federal government not deny any person equal protection of the laws. And for over a half century, the Court has ruled that a core aspect of equal protection is one person, one vote; every person must have an equal ability to influence the outcome of an election. In *Wesberry v. Sanders*, in 1964, the Supreme Court announced that as much as practicable, the Constitution requires that "one man's vote . . . is to be worth as much as another's."[10] In *Bush v. Gore*, in 2000, the Court stated, "Having once granted the right to vote on equal terms, the State may not . . . value one person's vote over that of another."[11]

The Electoral College is inconsistent with this basic principle of democracy: one person, one vote. Because every state has two senators, smaller states have disproportionate influence in choosing the president. Wyoming has a population of 584,153 and has three electoral votes, which means that each Wyoming elector represents 194,717 voters. California has a population of 38,800,000 and has fifty-five electoral votes, so each elector represents 705,454 voters. Each presidential vote in Wyoming is worth 3.6 times more than each vote in California. Courts thus can and should declare that the guarantee of equal protection found in the Fifth Amendment modifies Article II of the Constitution and requires that electors be allocated strictly on the basis of population.

At first blush there is likely discomfort with the courts fundamentally changing the system for the election of the president by declaring unconstitutional the method of choosing the president outlined in Article II. But the judicial role is most important when the political system is incapable of reforming itself to comply with the Constitution.[12] This is exactly why the Court's decisions concerning apportionment were so crucial. Prior to the 1960s, many state legislatures and congressional districts were badly malapportioned; within a state they varied widely in population. But those who benefited from this were not about to redraw legislative districts to vote themselves out of power. The Court articulated the one-person, one-vote rule: for any legislative body, all districts must be about the same in population.[13] Earl Warren remarked that the most important decisions during his tenure on the Court were those ordering reapportionment precisely because the political process was never going to solve the constitutional problem.[14]

The same is true with regard to the Electoral College. Amending the Constitution requires approval of two-thirds of both houses of Congress and then three-fourths of the states. There is no way that smaller states that benefit greatly from the Electoral College will ever approve a constitutional amendment to eliminate it. There have been constant proposed constitutional amendments to change the Electoral College; one commentator estimated that "nearly one-tenth of all constitutional amendments proposed in Congress have sought electoral college reform."[15] It is especially important for the Court to act because the political process will never deal with the clear unconstitutionality of the Electoral College.

The problem of the Electoral College is compounded by state laws that provide that electoral votes are awarded on a winner-take-all basis. In all states except Nebraska and Maine, the candidate who wins the popular vote in a state—even by the narrowest margin—gets all of the electoral votes from that state. This, too, greatly increases the chances of the Electoral College choosing a president who lost the popular vote.

Effectively winner-take-all meant that a vote for, say, Donald Trump in California or Hillary Clinton in Texas had absolutely no effect. Nebraska and Maine allocate electoral votes by congressional district, with the elector for each congressional district voting for the candidate who got the majority of the votes there and the remaining electors chosen statewide. This means that there is a much more proportional allocation of electoral votes in

Nebraska and Maine compared to all other states where it is winner-take-all.

At the very least, the courts should declare winner-take-all—provided by state law and not by the Constitution—unconstitutional. This would not entail declaring the Electoral College itself unconstitutional, just striking down state laws that allocate electors. This would greatly increase the chances that the winner of the popular vote would be chosen as president. That is what should happen in a democracy. Moreover, even apart from the Constitution, there is a strong argument that winner-take-all has a significant racially discriminatory effect against minority voters and thus violates section 2 of the Voting Rights Act, which prohibits electoral systems that limit or dilute the ability of racial and language minorities to elect candidates of their choice. Matthew Hoffman explains: "Voting in presidential elections is highly polarized along racial lines. Consequently, choosing presidential electors through the winner-take-all system results in a paradigmatic example of the kind of discrimination that section 2 was meant to eliminate. Its all-or-nothing character prevents the formation of politically cohesive blocs of African-American voters—and possibly blocs of other minority voters as well—even in states where they clearly could choose one or more electors under an alternative system."[16]

It is hard to even come up with a justification for a system for electing the president that is so inconsistent with basic principles of democratic governance. A primary justification advanced in recent years is that the Electoral College causes presidential candidates to pay attention to smaller states.[17] The concern is that there would be little reason for those running for president to campaign in smaller states that would have minimal impact on the overall national vote. I question whether this is sufficient to justify the profoundly anti-democratic Electoral College. Moreover, the reverse argument is currently in effect: the Electoral College system means that candidates will largely ignore and not campaign in states where it is obvious who is going to win. I live in California and rarely were there ads from either candidate in the weeks leading up to the 2016 presidential election. I am sure the same was true in Texas. But when I was in Ohio weeks before the election, ads for the candidates were everywhere. Any system of election will influence where campaigning is done, but that is not a reason to keep the Electoral College.

We are now governed by a president who lost the popular vote by three million votes. It does not matter whether it is a Republican or Democrat who benefits. The Electoral College is inconsistent with the promise of democratic rule found in the Preamble. The Constitution should be interpreted to mean that the requirement for equal protection found in the Fifth and Fourteenth Amendments modifies the text of Article II, which allocates representatives in the Electoral College. If nothing else, courts should invalidate state laws requiring winner-take-all and require allocation of electors proportionate to population. Never again should there be a president who lost the popular vote.

PARTISAN GERRYMANDERING

Partisan gerrymandering—where the political party controlling the legislature draws election districts to maximize seats for that party—is nothing new. In fact, the practice is named for Elbridge Gerry, the Massachusetts governor who, in 1812, signed a bill that redrew the state senate election districts to benefit his Democratic-Republican Party. But what has changed are the sophisticated computer programs and other techniques that make partisan gerrymandering far more effective than ever before. The political party that controls the legislature now can draw election districts to gain a much more disproportionate number of safe seats for itself. Through the use of "map-drawing software, highly detailed data about voting patterns, and sophisticated statistical analyses and tools, incumbents [draw] electoral districts to ensure continued control over legislatures under virtually any conceivable voting pattern. Voters no longer choose their representatives; maps crafted by party leaders and their consultants choose representatives, depriving the people of a meaningful voice in government."[18]

This is exactly what occurred in Wisconsin, where Republicans took advantage of their control of the legislature to give themselves a much greater number of seats relative to their voting strength. The Republicans employed two gerrymandering techniques in order to lessen the effect of votes for Democrats statewide: cracking—"dividing a party's supporters among multiple districts so that they fall short of a majority in each one"—and packing—"concentrating one party's backers in a few districts that they win by overwhelming margins."[19]

The gerrymandering worked. As the federal court explained: "In 2012, the Democrats received 51.4 percent of the statewide vote, but that percentage translated into only 39 Assembly seats. A roughly equivalent vote share for Republicans (52 percent in 2014), however, translated into 63 seats—a 24 seat disparity."[20] Put another way, "in 2012, the Republicans won 61 percent of Assembly seats with only 48.6 percent of the statewide vote. . . . In 2014, the Republicans garnered 52 percent of the statewide vote but secured 64 percent of Assembly seats. . . . Thus, the Republican Party in 2012 won about 13 Assembly seats in excess of what a party would be expected to win with 49 percent of the statewide vote, and in 2014 it won about 10 more Assembly seats than would be expected with 52 percent of the vote."[21]

The same is true in many other states. In North Carolina, essentially a purple state, Republicans were able to convert a slim majority in the votes cast for the state legislature into a supermajority of the seats in both houses and ten of thirteen congressional seats.[22] In Pennsylvania, where the voters are fairly evenly split between the parties, gerrymandering has meant that Republicans have thirteen of the state's eighteen seats in the U.S. House of Representatives.[23]

Partisan gerrymandering is inconsistent with basic principles of democratic government, as well as constitutional guarantees of equality in voting. Democracy involves voters choosing their elected officials, but partisan gerrymandering has elected officials choosing their voters.

Justice Ginsburg, writing for the Court in *Arizona State Legislature v. Arizona Redistricting Commission* (2015), explained that independent redistricting commissions are desirable because they "impede legislators from choosing their voters instead of facilitating the voters' choice of their representatives."[24]

With partisan gerrymandering, in order to protect its own control of the legislature, one political party hijacks the power of the state in order to "ma[k]e fruitless" another party's efforts to mobilize and elect representatives.[25] By its very definition, as the Supreme Court explained, partisan gerrymandering is "the drawing of legislative district lines to subordinate adherents of one political party and entrench a rival party in power."[26]

With partisan gerrymandering it is not "We the People" choosing our representatives; elections do not reflect the will of the "great body of society," which James Madison described as the core of democratic self-government,[27] but rather the will of the partisan incumbents who draw the maps. In *Federalist* No. 37, James Madison explained: "The genius of republican liberty seems to demand . . . not only that all power should be derived from the people, but that those intrusted with it should be kept in dependence on the people."[28] But partisan gerrymandering prevents that from happening.

Justice John Paul Stevens expressed this well when he stated in a dissent: "[The] danger of a partisan gerrymander is that the representative will perceive that the people who put her in power are those who drew the map rather than those who cast ballots, and she will feel beholden not to a subset of her constituency, but to no part of her constituency at all. The problem, simply put, is that the will of the cartographers rather than the will of the people will govern."[29] Even Justice Antonin Scalia, who wrote the opinion that partisan gerrymandering cannot be challenged in the federal courts, spoke of "the incompatibility of severe partisan gerrymanders with democratic principles."[30]

As Justice Black explained: "No right is more precious in a free country than that of having a choice in the election of those who make the laws under which, as good citizens, they must live. Other rights, even the most basic, are illusory if the right to vote is undermined."[31] Partisan gerrymandering undermines the right to vote by rigging the outcome of legislative elections.

Partisan gerrymandering thus very much undermines democratic rule and electoral accountability. In 2014 and 2016, House incumbents were reelected, respectively, in 95 percent and 97 percent of all the races.[32] This figure has not fallen below 85 percent in over half a century.[33] A stunning illustration of the effects of partisan gerrymandering is that in December 2016, Democrat Doug Jones was elected senator in Alabama over Republican Roy Moore, but Jones lost in six of the seven congressional districts in the state. The only district Jones carried was one that was created to pack African American voters: it encompasses much of rural western Alabama's African American population, with tentacles to include predominately black areas of Montgomery and Birmingham.[34]

California and Arizona are among a minority of states that have independent commissions to draw election districts. In a majority of the states, the political party that controls the state legislature draws districts for both the U.S. House of Representatives and the state legislature. They inevitably do so in a way that maximizes their political control. To be clear, both Democrats and Republicans do this when they can.

Unfortunately, up until now, the Supreme Court has refused to deal with this serious threat to democratic governance. Initially, in 1986, the Court, in *Davis v. Bandemer*, held that challenges to gerrymandering are justiciable and that substantial vote dilution through gerrymandering denies equal protection.[35] The Court said that gerrymandering is unconstitutional if it involves "intentional discrimination against an identifiable political group and an actual discriminatory effect on that group."[36]

But in *Vieth v. Jubelirer*, in 2004, the Court dismissed a challenge to partisan gerrymandering, and a plurality of four justices said that such suits are inherently nonjusticiable political questions.[37] Republicans controlled the Pennsylvania legislature, and they drew election districts to maximize Republican seats. In *Vieth*, the plurality concluded that *Davis v. Bandemer* had proven impossible to implement. The plurality opinion, written by Justice Scalia, concluded that challenges to partisan gerrymandering are "political questions" that cannot be adjudicated by the courts. Justice Scalia, joined by Chief Justice Rehnquist and Justices O'Connor and Thomas, said that there are no judicially discoverable or manageable standards and no basis for courts ever to decide that partisan gerrymandering offends the Constitution.

Justice Kennedy, concurring in the judgment (agreeing with the result of Justice Scalia's decision, but not with the reasons), provided the fifth vote for the majority. He agreed to dismiss the case because of the lack of judicially discoverable or manageable standards, but he said that he believed that such standards might be developed in the future. Thus, he disagreed with the majority opinion that challenges to partisan gerrymandering are always political questions; he said that when standards are developed, such cases can be heard. Justices Stevens, Souter, and Breyer wrote dissenting opinions, which Justice Ginsburg joined, arguing that there are standards that courts can implement.

The Court offered no more clarity in a subsequent decision, *League of United Latin American Citizens v. Perry*, in 2006, where it again dismissed a challenge to partisan gerrymandering.[38] After Republicans gained control of the Texas legislature in 2002, they redrew districts for Congress so as to maximize likely seats for Republicans. The redistricting was very successful. The Texas congressional delegation went from seventeen Democrats and fifteen Republicans after the 2002 election to eleven Democrats and twenty-one Republicans in the 2004 election. Many lawsuits were brought and again the Court, in a 5–4 decision, with no majority opinion, dismissed the case.

But in November 2016, a three-judge court in Wisconsin found the state's partisan gerrymandering to be unconstitutional.[39] This was the first court to find gerrymandering to be unconstitutional since the Supreme Court decisions a decade earlier. The three-judge federal court, in a lengthy opinion by Judge Kenneth Ripple of the Seventh Circuit, said that it now is possible to measure the effects of partisan gerrymandering by quantifying an "efficiency gap." The court explained that "the efficiency gap is the difference between the parties' respective wasted votes in an election, divided by the total number of votes cast."

The court applied this through a three-part test: First, plaintiffs have to establish that a state had an intent to gerrymander for partisan advantage. Second, the plaintiffs need to prove a partisan effect, by proving that the efficiency gap for a plan exceeds a certain numerical threshold. Third, and finally, if the plaintiffs meet these requirements, then the burden is on the defendants to rebut the presumption by showing that the plan "is the necessary result of a legitimate state policy, or inevitable given the state's underlying political geography." If the state is unable to rebut the presumption, then the plan is unconstitutional.

The three-judge court used this test and concluded in a 2–1 decision that the election districts for the Wisconsin legislature were drawn with the purpose and effect of enhancing Republican seats and decreasing those for Democrats. The court found no legitimate purpose for this disparity and found the partisan gerrymandering to be unconstitutional.

The Supreme Court granted review of the case, *Gill v. Whitford*, and heard oral arguments in October 2017. But in June 2018, the Court reversed the lower court on procedural grounds.[40] The Court said that the plaintiffs in the suit lacked standing because they failed to allege that they resided in districts that had been subjected to gerrymandering. The Court left open the possibility of the plaintiffs doing this. But with Anthony Kennedy gone from the Court, it is hard to see five votes to declare partisan gerrymandering unconstitutional for the foreseeable future.

There is strong nonpartisan support for eliminating partisan gerrymandering. A Harris Poll found that "over seven in ten Americans believe (71 percent—48 percent strongly so) that those who stand to benefit from redrawing congressional districts should not have a say in how they are redrawn."[41] The Harris Poll revealed "comparable views when compared by both political affiliation (74 percent Republicans, 73 percent Democrats, 71 percent independents) and underlying political philosophy (69 percent Conservative, 71 percent Moderate, 73 percent Liberal)." Indeed, partisan gerrymandering long has been condemned. As an amicus brief filed by historians in the Supreme Court explained: "Contrary to some misconceptions, although partisan gerrymanders have occurred at various times, they never have been regarded as an acceptable feature of American democracy. Rather, consistently since its inception, partisan gerrymandering has been forcefully denounced as unconstitutional, as a form of corruption that threatens American democracy, and as an infringement on voters' rights."[42]

But as with the Electoral College and also challenges to malapportionment of legislatures described above, the legislative process will not fix the problem. Legislators who benefit from partisan gerrymandering are not about to vote for an alternative election system that has a likelihood of taking them and their political party out of power.

Partisan gerrymandering is undesirable whether done by Democrats or Republicans. The Supreme Court should hold that challenges to it can be heard in the federal courts and explain that districting is unconstitutional when it disproportionately favors a political party with no other explanation besides partisanship. This is a chance for the Court to take a huge step to having our democratic process work.

RACIAL DISCRIMINATION IN VOTING

The United States has a long and disgraceful history of race discrimination with regard to voting. After the Civil War, the Fourteenth Amendment was ratified in 1868; it includes a provision that no state may deny any person equal protection of the laws. Two years later, the Fifteenth Amendment was ratified to explicitly deal with the problem of race discrimination in voting. It states: "The right of citizens of the United States to vote shall not be denied or abridged by the United States or by any State on account of race, color, or previous condition of servitude."

As a result of these amendments and Reconstruction, more than half a million African American men in the South became voters in the 1870s. (Women, of course, did not get the right to vote until the Nineteenth Amendment was ratified in 1920.) There was a dramatic effect to this enfranchisement of black men. In Mississippi, for example, former slaves were half of the state's population, and Mississippi elected two black U.S. senators and a number of black state officials, including a lieutenant governor.[43]

Because of the Hays-Tilden compromise that decided the 1876 election, Reconstruction was ended and northern troops were withdrawn from the South. After a very close election with winner in doubt, Democrats agreed to support the election of Republican Rutherford B. Hayes in exchange for the end of Reconstruction, which had included military rule over the former rebel states. Southern states quickly adopted laws to deny rights to former slaves and segregate every aspect of life. Southern states also adopted many laws designed to keep blacks from voting.[44] Poll taxes were adopted, requiring that individuals pay a fee in order to vote. Georgia initiated the poll tax in 1871 and made it cumulative in 1877 (requiring citizens to pay all back taxes before being permitted to vote). Every southern state then enacted a poll tax. It is estimated that the Georgia poll tax probably reduced overall turnout by 16 to 28 percent, and black turnout by half.[45]

Literacy tests were adopted, where a person seeking

to register to vote had to read a section of the state constitution to a county clerk and then explain it. The clerk, who was always white, had discretion to decide whether the person was sufficiently literate. This excluded almost all black men from voting because a significant percentage could not read, and for those who could, the clerk could still deem their literacy inadequate.[46] Southern states also enacted a "grandfather clause" that created an exception to the literacy tests for those whose grandfathers were qualified to vote before the Civil War. Obviously, this benefited only white citizens.

These actions worked. For example, in Mississippi, the percentage of black voting-age men registered to vote fell from over 90 percent during Reconstruction to less than 6 percent in 1892.[47]

Beyond the laws that kept African Americans from voting, there was intimidation directed at those who tried to register and vote. As a result, just 3 percent of voting-age black men and women in the South were registered to vote in 1940.[48] In Mississippi, less than 1 percent were registered.

The civil rights movement worked to combat race discrimination in voting and increase black voter registration. Still, in 1964, only about 43 percent of adult black men and women in the South were registered to vote.[49] In Alabama, only 23 percent of African Americans were registered to vote, and in Mississippi less than 7 percent of voting-age blacks were registered.[50]

The key change occurred when Congress passed the Voting Rights Act of 1965, one of the most important civil rights statutes adopted in American history. Unfortunately, the Supreme Court in its recent decision in *Shelby County v. Holder* invalidated a crucial provision in the law, tremendously decreasing its ability to deal with continued racial discrimination in voting.[51]

Section 2 of the Voting Rights Act prohibits voting

practices or procedures that discriminate on the basis of race or against certain language minority groups. Under the 1982 amendments to section 2, the act is violated by state or local laws that have the effect of disadvantaging minority voters. Lawsuits can be brought to challenge state or local actions that are alleged to violate section 2.

But Congress, in adopting the Voting Rights Act, concluded that allowing lawsuits to challenge election procedures was not adequate to stop discrimination in voting. Such litigation is expensive and time-consuming. Congress was also aware that southern states especially often invented new ways of disenfranchising minority voters. The arcade game Whack-A-Mole seems an apt analogy to what went on in many states. A law would be adopted to limit voting by racial minorities; it would be challenged and struck down, only to be replaced by a new voting restriction. Section 5 of the Voting Rights Act was adopted to prevent such actions.

It applies to jurisdictions with a history of race discrimination in voting and requires that there be preapproval—termed "preclearance"—of any attempt to change "any voting qualification or prerequisite to voting, or standard, practice, or procedure with respect to voting" in any "covered jurisdiction." The preapproval must come from either the U.S. attorney general, through an administrative procedure in the Department of Justice, or a three-judge federal court in the District of Columbia, through a request for a declaratory judgment.

In *South Carolina v. Katzenbach* (1966), the Supreme Court upheld the constitutionality of section 5 of the Voting Rights Act and spoke of the "blight of racial discrimination in voting."[52] The Court found that section 5 was a constitutional exercise of Congress's power to enforce the Fifteenth Amendment's prohibition of race discrimination in voting. Section 4(b) of the act determines which jurisdictions are required to get preclearance.

Congress has repeatedly extended section 5, including for five years in 1970, for seven years in 1975, and for twenty-five years in 1982. In 1982, Congress revised the formula in Section 4(b) for determining which jurisdictions were required to obtain preclearance before changing their election systems. After each reauthorization, the Court again upheld the constitutionality of sections 4(b) and 5.[53]

These provisions were scheduled to expire again in 2007. In 2005–2006, the House and Senate Judiciary Committees held twenty-one hearings, listened to ninety witnesses, and compiled a record of over fifteen thousand pages. Representative Sensenbrenner, a Republican from Wisconsin and then chair of the House Judiciary Committee, described this record as "one of the most extensive considerations of any piece of legislation that the United States Congress has dealt with in the 27½ years that I have been honored to serve as a Member of this body."[54]

Congress then voted overwhelmingly—98–0 in the Senate and 390–33 in the House—to extend section 5 for twenty-five years. It did not change sections 4(b) or 5. Congress expressly concluded that voting discrimination persists in the covered jurisdictions and that without section 5, "minority citizens will be deprived of the opportunity to exercise their right to vote, or will have their votes diluted, undermining the significant gains made by minorities in the last 40 years."[55]

The record before Congress supported this conclusion. For example, between 1982 and 2006, the section 5 preclearance requirement blocked 750 discriminatory changes in election systems in covered jurisdictions.[56] Another 205 discriminatory changes were withdrawn. Countless changes were not adopted because of the recognition that preclearance was unlikely. The continued discrimination in covered jurisdictions is further evidenced by

650 successful court challenges under section 2 of the Voting Rights Act in these places. University of Michigan law professor Ellen Katz did extensive studies and found that covered jurisdictions have only 25 percent of the country's population but account for 56 percent of the successful suits under section 2.[57]

Nor is this over. Before the 2012 elections, of the twelve states with the largest Hispanic populations, seven adopted restrictive voting laws.[58] Of the ten states with the largest African American populations, five adopted restrictive voting laws.[59]

Despite this, in *Shelby County v. Holder*, the Supreme Court, in a 5–4 decision, declared section 4(b) of the Voting Rights Act unconstitutional.[60] As explained above, this is the provision that determines which jurisdictions need to get preclearance. Without section 4(b), section 5 is meaningless; no jurisdictions need to get preclearance.

Shelby County, Alabama, which is south of Selma, is a jurisdiction, and in a state with a long history of race discrimination in voting. Because of this history, it is a jurisdiction covered by section 5, and it challenged the constitutionality of these provisions of the Voting Rights Act. It lost in both the district court and the federal court of appeals. The U.S. Court of Appeals for the District of Columbia Circuit, in a 2–1 decision, concluded that Congress found "widespread and persistent racial discrimination in voting in covered jurisdictions" and that section 5's "disparate geographic coverage is sufficiently related to the problem it targets."[61]

But the Supreme Court, 5–4, held section 4(b) unconstitutional and thereby also effectively nullified section 5 because it applies only to jurisdictions covered under section 4(b). It is the first time since the nineteenth century that the Court has declared a federal civil rights statute unconstitutional. Chief Justice Roberts wrote for the Court and stressed that the formula in section 4(b), last modified in 1982, rests on data from the 1960s and 1970s and that race discrimination in voting has changed since then. The Court declared: "Nearly 50 years later, things have changed dramatically. Shelby County contends that the preclearance requirement, even without regard to its disparate coverage, is now unconstitutional. Its arguments have a good deal of force. In the covered jurisdictions, '[v]oter turnout and registration rates now approach parity. Blatantly discriminatory evasions of federal decrees are rare. And minority candidates hold office at unprecedented levels.' The tests and devices that blocked access to the ballot have been forbidden nationwide for over 40 years."[62] Thus, "coverage today is based on decades-old data and eradicated practices."[63]

The Court stressed the intrusion on the covered states, as they could not exercise the power to choose how to hold elections, but instead the "States must beseech the Federal Government for permission to implement laws that they would otherwise have the right to enact and execute on their own, subject of course to any injunction in a section 2 action."[64] The Court also emphasized that sections 4(b) and 5, by requiring only some states to get preclearance, violated the principle of equal state sovereignty. The Court stated: "Not only do States retain sovereignty under the Constitution, there is also a 'fundamental principle of *equal* sovereignty' among the States. . . . Despite the tradition of equal sovereignty, the Act applies to only nine States (and several additional counties)."[65]

Justice Ginsburg wrote a dissent, joined by Justices Breyer, Sotomayor, and Kagan. The dissent stressed that race discrimination in voting remains and was documented by Congress. The dissent argued that the Court should be deferential to this judgment and the exercise of power by Congress. Justice Ginsburg stated:

> In the Court's view, the very success of section 5 of the Voting Rights Act demands its dormancy. Congress was of another mind. Recognizing that large progress has been made, Congress determined, based on a voluminous record, that the scourge of discrimination was not yet extirpated. The question this case presents is who decides whether, as currently operative, section 5 remains justifiable, this Court, or a Congress charged with the obligation to enforce the post–Civil War Amendments "by appropriate legislation." With overwhelming support in both Houses, Congress concluded that, for two prime reasons, section 5 should continue in force, unabated. First, continuance would facilitate completion of the impressive gains thus far made; and second, continuance would guard against backsliding. Those assessments were well within Congress' province to make and should elicit this Court's unstinting approbation.[66]

What is most curious about the Court's majority opinion is that it is unclear as to what constitutional provision or principle it felt was violated by section 4(b) of the Voting Rights Act. The fact that Congress relied on old data does not make the law unconstitutional, especially since it held exhaustive hearings finding continued discrimination in voting. The Court said that it found section 4(b) of the Voting Rights Act unconstitutional because it fails to treat all states the same; what the Court terms the principle of "equal sovereignty." But the text of the Constitution mentions no such principle, and the Congress that ratified the Fourteenth and Fifteenth Amendments did not believe in this as it imposed Reconstruction on the South. Countless federal laws treat some states differently from others.[67] The five most conservative justices who express such adherence to the text and the original meaning found a constitutional right for state governments that appears nowhere in the text and is contrary to the original understanding of the Fourteenth Amendment.

In theory, Congress can enact a new version of section 4(b) based on contemporary data. In reality, it is hard to imagine Congress being able to ever agree on a new formula to require that some of their jurisdictions get preclearance. Moreover, it would seem that any formula that treats some states differently from others would violate the Court's principle of equal state sovereignty. My hope is that Congress will try to adopt a new version of section 4(b) based on current data, though I recognize that this will take a Congress where Democrats are in the majority. More important, the Supreme Court hopefully someday will reverse *Shelby County*.

In the meantime, though, it is having the predicted effect of making it harder to deal with race discrimination in voting. Soon after it was adopted, states such as Texas and North Carolina put into place election systems that had been denied preclearance because of their discriminatory effects against minority voters.

Chief Justice John Roberts, in writing an opinion striking down a federal campaign finance law, declared, "There is no right more basic in our democracy than the right to participate in electing our political leaders."[68] It is tragically perverse that Chief Justice Roberts and the Court's conservative majority used this right to strike down laws limiting the ability of corporations and the wealthy to spend money in election campaigns but are untroubled when those who are kept from participating are the poorer in society and racial minorities. "We the People" today, unlike in 1787, includes those of all races; the progressive agenda must be to make this a constitutional reality.

5

PROVIDING EFFECTIVE GOVERNANCE

As I explained in chapter 3, it is quite understandable that the Preamble stressed the Constitution's purpose of providing effective governance. Above all, the Constitution was developed to replace the failed government of the Articles of Confederation. Thus, the Constitution should be interpreted to empower the federal government, while also ensuring checks and balances to prevent abuses of power.

The Constitution structures American government around two principles: federalism (allocating power between the federal government and the states) and separation of powers (dividing authority among the three branches of the federal government). In this chapter, I want to present a progressive vision of each.

FEDERALISM

Federalism refers to the allocation of power between the national government and the states. Ultimately, the question is, what should be the scope of federal power, and to what extent should the existence of states be a limit upon it? I believe that the progressive vision should be—as it has been throughout American history—to broadly define the scope of federal power to deal with society's most serious needs.

This is in sharp contrast to the conservative vision of federalism. Since the country's earliest days, "states' rights" has been used by conservatives as a political argument in support of conservative causes. During the early nineteenth century, John Calhoun argued that states had independent sovereignty and could interpose their authority between the federal government and the people to nullify federal actions restricting slavery.[1] During Reconstruction, southern states claimed that the federal military presence was incompatible with state sovereignty and federalism.

In the early twentieth century, federalism was successfully used as the basis for challenging federal laws regulating child labor, imposing the minimum wage, and protecting consumers.[2] During the Depression, conservatives objected to President Franklin Roosevelt's proposals, such as Social Security, on the grounds that they usurped functions properly left to state governments.[3]

During the 1950s and the 1960s, objections to federal civil rights efforts were phrased primarily in terms of federalism. Southerners challenged Supreme Court decisions mandating desegregation and objected to proposed federal civil rights legislation by resurrecting the arguments of John Calhoun.[4] Segregation and discrimination were defended less on the grounds that they were desirable practices, and more in terms of the states' rights to choose their own laws concerning race relations.

In the 1980s, President Ronald Reagan proclaimed a "new federalism" as the basis for attempting to dismantle federal social welfare programs.[5] In his first presidential inaugural address, President Reagan said that he sought to "restore the balance between levels of government." Federalism was thus employed as the basis for cutting back on many federal programs.

Over the course of American history, the Supreme Court has shifted back and forth between the progressive vision of broadly defining federal powers to equip the federal government with the authority to deal with social ills and the conservative view of narrowly defining federal powers, ostensibly to protect state governments. For the first century of American history, the Court adopted an expansive view of the scope of congressional power; from 1787 until the 1890s not one federal statute was declared unconstitutional as exceeding congressional authority or violating states' rights. But from the late nineteenth century until 1937, a conservative Court embraced federalism, adopted a much narrower construction of federal power, and invalidated many federal laws as exceeding the scope of this authority.

The pendulum shifted again in 1937; from then until 1995, not one federal law was declared unconstitutional as exceeding the scope of Congress's powers. Most notably, during this time, the Court rejected federalism challenges and upheld federal laws that advanced progressive aims, such as those protecting workers, enhancing civil rights, and safeguarding consumers.

But the composition of the Court changed with the appointment of deeply conservative justices, such as William Rehnquist, Antonin Scalia, and Clarence Thomas. They were joined by more moderate conservatives, Sandra Day O'Connor and Anthony Kennedy, in a series of decisions that struck down federal laws on federalism grounds. Although the Roberts Court thus far has not had many federalism decisions, it did strike down key provisions of the Patient Protection and Affordable Care Act on states' rights grounds, and four justices would have invalidated the entire law on federalism grounds.[6] I expect that with a conservative Supreme Court in place for years to come, federalism will be used—as it has been by conservatives throughout American history—to challenge progressive federal laws, especially in the areas of civil rights and environmental protection.

Initially, I want to show how the conservative approach to federalism on the Supreme Court has prevented unquestionably desirable laws from going into effect, doing so without in any way advancing the underlying goals of federalism, such as preventing tyranny or enhancing democratic rule. I then want to advance an alternative vision of federalism that I believe should guide progressives: federalism should be defined to empower government at all levels to deal with society's serious ills.

As mentioned above, for the first century of American history the Supreme Court broadly defined the scope of Congress's powers and did not invalidate any law on the ground that it exceeded its authority.[7] But for approximately forty years, from the mid-1890s through 1936, the Court regularly declared unconstitutional federal, state, and local laws protecting employees, consumers, and the public. A very conservative Court struck down over two hundred laws, most regulating business in various ways. Federal statutes were invalidated on the grounds that they invaded states' rights, while state and local laws were declared unconstitutional for interfering with freedom of contract. Both liberals and conservatives—later Supreme Court justices and academics alike—largely agree that these decisions were terribly misguided.

How did this happen? By the late nineteenth century, scholars and judges increasingly espoused a belief in a laissez-faire, unregulated economy.[8] In part, this was based on a philosophy of social Darwinism, the belief that society would thrive with the least government regulation so as not to interfere with allowing the "best" to advance and prosper. In part, it was based on a belief that government regulations unduly interfered with the natural rights of people to own and use their property and with a basic liberty interest in freedom of contract. And, in part, support for a laissez-faire philosophy simply reflected hostility by businesses to the increased government regulation that accompanied the industrial revolution—regulation that was designed to protect workers, unions, consumers, and competitors.

The Court's decisions in this time period were also very inconsistent. The Court was conservative both economically and morally, so laws regulating corporations were routinely struck down but laws based on moral judgments—regulating gambling, obscenity, prostitution—were always upheld. The justices read their conservative values into the Constitution, and ultimately the results kept Congress and the states from dealing with the economic and social crisis of the Great Depression.

The paradigm example of this was the Court's tragic decision in *Hammer v. Dagenhart*, in 1918, which declared unconstitutional the first federal statute limiting child labor.[9] Industrialization in the late nineteenth century caused a great increase in the use of child labor in the United States. Factory owners, for example, used child labor where possible because children were seen as more manageable, less expensive, and less likely to strike. By 1900, "children worked in large numbers in mines, glass factories, textiles, agriculture, canneries, home industries, and as newsboys, messengers, bootblacks, and peddlers."[10] It is estimated that in the early years of the twentieth century, approximately two million children aged sixteen and younger worked in the fields, mines, mills, and factories of the United States. Unhealthy and dangerous working conditions were common; many children were injured or killed, while many left school, still illiterate, to take jobs.

Some states enacted laws limiting child labor, but others did not. States that restricted the use of child labor found themselves at a competitive disadvantage compared to states that did not impose limits. Some factories relocated to states where child labor was unregulated because goods could be produced more cheaply by children, who were paid significantly lower wages than adult workers.

Constant exposés by journalists, labor, and progressives showed the great harm to children and created pressure for federal action. In 1916, Congress passed the Keating-Owen Act, which prohibited interstate commerce of any merchandise that had been made by children under the age of fourteen or that had been made in factories where children between the ages of fourteen and sixteen worked for more than eight hours a day, worked overnight, or worked more than six days a week. Article I, Section 8, of the Constitution gives Congress the power "to regulate Commerce . . . among the several States," and that is exactly what Congress did in this law: it did not eliminate child labor, but simply forbade the shipment of interstate commerce of goods made by child labor under certain circumstances. From the perspective of social policy, it is impossible to imagine opposing such a law.

But in *Hammer v. Dagenhart*, the Court declared the law unconstitutional on federalism principles, as a violation of the Tenth Amendment, which states: "The powers not delegated to the United States by the Constitution, nor prohibited by it to the States, are reserved to the States respectively, or to the people." By its terms, the Tenth Amendment is an important reminder and embodiment of a basic principle of American government: Congress can act only if it is granted the power to do so by the Constitution, but state and local governments can do anything except what is prohibited by the Constitution. That is all the Tenth Amendment says, and for the first century of American history that is how the Supreme Court interpreted it.

In *Hammer v. Dagenhart*, however, the Supreme Court

said that the Tenth Amendment meant much more than this.[11] The Court held that Congress violated the Tenth Amendment if it attempted to control the production of goods, even though it was exercising its constitutional power to regulate commerce among the states. The Court concluded that the Tenth Amendment reserves control of production to the states for their exclusive control. The Court did not question that Congress had the authority to regulate shipments in interstate commerce, but it said that this power could not be used to control production and ban child labor. It is a highly dubious conclusion; there is nothing in the text of the Tenth Amendment or anything about its history that implies this, and it is socially undesirable. The Court said that regulating the hours of labor of children was entrusted "purely [to] state authority."[12] Thus, the federal effort to limit child labor—surely an important, even essential, government action—was deemed unconstitutional.

The practical problem with the Court's approach to leave this to "state authority" was that economic pressure from states that did not prohibit child labor would keep other states from being able to do so. States that wanted to outlaw child labor would find it difficult to have their businesses be competitive as long as other states allowed cheap child labor. Over time, the economic pressures would be great for all states to allow it. Economic pressures realistically limited state choices as much as any federal regulation.

This argument as to the need for federal regulation was made to the Supreme Court and expressly rejected. The Court said that Congress could not act to prevent unfair competition among the states. The Court spoke in apocalyptic terms as to the consequences if Congress was accorded such regulatory power: "The far-reaching result of upholding the act cannot be more plainly indicated than by pointing out that if Congress can thus regulate matters entrusted to local authority by prohibition of the movement of commodities in interstate commerce, all freedom of commerce will be at an end, and the power of the States over local matters may be eliminated, and thus our system of government be practically destroyed." It is hard to believe that a majority of the justices really believed that allowing Congress to ban child labor would practically destroy the entire system of government.

The decision cannot be understood as anything other than a reflection of the ideology of the justices at the time and their hostility to regulation of business, even when it was a law to protect children.

This case is typical of this era, when the conservative Court used federalism to strike down many progressive laws. This especially occurred during FDR's first term, when the Court invalidated many New Deal laws meant to revitalize the economy and protect workers and consumers.

For example, in *Carter v. Carter Coal Co.* (1936), the Court declared unconstitutional the Bituminous Coal Conservation Act of 1935.[13] The law contained detailed findings as to the relationship between coal and the national economy and declared that the production of coal directly affected interstate commerce. The law provided for local coal boards to be established to determine prices for coal and to determine, after collective bargaining by unions and employers, wages and hours for employees. A shareholder in the Carter Coal Company sued the company in order to stop it from complying with the law.

The Supreme Court declared the law unconstitutional. The Court focused on the unconstitutionality of federal regulation of wages and hours. The Court said that "the employment of men, the fixing of their wages, hours of labor and working conditions, the bargaining in respect of these things—whether carried on separately or collectively," are all aspects of production and could not be regulated by Congress.[14]

The Court again emphasized that this narrow definition of commerce was essential to protect the states. The Court lamented: "Every journey to a forbidden end begins with the first step; and the danger of such a step by the federal government in the direction of taking over the powers of the states is that the end of the journey may find the states so despoiled of their powers, or—what may amount to the same thing—so relieved of responsibilities . . . as to reduce them to little more than geographic subdivisions of the national domain."[15]

In *A. L. A. Schecter Poultry Corp. v. United States* (1936), often referred to as the "sick chicken case," the Court declared a federal law unconstitutional based on an insufficient direct effect on interstate commerce.[16] The National Industrial Recovery Act of 1933, a key piece of New Deal legislation, authorized the president to approve "codes of fair competition" developed by boards of various industries. Pursuant to this law, the president approved a live-poultry code for New York City. In part, the code was designed to ensure quality poultry by preventing sellers from requiring buyers to purchase the entire coop of chickens, including sick ones. The code also regulated employment by requiring collective bargaining, prohibiting child labor, and establishing a forty-hour workweek and a minimum wage.

The Supreme Court declared the entire code unconstitutional because there was not a sufficiently "direct" relationship to interstate commerce. Although the Court acknowledged that virtually all the poultry in New York was shipped from other states, it said that the code was not regulating the interstate transactions; rather, the code concerned the operation of businesses within New York. The Court emphasized that Congress only could regulate when there was a direct effect on interstate commerce.

The Court once again explained that this distinction was essential in order to protect state governments and, ultimately, the American system of government. It declared that enforcing the distinction between direct and indirect effects on commerce "must be recognized as . . . essential to the maintenance of our constitutional system."[17]

In 1936, *Railroad Retirement Board v. Alton R. R. Co.* the Court declared unconstitutional the Railroad Retirement Act of 1934, which provided a pension system for railroad workers.[18] Also in 1936, the Court struck down another key piece of New Deal legislation: the Agricultural Adjustment Act of 1933, which sought to stabilize production in agriculture by offering subsidies to farmers to limit their crops. By restricting the supply of agricultural products, Congress sought to ensure a fair price and thus to encourage agricultural production. If the supply of a product was too great, prices would plummet, no profit could be gained, and future production would then be curtailed. In *United States v. Butler* (1936), it declared the Agricultural Adjustment Act (1933) unconstitutional on the grounds that it violated the Tenth Amendment because it regulated production; the regulation of production, according to the Court, was left to the states.[19]

The result of these doctrines was that for forty years, including for the first years of the Depression, Congress was greatly limited in its ability to regulate the economy because the Court had so narrowly construed the scope of congressional powers. What is striking, in hindsight, is that all of these laws were highly desirable: limiting the use of child labor, creating a minimum wage in the coal industry, preventing the shipment of diseased chickens, providing a pension for railroad workers, stabilizing agricultural production. All ultimately came to be approved without controversy. Yet all were initially struck down by conservative justices in the name of federalism.

By the mid-1930s, enormous pressure was mounting for the Court to abandon this approach. The Depression created a widespread perception that government economic regulations were essential. Strong political pressure mounted for change. Four of the justices—Pierce Butler and George Sutherland (appointed by Warren Harding), James McReynolds (appointed by Woodrow Wilson), and Willis Van Devanter (appointed by William Howard Taft)—were very conservative and virtually always voted to invalidate New Deal programs and progressive state laws. They were referred to in the press as "the Four Horsemen," after the allegorical figures of the Apocalypse associated with death and destruction. They often found a fifth vote in Owen Roberts, who had been appointed by Herbert Hoover and, in 1936, was the youngest justice on the Court at age sixty-one.

After Franklin Roosevelt was elected to a second term as president in 1936, he proposed a plan to pack the Court: the president could appoint one additional justice for every justice on the Court who was over age seventy, up to a maximum of fifteen justices.[20] That would have allowed Roosevelt to quickly appoint enough justices to have a sympathetic majority on the Court to uphold New Deal programs.

Roosevelt's plan met substantial opposition in Congress, even from a Congress that was controlled by Democrats. But in 1937, even without that failed scheme, the Court dramatically reversed course and rejected the prior forty years of jurisprudence. In two cases—one involving freedom of contract and one involving the scope of Congress's commerce power—Justice Owen Roberts switched sides and cast the fifth vote to uphold the laws.[21] Perhaps this was a reaction to the Court-packing plan, or perhaps he made up his mind in these cases before even learning about that threat. Very soon after, the conservative justices began leaving the Court and President Franklin Roosevelt was able to appoint justices committed to upholding New Deal programs.

From 1937 until 1995, not one federal law was declared unconstitutional on the grounds of exceeding the scope of Congress's powers. The Supreme Court broadly defined the scope of federal authority to deal with national problems and rejected the idea that the Tenth Amendment reserved a zone of activities to the states. The progressive vision of federalism was the law.

But in the 1990s, the new conservative majority of the Court, in a series of 5–4 rulings, returned to the repudiated states' rights jurisprudence of the earlier era. The appointments of Richard Nixon, Ronald Reagan, and George H. W. Bush created a conservative five-justice majority to return to strike down federal laws in the name of states' rights: William Rehnquist (appointed by Richard Nixon and as Chief Justice by Ronald Reagan), Sandra Day O'Connor, Antonin Scalia, and Anthony Kennedy (all Reagan appointees), and Clarence Thomas (a Bush appointee). What is most striking about these states' rights decisions is that they have all declared unconstitutional federal laws that are unquestionably socially desirable: preventing guns near schools, allowing victims of rape and domestic violence to sue, requiring states to clean up nuclear waste, mandating state and local governments to do background checks before issuing permits for firearms, and expanding Medicaid coverage for the poor.

In *United States v. Lopez*, in 1995, by a 5–4 margin, the Supreme Court declared unconstitutional the Gun-Free School Zones Act of 1990, which made it a federal crime to have a gun within one thousand feet of a school.[22] Splitting along ideological lines, the Court ruled that the relationship to interstate commerce was too tangential and uncertain to uphold the law as a valid exercise of Congress's commerce power. Chief Justice Rehnquist wrote the opinion of the Court and was joined by Justices O'Connor, Kennedy, Scalia, and Thomas. Justices Stevens, Souter, Ginsburg, and Breyer dissented. For the first time in almost sixty years, the Court declared unconstitutional a federal law on grounds that it exceeded the scope of Congress's commerce power. Guns near schools are inherently a bad thing. It is hard to identify what is gained by declaring this law unconstitutional. The Supreme Court frequently has said that states' rights are important as a way to prevent tyranny, to safeguard individual liberties, and to allow states to serve as laboratories for experimentation. But prohibiting guns near schools is hardly tyrannical, and even staunch advocates of gun rights must have pause when it comes to guns near schools. Nor does it make sense to allow states to experiment with this.

Five years later, in *United States v. Morrison* (2000), the Court followed *Lopez* and declared unconstitutional a federal law intended to help women who were victims of violence.[23] The federal Violence Against Women Act (1994) allowed victims of gender-motivated violence to sue for money damages. Congress enacted the Violence Against Women Act based on detailed findings of the inadequacy of state laws in protecting women who are victims of domestic violence and sexual assault. Congress found that gender-motivated violence costs the American economy billions of dollars a year and is a substantial constraint on freedom of travel by women throughout the country. Congress also concluded that state courts were not receptive to claims by women who were victims of gender-motivated violence.

The case was brought by Christy Brzonkala, who was raped by football players while she was a freshman at

Virginia Polytechnic Institute. The players were not criminally prosecuted and ultimately even avoided sanctions by their university. Brzonkala filed suit against her assailants and the university under the civil damages provision of the Violence Against Women Act.

In a 5–4 decision, again split along ideological lines, the Court held that Congress lacked the authority to authorize such suits. The Supreme Court expressly rejected the argument that Congress could act based on its finding that violence against women costs the American economy billions of dollars a year. Chief Justice Rehnquist emphasized that Congress was regulating noneconomic activity that has traditionally been dealt with by state laws and thus exceeded the scope of its commerce clause power.

Again, it is unquestionably desirable to allow victims of rape or domestic violence to be able to sue where they have a realistic chance of success. Congress explicitly found that state courts are often hostile to such claims. Yet the Court declared this law unconstitutional.

In its most recent decision concerning the scope of Congress's commerce power, the five most conservative justices again took a very restrictive view. The case, *National Federation of Independent Business v. Sebelius* (2012), involved the constitutionality of the Patient Protection and Affordable Care Act.[24]

Congress found that there were fifty million Americans without health insurance and the Affordable Care Act sought to remedy that. Insurance companies are required to provide coverage to all and can no longer deny policies based on preexisting conditions, or charge higher premiums based on health conditions, or impose yearly or lifetime caps on payments. But Congress knew that just imposing these restrictions on insurance companies would be self-defeating; if people could wait until they were very sick to obtain insurance and could do so without any additional cost, fewer healthy people would purchase it. The costs of health insurance would dramatically increase. The individual mandate sought to remedy this by expanding the risk pool as much as possible. Subject to some exceptions, such as those with income below a specified level and those who have religious objections to receiving medical care, the rest of the population has to buy insurance or pay a penalty. The idea actually originated with a conservative think tank, the Heritage Foundation—which developed it as an alternative to a single-payer plan favored by liberals. Massachusetts became the first state to adopt an individual mandate when its Republican governor, Mitt Romney, signed it into law.

Five justices—Chief Justice Roberts and Justices Scalia, Kennedy, Thomas, and Alito—said that the individual mandate was not a constitutional exercise of Congress's commerce clause power. They said that Congress under the commerce clause can regulate *economic activity* that, taken cumulatively, has a substantial effect on interstate commerce. They saw the individual mandate as regulating *inactivity*, regulating those not engaged in commerce, and thus exceeding the scope of Congress's power.

This is misguided because all of us are engaged in economic activity with regard to health care; as Justice Ginsburg pointed out in her dissent, over 99 percent of people will receive medical care in their lifetimes and 60 percent of the uninsured do so each year. Everyone is engaged in economic activity with regard to health care in that they are either purchasing insurance or self-insuring. Congress is regulating the latter economic behavior because of its ill effects on the economy and society.

However, the Court upheld the individual mandate based on a different congressional power: Congress's authority to tax and spend for the general welfare. Chief

Justice Roberts, joined by Justices Ginsburg, Breyer, Sotomayor, and Kagan, said that the individual mandate is a tax and within the scope of Congress's taxing power. He explained that the mandate is calculated like a tax; for example, in 2014, it was 1 percent of income or $95 for those who do not purchase insurance. It is collected by the Internal Revenue Service and the funds go to the federal treasury; it generated about $4 billion in 2014. The Court said that it was irrelevant that the Obama administration never called it a tax; the labels used by the government are not determinative.

The Court, though, did strike down a key part of the Affordable Care Act that was meant to increase medical care coverage for the poorest in society. Under the ACA, states were required to provide coverage via Medicaid for all those within 133 percent of the federal poverty level. The federal government would pay 100 percent of these costs until 2019 and 90 percent thereafter. Any state that failed to comply would lose all of its Medicaid funds. In a 7–2 ruling, the Court held that the act exceeded the scope of Congress's spending power and violated the Tenth Amendment by denying all Medicaid funding to states that did not comply with the new conditions outlined in the ACA.

The Court said that it was unduly coercive to tie existing Medicaid funds to a failure to comply with the new ACA requirement. The Court held that there were two Medicaid programs, the old one and the new requirements, and said that it was impermissible to tie existing funds to the failure to comply with new requirements. But why see this as two programs rather than one? Moreover, why see this as Congress coercing, or to use Chief Justice Roberts's word, "dragooning," the states? Admittedly, given the huge amount of money involved, any state would face a hard choice to turn it down, but no state is forced to take federal Medicaid money. Why shouldn't Congress be able to condition federal dollars on compliance with its terms, especially when the conditions are entirely about fulfilling the purpose of the Medicaid program in ensuring health care for those who cannot afford it? Countless federal statutes provide funds to state and local governments on the condition that they comply with requirements. This is the first time in history that the Court ever found conditions on federal funds to be so coercive as to be unconstitutional.

This decision rests on another Rehnquist-era decision where the Court returned to the view that the Tenth Amendment leaves a zone of activities to the states. In *New York v. United States,* in 1992, the Court invalidated the 1985 Low-Level Radioactive Waste Policy Amendments Act, which created a statutory duty for states to provide for the safe disposal of radioactive waste generated within their borders.[25] The act provided monetary incentives for states to comply with the law and allowed states to impose a surcharge on radioactive waste received from other states. Additionally, and most controversially, to ensure effective state government action, the law provided that states would "take title" to any nuclear waste within their borders that was not properly disposed of by January 1, 1996, and then would "be liable for all damages directly or indirectly incurred."

The Supreme Court ruled that forcing states to accept ownership of radioactive waste would impermissibly "commandeer" state governments, and requiring state compliance with federal regulatory statutes would impermissibly impose on states a requirement to implement federal legislation. The Court concluded that it was "clear" that because of the Tenth Amendment and limits on the scope of Congress's powers under Article I, "the Federal Government may not compel the States to enact or administer a federal regulatory program."

Notice again that each of the laws involved in these cases is unquestionably desirable: preventing guns near schools, allowing victims of gender-motivated violence to sue, providing Medicaid coverage for the poor, cleaning up nuclear waste. Most important, none of these decisions serve the underlying values of federalism, such as preventing tyranny or facilitating states being laboratories for experimentation. We should not want to experiment with guns near schools, or deny women who have been raped or assaulted the chance to sue, or leave the poor without medical care, or fail to clean up nuclear waste. In each of these decisions, the Court failed the Preamble's promise of effective governance.

There is an alternative progressive vision of federalism: define it to empower government at all levels to deal with social problems.[26] A key advantage of having multiple levels of government is the availability of alternative actors to solve important problems. If the federal government fails to act, state and local government action is still possible. If states fail to deal with an issue, federal or local action is possible. In other words, a tremendous advantage of federalism is its redundancy—multiple levels of government over the same territory and population, each with the ability to act. From this perspective, federalism needs to be reconceptualized as being primarily about empowering varying levels of government and much less about limiting government.

Sometimes effective government requires concerted effort at all three levels: federal, state, and local. Environmental protection is an example of this, where federal laws have been essential, but where local conditions and problems have necessitated independent state and local action. Sometimes, though, one level of government must act because of the failure at other levels. During the 1950s and the 1960s, it was obvious that southern states would not act to end segregation and systematic discrimination against African Americans. The Supreme Court's decisions and laws such as the Civil Rights Act of 1964 and the Voting Rights Act of 1965 were essential federal actions. In the 1990s and again now, as the federal government has abandoned the poor and the war on poverty, it is imperative that state and local governments act to ensure that people have food, shelter, and medical care. Today, as the federal government is hostile to environmental regulation and denying the problem of climate change, it is essential that state governments act.

Although this view of federalism should be apparent from the very structure of American government, it is virtually absent from the Supreme Court's federalism decisions. What would it mean in practical terms? The Court should return to the approach of federalism that it followed from 1937 to 1992: Congress should be able to regulate under the commerce clause so long as there is a rational reason for believing that an activity has a substantial effect on interstate commerce.

Critics will invoke the importance of state governments. But the structure of government is a means to an end—the effective governance promised in the Preamble—and not an end in itself. Defenders of federalism argue that dividing power vertically among levels of government can be seen as a way of checking authority and decreasing the possibility of tyranny.

There are several responses to this. First, the best check against tyranny is judicial review safeguarding individual liberties. "Tyranny" is both a loaded and an ambiguous word. In a world where we witness truly tyrannical and abusive rule, the mere invocation of the concept has enormous rhetorical power. But it is essential to consider what really constitutes tyranny. The examples that come to mind can be best dealt with by ensuring the availability of courts to invalidate unconstitutional government conduct.

Second, empowering multiple levels of government is itself a safeguard against tyranny. Generally, each level of government has the ability to expand individual rights. States can provide more rights and greater protection of equality than the federal government, but never less.

Finally, as mentioned above, it must be noted that the Supreme Court's decisions about federalism have had nothing to do with preventing tyranny. Forcing states to clean up their nuclear waste or prohibiting guns near schools are desirable government actions; they are not in any way tyrannical. If the ultimate concern behind federalism is preventing tyranny, then the Supreme Court should focus on this value directly and invalidate laws only where there is a real risk of abuse of power.

Ultimately, I believe that the progressive vision of federalism as empowering government will do a much better job of fulfilling the Preamble's goal of effective governance than the conservative approach of using federalism to strike down desirable federal laws. I have no doubt that this will be important in the years to come as conservatives turn to federalism to strike down federal laws concerning civil rights, consumer safeguards, and environmental protection.

SEPARATION OF POWERS

The other key structural aspect of the Constitution is separation of powers. Here, especially, there is a need for an approach to fulfill the Preamble's goal of effective government while also preventing abuses of power. Two features should be especially important for the progressive vision of separation of powers: ensuring that two branches of government should have to be involved in virtually all major government actions and allowing checks to prevent abuses of power.

The Constitution is based on a simple vision of shared and separated powers. For almost every major government action, at least two branches of government must be involved. Enacting a law requires involvement of both Congress and the president. Enforcing a law requires a prosecution by the executive and a conviction by the courts; searching or arresting someone requires approval by the courts and execution by the executive; filling key government positions—federal judges, ambassadors, cabinet secretaries—requires appointment by the president and confirmation by the Senate; undertaking treaty obligations requires negotiation by the president and ratification by the Senate; and going to war requires a declaration by Congress and implementation by the president as commander in chief.

To be sure, there are some areas where the Constitution assigns power to only one branch, unchecked by any other. For example, the president alone has the power to pardon; there is no oversight of pardons by any other branch of government. Congress may impeach and remove the president, the vice president, federal judges, and other officers of the United States. Impeachment and removal decisions are not reviewable by any other branch of government.[27] Congress's choice to propose a constitutional amendment for consideration by the states is not reviewable by the courts or the executive branch.

However, even these areas of seemingly unilateral executive authority must be understood as part of an overall system of checks and balances. For example, the president's pardon power is a final check to make sure that no one is incarcerated in violation of the Constitution and laws of the United States, and impeachment acts as a check on abuses by the other branches of government. Impeachment has the added protection of requiring a two-thirds vote of the Senate to remove a person from office. Constitutional amendments must be approved by two-thirds of both houses of Congress and by three-fourths of the states.

The Constitution thus embraces an approach to government power that is both simplistic and elegant. Traditional discussions of presidential power have recognized this basic constitutional framework. For example, the Supreme Court often invokes Justice Robert Jackson's famous description of presidential power in *Youngstown Sheet & Tube Co. v. Sawyer* (1952).[28] In *Youngstown*, the Court declared unconstitutional President Truman's seizure of the steel industry to prevent a work stoppage during the Korean War.

Justice Jackson's concurring opinion delineated three zones of presidential authority.[29] First, Jackson said that "when the president acts pursuant to an express or implied authorization of Congress, his authority is at its maximum, for it includes all that he possesses in his own right plus all that Congress can delegate."[30] Under such circumstances, the president's acts are presumptively valid.

Jackson's second zone covers circumstances "when the president acts in absence of either a congressional grant or denial of authority, he can only rely upon his own independent powers, but there is a zone of twilight in which he and Congress may have concurrent authority, or in which its distribution is uncertain."[31] Jackson said that it is impossible to formulate general rules as to the constitutionality of actions in this area; rather, constitutionality is likely "to depend on the imperatives of events and contemporary imponderables rather than on abstract theories of law."[32]

Third, Jackson argued that "when the President takes measures incompatible with the expressed or implied will of Congress, his power is at its lowest ebb."[33] Only if the law enacted by Congress is unconstitutional will such presidential action disobeying federal law be allowed. In other words, for Justice Jackson, presidential power is at its weakest if the president is violating a statute and at its strongest when in compliance with a statute. This formulation is consistent with a system that values shared powers and checks and balances. It emphasizes the need for two branches of the federal government to act.

Over the last several decades both Republican and Democratic presidents have claimed the authority to take actions that could not be checked by other branches of government.

The Nixon administration repeatedly asserted broad, uncheckable power. For example, the administration claimed the power to impound federal funds allocated and appropriated by Congress.[34] This led Congress to adopt the Impoundment Control Act of 1974, which effectively forbids the practice.[35] The Nixon administration also asserted the authority to engage in warrantless wiretapping for the sake of domestic security. In 1972, the Supreme Court unanimously ruled that the president could not authorize such warrantless electronic surveillance.[36]

The claim of expansive, uncheckable presidential power grew during the Reagan presidency, most notably during the major scandal of the Reagan administration: Iran-Contra. Several high-level members of the Reagan administration intentionally violated the Boland Amendment, which prohibited the use of federal money to aid the Contras, an anticommunist guerrilla organization in Nicaragua. Some have argued that the Boland Amendment was an impermissible restriction on the president's power to conduct foreign policy. For example, a Republican minority report to the House committee investigating the Iran-Contra affair declared: "The Constitution gives the President some power to act on his own in foreign affairs . . . Congress may not use its control over appropriations, including salaries, to prevent the executive or judiciary from fulfilling Constitutionally mandated obligations."[37]

Democratic presidents, too, at times asserted unreviewable power. President Bill Clinton argued that he could not be civilly sued, even for actions that occurred prior to taking office (a position that the Supreme Court unanimously rejected).[38] President Barack Obama claimed authority to impose a Clean Power Plan, including restrictions on greenhouse gas emissions from coal-fired utility plants (subsequently repealed by the Trump administration).[39]

But no administration did more to assert unreviewable executive power than that of President George W. Bush. Its repeated assertion of broad, uncheckable executive power shows the need for the progressive approach to separation of powers: two branches generally must be involved in major federal government actions.

One of the most disturbing acts of the Bush administration was its claim of authority to detain individuals without judicial review. For example, it claimed a power to suspend the Bill of Rights by detaining José Padilla, an American citizen apprehended in the United States, without complying with the Fourth, Fifth, and Sixth Amendments. Padilla was apprehended at Chicago's O'Hare Airport in May 2002 and accused of planning to build and detonate a "dirty bomb" in the United States.[40] Authorities imprisoned Padilla for almost four years before indicting him for any crime.

But Padilla's case is not the only instance where the Bush administration claimed the power to detain people without judicial review. Numerically, the most significant presidential claim of authority to detain without judicial review involved the detention of over seven hundred people as prisoners at a military facility in Guantanamo. The Bush administration argued that there could be no judicial review of its actions with respect to the detentions in

Guantanamo,[41] a position rejected by the Supreme Court.[42]

The Bush administration also claimed the authority to engage in electronic surveillance without a judicially issued warrant or even probable cause. In December 2005, the *New York Times* revealed that the National Security Agency was intercepting electronic communications by telephone and email between the United States and foreign countries without warrants or probable cause.[43] The Bush administration acknowledged and vehemently defended this warrantless wiretapping.[44] However, the Fourth Amendment dictates that searches, including wiretapping and intercepting electronic communications, require a judicially approved warrant. Federal statutes explicitly state that the government may engage in electronic eavesdropping only after obtaining a warrant either from a federal district court or from the Foreign Intelligence Surveillance Court (FISC).[45]

President Bush claimed two sources of power for engaging in warrantless surveillance: his power as commander in chief and his authority under the Authorization for Use of Military Force (AUMF) joint resolution after September 11.[46] Neither source provides for such authority.

The president, as commander in chief, has no power to violate the Bill of Rights. Indeed, if the president can authorize wiretapping without a warrant, he could authorize searches of homes without complying with the Fourth Amendment. Under this reasoning, the president could suspend freedom of speech or the press as commander in chief. If presidential power can trump the Fourth Amendment's requirement for a warrant, there is no reason why it cannot be used to override any other constitutional provision.

Nor does the AUMF provide a basis for such presidential power. Congress authorized the use of troops and arms to respond to the terrorists; the resolution has nothing to do with eavesdropping. Authorizing "military force" does not include every other action that the government wants to take in the name of the war on terrorism. The AUMF is not an indefinite blank check.

One more example: in 2002, the Department of Justice Office of Legal Counsel issued a memorandum that stated that the president could authorize torture of human beings in violation of treaties ratified by the United States and federal statutes that prohibit such conduct.[47] The so-called torture memo argued that the antitorture statutes could not prohibit the president from ordering the use of torture in interrogations of enemy combatants because such a prohibition would violate the president's constitutional powers.[48] The memo based this conclusion on a broad assertion of presidential war powers that recognized no ability of statutes or treaties to impose limits.[49]

The Department of Justice ultimately withdrew the torture memo.[50] But as Professor Neil Kinkopf notes, "The withdrawing memo, however, does not repudiate or even question the substance of the Torture Memo's reasoning on the issue of presidential power."[51] The significance of the torture memo in terms of the Bush administration's views of executive power cannot be overstated. Top officials were claiming that the U.S. government could torture human beings, notwithstanding laws and treaties specifically forbidding torture. This is an assertion of executive power that recognizes no limits and acknowledges no checks and balances.

And as a result, the government engaged in torture. A report of the Senate Intelligence Committee, released in December 2014, describes horrific, sadistic brutality inflicted on prisoners. It also leaves no doubt that both U.S. criminal statutes and international treaties were violated. The 499-page report describes in detail what was done. It is sickening and saddening. The report tells of a man chained to a wall in the standing position for 17 days and of detainees kept awake for nearly 180 hours in standing or stress positions. The report documents repeated waterboarding, which international law has long defined as torture, including one man who was waterboarded 183 times. It tells of detainees being immersed in ice baths and of the killing of an Afghan, Gul Rahman, who died of suspected hypothermia in November 2002 after he was beaten, stripped naked from the waist down, and left chained to a concrete floor in near-freezing temperatures. The report details forced rectal feeding, which is described as intensely painful and obviously is enormously degrading; it is rape.

At the risk of stating the obvious, checking executive power was a central goal of the Constitution. Having endured the tyranny of the king of England, the founders structured the Constitution with checks and balances as a crucial way to preserve democracy. James Madison wrote, "No political truth is certainly of greater intrinsic value or is stamped with the authority of more enlightened patrons of liberty than that . . . the accumulation of all powers, legislative, executive, and judiciary, in the same hands, whether of one, a few, or many, and whether hereditary, self-appointed, or elective, may justly be pronounced the very definition of tyranny."[52]

All of which is to say that the progressive vision of constitutional law should oppose unilateral, unchecked executive power, no matter what the political party of the president.

At the same time, progressives should oppose the conservative assertion of a "unitary executive" that prevents checks on the president. The conservatives' claim is that all executive power must reside in or be accountable to the president.[53] This theory is very problematic when it prevents desirable checks on the president.

In light of the events of the Watergate cover-up and investigation, Congress adopted the Ethics in Government Act of 1978.[54] Title 6 of the act allowed for the appointment of an "independent counsel" to investigate and prosecute wrongdoing by high-level federal government officials. If the attorney general determined that further investigation or prosecution is warranted, a panel of federal court judges "shall appoint an independent counsel and shall define that independent counsel's prosecutorial jurisdiction." The law provides that the panel shall consist of three federal court judges: one must be a judge of the U.S. Court of Appeals for the District of Columbia Circuit, and no two of the judges can be from the same court.

The Court, by a 7–1 margin, in an opinion by Chief Justice Rehnquist, upheld the law. Justice Scalia wrote a lone dissent. He argued that the Constitution presumes that all executive powers are within control of the president, and therefore having an independent special prosecutor is unconstitutional because the president must command all criminal investigations.[55] He emphasized that the power to prosecute is "a quintessentially executive activity" and that it usurps presidential power for Congress to vest this authority in the independent counsel.[56] It "effects a revolution in our constitutional jurisprudence" to allow the independent counsel once it has been determined that "(1) purely executive functions are at issue here, and (2) those functions have been given to a person whose actions are not fully within the supervision and control of the President."[57]

Subsequently, conservatives have embraced the Scalia dissent, even though it was the sole dissent in a 7–1 decision.[58] But the progressive vision of separation of powers should reject this and favor checks and balances. For example, long before the Trump administration, I believed that an independent counsel to investigate alleged wrongdoing by the president or high-level officials is not only constitutional but essential. The events in the first year of the Trump presidency very much confirm this.

The Supreme Court's most recent decision about presidential power, *Trump v. Hawaii*, is enormously troubling.[59] As a candidate, Donald Trump repeatedly declared that he wanted a total ban on Muslims entering the United States. On January 27, 2017, a week after taking office, President Trump issued an executive order suspending immigration from seven counties. They shared three things in common: they all have populations that are more than 90 percent Muslim, Donald Trump has no economic investments in any of them, and none has ever been linked to terrorist activity in the United States. After courts issued a preliminary injunction against this and a similar executive order, President Trump issued a new version of the travel ban by proclamation.

The Court in, in a 5–4 decision, upheld this. Chief Justice Roberts wrote for the Court. He said that the president has broad powers in immigration, so restrictions only have to meet a rational basis test. Under the rational basis test, a government action is upheld if it is rationally related to a legitimate government purpose. Quite importantly, the government's actual purpose is irrelevant; all that is required is a conceivable legitimate purpose for the government's action. In other words, the actual discriminatory purpose behind the travel ban became irrelevant. The Court found a conceivable national security purpose. But this means there is virtually no check on presidential policies—even discriminatory ones—in the area of immigration.

As the dissent pointed out, the Court's decision was sadly very similar to the infamous ruling in 1944 in *Korematsu v. United States*, where the Court upheld the evacuation of Japanese Americans from the West Coast during World War II. Although Chief Justice Roberts denied the analogy and repudiated *Korematsu,* there are striking similarities. In both cases, the Court showed great deference to the president, even with no evidence of danger. Not one Japanese American ever was indicted or convicted of espionage or a crime against national security. No evidence links anyone from the banned countries in Trump's immigration order to terrorism in the United States. Both policies were based on prejudice. In each, the Court allowed danger to be determined by ancestry or country of residence and not individualized evidence.

Progressives, whether there is a Democratic or a Republican president, should embrace the importance of checks and balances that are at the core of the Constitution's structure.

6

ESTABLISHING JUSTICE

The Preamble says that the Constitution exists to "establish Justice." As described in chapter 3, many provisions of the Constitution and several of the amendments are focused on the critically important area of criminal justice. In attempting to fulfill the Preamble's promise of justice, the Constitution—and especially the Bill of Rights—address three important aspects of the criminal justice system: policing, trials, and punishment. Yet in each area, the Constitution's promise has not been realized. A key part of the progressive agenda for the Constitution must be to improve justice for those investigated, tried, and convicted of crimes.

POLICING

As has been tragically shown by police killings of unarmed African American men and articulated by the Black Lives Matter movement, criminal justice reform must involve better oversight and control of the police to prevent abuses. Statistics show that African Americans and Hispanics are more likely to be stopped by police than whites for the same behavior, more likely to be arrested, and more likely to be subjected to police violence.[1] As President Obama explained: "A large body of research finds that, for similar offenses, members of the African American and Hispanic communities are more likely to be stopped, searched, arrested, convicted, and sentenced to harsher penalties."[2] In 2016, black males aged fifteen to thirty-four were nine times more likely than other Americans to be killed by law enforcement officers.[3] They were also killed at four times the rate of young white men.[4] Hispanic men are nearly twice as likely to be killed by police as white men.[5] Overall, civilian deaths from shootings and other police actions are vastly higher in the United States than in other developed nations.[6] And there is a serious problem of excessive police force, especially directed at racial minorities, that doesn't result in death.

Despite protests and public attention to this issue, we have largely overlooked how the Supreme Court, through a series of decisions, has contributed to the problem by making it very difficult to sue police and to hold officers and the governments that employ them accountable for wrongdoing. I believe that "establishing Justice" with regard to policing requires doing much more to be able to hold police accountable.

The Constitution and the courts are crucial here because the political process continually fails to prevent and remedy police misconduct. There are many explanations for this. Generally, public pressure is for more aggressive law enforcement, not for the protection of rights of suspects and criminal defendants. After all, when was the last time that any state or city adopted a law to expand the rights of criminal suspects or criminal defendants? When was the last time a state ever adopted a law trying to create more protection for prisoners' rights? The political pressure virtually always has been in one direction: for aggressive, even overaggressive, law enforcement. As discussed later in this chapter, this is reflected in the tremendous overcriminalization in the United States. The

United States has 5 percent of the world's population, but it has 25 percent of the world's prisoners.

Also, the political process does not work because of the identity of the victims of police misconduct. The victims are disproportionately individuals of color, and the political process, historically, has been far less responsive to their needs. In 1938, in a famous footnote, the Supreme Court explained that the political process does not provide an adequate safeguard for "discrete and insular" minorities.[7] This includes when discrete and insular minorities are the victims of police abuse.

Another problem with focusing on the political process is that it does not deal with the day-to-day violations of rights that are largely invisible to the public. Actors in the political process, to be sure, hear about the high-profile shootings and deaths. But it rarely comes to the public's attention when the police engage in illegal stops and abusive frisks. When it does, rarely does it produce concern, let alone outrage.

If the political process is not the solution, it is essential to turn to the courts. There are two primary ways of suing police and their departments: suits for injunctions or for damages. But the Supreme Court has made both exceptionally difficult. Suing cities and police departments for injunctive relief to halt abusive practices is one possible mechanism for achieving police accountability. But the decision in a key 1982 case, *City of Los Angeles v. Lyons*, is the case that makes this very difficult, even when there are systemic policies in a police department that violate the Constitution.[8]

Adolph Lyons was a twenty-four-year-old African American man. He was stopped by police officers about two o'clock in the morning for having a burned-out taillight. An officer ordered him out of the car. The officer slammed Lyons' hands above his head. Lyons complained that the keys in his hand were cutting into the skin of his palm. At that point, the officer administered a chokehold on Lyons and rendered him unconscious. When Lyons awoke, he had urinated and defecated. He was spitting blood and dirt. He was given a traffic ticket and allowed to go. He did some research and discovered at that point that sixteen people in Los Angeles died from the use of police chokeholds. Almost all, like him, were African American men. When the police chief, Daryl Gates, was asked at a press conference why it was that virtually all who died from the chokehold were African American, Gates said that it was because of physiological differences between "black people" and "normal people."[9]

Lyons sued the city of Los Angeles for an injunction to stop police officers from using the chokehold except when necessary to protect the officer's life or safety. The U.S. Supreme Court, in a 5–4 decision, ruled that Lyons lacked standing to sue for an injunction because he could not show that he personally was likely to be choked by the police again in the future. The Court said a plaintiff who is seeking an injunction must show a likelihood of future harm. This makes it enormously difficult to get an injunction against abusive police behavior. I have been part of so many conversations with lawyers over the last thirty years where they are seeking to enjoin an unconstitutional police practice, but they cannot bring a suit because they cannot think of a way to get around *City of Los Angeles v. Lyons.*

Alternatively, officers and the cities that employ them can be sued for money damages. Such relief is crucial for compensating victims of police misconduct and also for deterring future wrongdoing. But there are many obstacles to bringing a successful suit against the police or police departments for money damages. For the day-to-day violations—the illegal stops and searches—it is unlikely that there is enough possibility of money damages to interest a lawyer in taking the case. And in those situations, as well as in more serious cases, it is often going to be the word of the police officer against that of the person who claims a violation of rights. Often the plaintiff in a civil suit would be somebody who has been convicted of a crime.

The obstacles I want to focus on with regard to civil suits are those that the Supreme Court has created. The Court has made it enormously difficult to sue officers or cities for money damages. With regard to suing individual officers who engage in misconduct, the Supreme Court has said that *every* government official who is sued for money damages—local, state, or federal—has the ability to invoke "immunity" as a defense. It does not matter if it is a suit against a federal or state or local official for money damages; there always is an immunity defense.[10]

For some actions, there is absolute immunity: a complete bar to money damages. Even if the constitutional violation is egregious and the harms inflicted are grave, there is no liability when there is absolute immunity. For example, police officers have absolute immunity to a suit for money damages for testimony they give as a witness. *Briscoe v. LaHue*, in 1983, said a police officer cannot be civilly sued for money damages *even if the officer commits perjury on the witness stand that leads to the conviction of an innocent person.*[11]

Prosecutors have absolute immunity for all of their prosecutorial tasks. A prosecutor who knowingly uses perjured testimony that leads to the conviction of an innocent person cannot be sued for money damages. *Imbler v. Pachtman*, in 1976, involved a prosecutor who did just that and it resulted in the conviction of an innocent person who spent nine years in prison.[12] Nonetheless, the Supreme Court said that the prosecutor had absolute immunity and could not be sued for money damages.

More recently, the Court reaffirmed and extended

absolute immunity for police officers in *Van de Kamp v. Goldstein* (2009).[13] Tommy Lee Goldstein spent twenty-three and a half years in prison for murders he did not commit. At the time of his trial, there was no physical evidence linking him to the murder. There were no eyewitnesses. There was no confession. The only testimony against him at trial was from two people who, at different points, shared a jail cell with him and said they heard Goldstein admit to the murders. One recanted his testimony. The other was a longtime police informant, ironically with the name "Edward Fink." Fink had a long history of making deals with the police to get a reduction of charges and sentences in exchange for giving testimony against those with whom he had shared a jail cell. Fink testified that, when he was in a cell with Goldstein in Long Beach, he heard Goldstein admit to the murders. Goldstein's lawyers asked the deputy district attorney if Fink had ever made a deal for giving testimony in exchange for a reduction in charges and sentences and if there was such a deal here. The deputy district attorney said no. Goldstein was convicted, and, as I said, he spent twenty-three and a half years in prison.

Ultimately, a federal judge granted his habeas corpus petition. A federal judge said there was no credible evidence at all that Goldstein committed the murder, and, in fact, it turned out that, though not disclosed to Goldstein's lawyers, there was a deal in place for that case for Fink to get a reduction of charges and sentences in exchange for testimony. Goldstein, after being released from custody, knew he could not sue the deputy district attorney because of prosecutorial immunity. Instead, he sued the then district attorney, John Van de Kamp, saying that the district attorney's office failed to implement a policy to ensure that such exculpatory impeachment evidence was disclosed, as is constitutionally required.[14] The Ninth Circuit said this was an administrative failure and therefore not protected by absolute prosecutorial immunity. But the Supreme Court, in an opinion by Justice Stephen Breyer, unanimously said the district attorney was protected by absolute immunity. The Court said all of the administrative choices were linked to what happened in the courtroom and thus there could be no liability.

When government officials are not protected by absolute immunity, that does not necessarily mean that they can be sued. They then have what is called "qualified immunity." Qualified immunity, according to the Supreme Court, means that the government official can be held liable only if he or she violates a clearly established right that every reasonable officer knows and it has to be a right established beyond dispute. In case after case over the last decade, the Supreme Court has found qualified immunity to protect police officers who use excessive force. For example, a decade ago, there was *Brosseau v. Haugen* (2004).[15] The case involved a police officer who was chasing an individual. The person being chased got into a car and began to back out. The officer fired a number of shots into the car, seriously wounding the driver, though thankfully not fatally. The driver sued, saying this was excessive police force under the circumstances. The U.S. Court of Appeals for the Ninth Circuit said this was a question for a jury to decide. The Supreme Court reversed, stating that there were no cases on point that said a police officer can be held liable in these specific circumstances, and therefore, the officer was protected by qualified immunity.

Another case, from just a few years ago, is *Plumhoff v. Rickard* (2014).[16] A police officer stopped a car with a burned-out headlight. The officer asked the driver if he had been drinking. The driver said no. The officer asked the driver to get out of the car. Rather than do so, the driver sped away. A high-speed chase ensued; it went to almost one hundred miles an hour. At one point, the officers thought they had pinned the car they were chasing, but then the car got away. The officers fired three shots at the car. When the car still did not stop, the officers fired twelve more shots into the car. The driver and the passenger were killed. The estate of the driver sued the police, saying this was excessive police force in violation of the Fourth Amendment. The estate said there was no need to use deadly force when the underlying offense was a burned-out headlight. The officer could have let the car go. They had the license plate number. They could track down the driver and then arrest the driver for evading arrest and the high-speed chase.

The U.S. Court of Appeals for the Sixth Circuit said the case should go to a jury to decide whether there was excessive force. But instead, the Supreme Court said that the police officers could not be held liable. Once more, the Supreme Court was unanimous. Justice Alito wrote for the Court; there were two parts to his opinion. First, he said that there was no violation of the Fourth Amendment. He said that when there is a high-speed chase and the police perceive that innocent people might be in danger, the police can use deadly force and continue to use deadly force until the car stops. This now means that in a high percentage of all of these chases, the police can shoot and keep shooting until those in the car are dead. But then the Court went even further and said that even if there was a violation of the Fourth Amendment, the officers were protected by qualified immunity. The Court explained that there is no case on point that this behavior is unconstitutional.

The absolute and the qualified immunities together make it extremely difficult to civilly sue police officers for money damages when they violate the Constitution and even when they inflict great harms.

The other possible defendant, when it comes to suing

for money damages, is the city and the police department that employs the officers. But here, too, the Supreme Court has created significant obstacles to holding local governments liable. In 1978, in *Monell v. Department of Social Services*, the Court said that a local government can be held liable only if its own policies violate the Constitution.[17] A local government cannot be held liable on the grounds that someone it employs in the scope of work injures others. That is different than the usual rule in the law, which provides that employers are liable for the torts—the harms—inflicted by their employees in the scope of their duties. But it is not so when it comes to suits against local governments.

In the years since *Monell v. Department of Social Services*, the Supreme Court has made it ever more difficult to hold local governments liable. Often these cases have arisen in the context of police abuses. For example, in *Bryan County v. Brown*, in 1997, a sheriff decided to hire a relative who did not meet the usual criteria for hiring at the Sheriff's Department because of a police record and a serious history of violent behavior.[18] The sheriff knew about this, and he decided that he would not give a gun to this deputy sheriff. An incident arose where the officer, the deputy sheriff, pulled a car over. There was an exchange of words, and the officer yanked the passenger of the car, a woman, out with great violence. In fact, so much force was used that when the woman landed on her knees, permanent structural damage was done, and she had to have replacement knees on both of her legs.

The suit was brought against the police department. The Supreme Court previously had said that deliberate indifference in hiring, training, and supervision can be used to establish a municipal policy. The Supreme Court, however, ruled 5–4 that the local government could not be held liable. The Court said it was not foreseeable that this specific injury would result from deliberate indifference. To hold the city liable, it has to be foreseeable that the particular harm would result. It is extremely difficult to be able to prove such a result with the specificity required by the Supreme Court.

A more recent example is *Connick v. Thompson* (2011).[19] John Thompson spent eighteen and a half years in prison for a murder he did not commit. At the time of his trial, the deputy district attorney was given blood evidence apparently linking Thompson to the murder. Although the deputy district attorney was constitutionally required to make available that blood sample so the defense lawyers could do their own testing, he did not do so and did not disclose the existence of the blood evidence. Thompson was convicted and sentenced to death. Many years later, when this prosecutor was literally on his deathbed, dying of cancer, he told another deputy district attorney about the blood evidence and how it was hidden. That deputy district attorney had the obligation to come forward, but he also did not do so.

Just weeks before Thompson's scheduled execution, through a series of coincidences, his lawyers learned of this blood evidence. Thankfully, it was still there in the police evidence room. Testing was done. Not only did the blood not match Thompson's DNA; it did not even match his blood type. There was a new trial and Thompson was acquitted. He brought a civil suit against the jurisdiction, the New Orleans parish in Louisiana, for a violation of his rights in not disclosing evidence to the defense as is required by the Constitution. Thompson claimed there was a long pattern in New Orleans, through its prosecutor's office, of violating *Brady v. Maryland* (1963). The jury in the federal district court gave Thompson a large judgment. The U.S. Court of Appeals for the Fifth Circuit affirmed, but the Supreme Court, in a 5–4 decision, reversed.

Justice Clarence Thomas wrote the opinion for the Court. Justice Thomas said one incident is not enough to establish a municipal policy. Because the Court saw this as just one incident, Thompson could not recover anything from the city of New Orleans. Justice Ginsberg wrote a powerful dissent saying this was not just one incident. She said there were five different prosecutors who came to know of this blood evidence, and not one of them came forward. She said this was not the only constitutional violation in this case. She said the police had a witness that they did not disclose to the defense; the witness said that the assailant had short hair, but Thompson had a large afro at the time of the murder. Also, there was a great deal of evidence of other similar violations by this prosecutor's office. Nonetheless, the Court said there could be no liability.

So besides all the practical hurdles, the Supreme Court, by immunity doctrine and by requiring proof of a municipal policy, has made it extremely hard for individuals to recover money damages.

There is much that can be done to reform policing in the United States to better achieve justice. But a crucial step is to change the law to allow suits against police officers and prosecutors for constitutional violations. I am convinced that meaningful police reform, and therefore greater compliance with the constitutional provisions concerning this aspect of justice, will only happen if there is great accountability in the courts. This could happen by the Supreme Court reversing its earlier decisions or through legislation by Congress or at the state level.

TRIALS

Even though the Sixth Amendment guarantees the right to counsel in criminal cases, the major failing in criminal trials is not ensuring adequate counsel for those accused of crimes. *Gideon v. Wainwright* spoke eloquently of the vital importance of an attorney for ensuring a fair process and held that all citizens facing a possible prison sentence have the right to an attorney. But the Supreme Court created no enforcement mechanism, and the reality is that the poor often have grossly inadequate lawyers. Fulfilling the Preamble's promise of establishing justice requires remedying the tremendous inequities in the criminal justice system. It is long overdue for the Supreme Court to mandate that the government must provide *competent* counsel and to use a more realistic standard for determining when there is "ineffective assistance of counsel."

An adversary system of justice requires some semblance of equality between the two sides. *Gideon* was a crucial attempt to make that a reality. It holds that all facing the power of the state to take away their liberty, however poor, are entitled to representation. *Gideon* holds that the government must pay for and provide an attorney to those who cannot afford one and face the loss of their liberty by imprisonment. As the Court powerfully declared in *Gideon*:

> Reason and reflection require us to recognize that in our adversary system of criminal justice, any person haled into court, who is too poor to hire a lawyer, cannot be assured a fair trial unless counsel is provided for him. This seems to us to be an obvious truth. . . . The right of one charged with crime to counsel may not be deemed fundamental and essential to fair trials in some countries, but it is in ours. From the very beginning, our state and national constitutions and laws have laid great emphasis on procedural and substantive safeguards designed to assure fair trials before impartial tribunals in which every defendant stands equal before the law. This noble ideal cannot be realized if the

> poor man charged with crime has to face his accusers without a lawyer to assist him.[20]

Yet while *Gideon* is celebrated, the reality of its implementation must be lamented. In 2004, forty years after *Gideon v. Wainwright*, an American Bar Association study concluded: "Indigent defense in the United States remains in a state of crisis, resulting in a system that lacks fundamental fairness and places poor persons at constant risk of wrongful convictions. . . . Funding for indigent defense services is shamefully inadequate."[21] Over the last decade, the problem has undoubtedly gotten much worse as the severe recession caused budget crises in states across the country and cuts in funding for courts and all the services they provide; these were cuts that have often not been restored even as the economy has improved.[22]

As someone who handles criminal appeals, I have represented clients I believe to be innocent who were convicted because of ineffective assistance of counsel.[23] And I have represented clients who, I am convinced, received death sentences because of this.[24] In instances like these, I wonder whether these individuals really were better off because of *Gideon*. Perhaps if they had been left to represent themselves they would have done better or the courts might have looked more closely at their cases. *Gideon* creates such a strong presumption that the presence of counsel has insured adequate representation, when the reality is so very different. As Senator Patrick Leahy remarked: "Too often individuals facing the ultimate punishment are represented by lawyers who are drunk, sleeping, soon-to-be disbarred or just plain ineffective. Even the best lawyers in these systems are hampered by inadequate compensation and insufficient resources to investigate and develop a meaningful defense."[25]

What explains *Gideon*'s failure? Most of all, it has been

a failure to adequately fund the right to counsel that *Gideon* promised. My premise is a simple one: the quality of representation often matters in criminal cases, and money is often crucial in determining the quality of representation. Of course, there are instances where the outcome will be the same no matter how good or bad the defense lawyer. Of course, too, there are instances where the best-paid lawyer does a poor job or the inadequately compensated attorney is terrific. But that said, any one of us facing criminal charges would want the best lawyer we could get, and being able to pay for it matters.

The most powerful evidence of this comes from studies that have compared the outcomes of cases depending on how the lawyer is compensated. The Bureau of Justice Statistics found that those with publicly funded counsel are more likely to be convicted than those with privately paid attorneys.[26] It concluded: "Of defendants found guilty in federal district courts, 88 percent with publicly financed counsel and 77 percent with private counsel received jail or prison sentences; in large state courts, 71 percent with public counsel and 54 percent with private attorneys were sentenced to incarceration."[27]

Moreover, among those with publicly paid attorneys, the outcome varies depending on whether there is a public defender or appointed counsel, such as in federal court, whether there is a federal defender or an attorney appointed under the Criminal Justice Act (2003).[28] Professor Radha Iyengar concluded that "defendants with CJA panel attorneys are on average more likely to be found guilty and on average to receive longer sentences. Overall, the expected sentence for defendants with CJA panel attorneys is nearly eight months longer."[29]

The same difference has been found in state courts. James M. Anderson and Paul Heaton compared the outcomes in murder cases depending on whether there is a public defender and/or an appointed counsel in Philadelphia courts.[30] They found that compared to appointed counsel, public defenders reduce their clients' murder conviction rate by 19 percent and lower the probability that their client will receive a life sentence by 62 percent.[31] Public defenders, as compared to appointed counsel, reduce overall expected time served in prison by 24 percent.[32] To say the obvious, these are dramatic differences.

Many studies have been done in capital cases and they are remarkably consistent in documenting that a conviction and death sentence in a capital case is least likely with a privately paid lawyer, and that those with government-paid attorneys are much better off with public defenders than with appointed counsel.[33]

The advice to a person facing prosecution, especially for a serious crime, would be clear: if you can, hire your own attorney. Failing that, do all you can to get representation by a public defender rather than by a court-appointed attorney. Why? James Anderson and Paul Heaton offer a compelling explanation: "We find that, in general, appointed counsel have comparatively few resources, face more difficult incentives, and are more isolated than public defenders. The extremely low compensation for appointed counsel reduces the pool of attorneys willing to take the appointments and makes extensive preparation economically undesirable. Moreover, the judges selecting counsel may be doing so for reasons partly unrelated to counsel's efficacy. In contrast, the public defenders' steady salaries, financial and institutional independence from judges, and team approach to indigent defense avoid many of these problems. These longer-term institutional differences lead to the more immediate cause of the difference in outcomes: less preparation by appointed counsel."[34]

Simply put, the identity of the lawyer matters and the method of compensating the lawyer is often crucial in determining who will provide representation. It is in this context that the many studies done of the inadequacy of representation in criminal cases can be understood. The American Bar Association's Standing Committee on Legal Aid and Indigent Defendants (SCLAID) concluded: "Quality legal representation cannot be rendered unless indigent defense systems are adequately funded. Attorneys who do not receive sufficient compensation have a disincentive to devote the necessary time and effort to provide meaningful representation or even participate in the system at all. With fewer attorneys available to accept cases, the lawyers who provide services are often saddled with excessive caseloads, further hampering their ability to represent their clients effectively."[35] The committee further stated that "inadequate compensation for indigent defense attorneys is a national problem, which makes the recruitment and retention of experienced lawyers extraordinarily difficult."[36]

The Report of the National Right to Counsel Committee similarly concluded: "Inadequate financial support continues to be the single greatest obstacle to delivering 'competent' and 'diligent' defense representation."[37] It noted that "the most visible sign of inadequate funding is attorneys attempting to provide services while carrying astonishingly large caseloads. Frequently, public defenders are asked to represent far too many clients."[38] Appointed counsel are often paid so little that only those who cannot find other work are available and their compensation is so inadequate as to provide insufficient incentives for the needed work.[39]

This notion that one gets what one can pay for in representation is reflected in studies done of the quality of representation in capital cases. Professor Douglas Vick explained: "Several observers have noted that poor compensation will not attract the best attorneys to represent indigents in death penalty cases. . . . For example, as of

January 1990, the Alabama attorneys who represented defendants sentenced to death had been subject to disciplinary action, including disbarment, at a rate twenty times that of the Alabama bar as a whole. For those attorneys whose clients were executed, the rate of disciplinary sanctions was almost forty times that of the bar as a whole. One-quarter of the inmates on Kentucky's death row were represented at trial by attorneys who subsequently were disbarred or resigned rather than face disbarment. As of January 1990, nearly 13 percent of the defendants executed in Louisiana had been represented by lawyers who had been disciplined, while the disciplinary rate for the Louisiana bar as a whole was 0.19 percent. In Texas, the attorneys who represented defendants sentenced to death have been disciplined at a rate nine times that of the Texas bar as a whole; similar disparities exist in Georgia, Mississippi, and Florida."[40]

All of this has been exacerbated by the fiscal crisis facing state governments, and thus state courts, across the country. The Report of the National Right to Counsel Committee concluded: "The country's current fiscal crisis, which afflicts state and local governments everywhere, is having severe adverse consequences for the funding of indigent defense services, which already receives substantially less financial support compared to prosecution and law enforcement."[41] A study by the National Center for State Courts found that from 2008 to 2011, forty-two states cut their funding for their state court systems.[42] Funding for defense lawyers and all of the support they need has been cut from its previously inadequate levels.

By every measure, then, there are gross inadequacies in the provision of counsel to indigent defendants. The constitutional assurance of the right to counsel is rendered illusory, and innocent people are convicted as a result.[43]

Why has the promise of *Gideon* been so poorly realized? I believe two interrelated phenomena explain this. First, the Supreme Court imposed an unfunded mandate on state and local governments with the only realistic enforcement mechanism being the finding of ineffective assistance of counsel in individual cases. Second, the Court created a test for ineffective assistance of counsel that makes it very difficult for a convicted individual to get relief, even when counsel's performance is quite deficient.

As to the former, *Gideon* is atypical in American constitutional law because it involves the Court finding an affirmative constitutional right requiring the government to provide a "service" to individuals. The rights in the Constitution are generally thought to be negative liberties, prohibitions on what the government may do.[44] The Constitution forbids the government from abridging freedom of speech or denying equal protection of the laws or depriving a person of life, liberty, or property.

Gideon, though, creates an affirmative constitutional duty for the government to provide something to individuals: counsel in criminal cases where there is a possible prison sentence, if necessary at the government's expense. The Court, however, imposed this duty without providing a funding source. It was left to each state, and in many instances each county, to provide funds for attorneys for indigent criminal defendants.[45]

In the decades following *Gideon*, this burden increased tremendously as a result of an enormous increase in criminalization, prosecution, and incarceration. Nationally, five times more prisoners are incarcerated today than just a few decades ago.[46] "Between 1991 and 1999, the number of children with a parent in a federal or state correctional facility increased by more than 100 percent, from approximately 900,000 to 2,000,000."[47] The nation's incarceration rate is among the world's highest, and five to ten times higher than the rates in other industrialized nations.[48] In other words, whatever burden on state treasuries was envisioned by the *Gideon* Court, the dramatic growth in criminal laws and criminal prosecutions made it vastly greater than expected.

Among the many competing for scarce government resources, indigent criminal defendants are hardly a powerful political constituency. Professor Vick notes that, in the context of inadequate representation for those facing death sentences, "the individuals adversely affected by this crisis—those accused of aggravated murder—are the most hated and the least politically powerful in the country, and political actors, including judges, are not highly motivated to make unpopular decisions that would benefit them."[49] It is not surprising, then, that the result is the inadequacy in funding of defense counsel described above. The Supreme Court left it to the states to provide defense lawyers, and states often will choose the most inexpensive way to meet this obligation.

Actually, the problem is more subtle and more difficult. *Gideon* must mean more than just a right to a lawyer: to have any meaning, it must be that there is a right to competent counsel. The Supreme Court has recognized that the Sixth Amendment of the United States Constitution guarantees a criminal defendant *effective* assistance of counsel.[50] This means that no criminal defendant is to be left to the "mercies of incompetent counsel."[51] But whereas the existence of an attorney for a criminal defendant is easily achieved, ensuring competent counsel is far more difficult and elusive.

In theory, this can be defined and ensured in a systemic way. But in practice, the attempt to enforce a right to competent counsel on a systemwide basis has proven futile. There have been many challenges to the inadequacy of the system of providing criminal representation within a jurisdiction. Challenges in federal court to the inadequacy of criminal representation in state courts generally have been dismissed on procedural grounds.

Nor are such systemwide suits in state court likely to succeed. For example, in *Florida v. Public Defender, Eleventh Judicial Circuit* (2009), the public defender's office argued that inadequate funding led to excessive caseloads, which prevented it from carrying out its legal and ethical obligations to indigent defendants.[52] The court, though, ruled that the public defender was required to prove prejudice or conflict, separate from excessive caseload, on an individual basis to be relieved of the duty to represent indigent criminal defendants. Similarly, in *Kennedy v. Carlson*, a challenge to the inadequacy of the funding of public defenders in Minnesota was dismissed on the ground that the chief public defender failed to show injury in fact sufficient to establish a justiciable issue that indigent clients of the public defenders' office had received ineffective assistance of counsel due to insufficient funding.[53] As Catholic University law professor Cara Drinan notes: "Historically, structural litigation—which has been defined as 'a sustained pattern of cases against large power structures invoking the power of the courts to oversee detailed injunctive relief'—has been sparingly used in the indigent defense context. It is estimated that no more than ten of these suits were filed between 1980 and 2000. Moreover, early suits seeking to improve indigent defense failed to generate lasting reform."[54] State courts have not been receptive to such claims, and "to date, a federal forum has not been available to indigent defendants seeking to vindicate their Sixth Amendment right to counsel on a systemic basis."[55]

The primary mechanism, then, for enforcing *Gideon*'s promise has been the ability of an individual criminal defendant to argue that he or she received ineffective assistance of counsel. But the Supreme Court, in *Strickland v. Washington* (1984), made it very difficult for courts to find ineffective assistance of counsel, even when representation is very deficient.[56] Justice Sandra Day O'Connor, writing for the conservative majority, set a standard that means that only rarely will a conviction be overturned for inadequacy of representation. The Court said that a finding of ineffective assistance of counsel requires demonstrating first that the attorney's performance was so deficient "that counsel was not functioning as the 'counsel' guaranteed by the Sixth Amendment."[57] But even gross deficiency by a defense counsel is not sufficient to overturn a conviction or a sentence for ineffective assistance of counsel. Second, the defendant must show prejudice; that is, that defendant has to demonstrate that the "counsel's deficient performance more likely than not altered the outcome in the case."[58] In other words, relief for ineffective assistance of counsel requires that a convicted defendant show that the result of the trial likely would have been different if only the attorney had acted competently.

This is usually an insurmountable burden. It is so easy for later judges to say that they think that the judge or jury would have come to the same conclusion anyway. Justice Thurgood Marshall explained exactly this problem in his dissent in *Strickland*: "It is often very difficult to tell whether a defendant convicted after a trial in which he was ineffectively represented would have fared better if his lawyer had been competent. Seemingly impregnable cases can sometimes be dismantled by good defense counsel."[59]

My former colleague, Yale law professor Dennis Curtis, said that under *Strickland* an attorney will be found to be adequate so long as a mirror put in front of him or her at trial would have shown a breath. Professor Curtis overstates, but not by much. The Court's recent decision in *Cullen v. Pinholster* (2011) shows how difficult it is to prove ineffective assistance of counsel.[60]

Scott Lynn Pinholster was convicted of murder. His

defense lawyers had not been notified that the prosecutor planned to present aggravating circumstances in a penalty phase and therefore did not prepare to present mitigating evidence. Nonetheless, the judge allowed the penalty phase to go forward and the defense lawyers presented only one witness, Pinholster's mother.

After Pinholster was sentenced to death and exhausted his appeals in California state court, his new lawyers filed a writ of habeas corpus in federal court. The lawyers provided declarations showing substantial new evidence that supported the claim of ineffective assistance of counsel. The federal court granted a hearing, and the new evidence documented that the defense counsel at trial had undertaken no investigation of mitigating circumstances. Had they done so, they would have learned that Pinholster suffered from a brain injury, a seizure disorder, and personality disorders. The evidence also included testimony from family members and school officials about Pinholster's abuse as a child. All of this is powerful mitigating evidence that might have caused the jury to refrain from imposing the death penalty.

The federal district court granted the writ of habeas corpus, and ultimately the Ninth Circuit affirmed in an en banc decision (a decision of eleven judges on the court). The Supreme Court, though, in an opinion by Justice Clarence Thomas, reversed. The Court held that the federal district court should not have held the hearing on ineffective assistance of counsel. The Court ruled that the federal court on habeas corpus is limited to considering the evidence that was before the state court and cannot hold an evidentiary hearing. The result is that individuals who have substantial evidence of ineffective assistance of counsel, or of a prosecutor's failure to disclose exculpatory evidence or even of actual innocence, will be unable to present this material on habeas corpus. In theory, the criminal defendants can go to state court, but often state courts are unwilling to hear the evidence or simply deny claims without a hearing and with no more than a postcard.

Moreover, the Court concluded, 5–4, that the inadequacy of the defense lawyers was not sufficient to show ineffective assistance of counsel. The Court stressed the need for great deference to the state courts and concluded that Pinholster could not prove that he was prejudiced by the failings of counsel.[61] But if this total failure of defense counsel to investigate can be rationalized as a strategic choice of counsel and not prejudicial, there will be few instances in which ineffective assistance of counsel can be demonstrated.

Taken together, then, it is possible to explain the failure to implement *Gideon*: the Supreme Court created a mandate without ensuring adequate funding; state and local governments lacked political or legal incentives to provide sufficient resources; systemic litigation was unsuccessful, leaving the only remedy as the determination of ineffective assistance of counsel in individual cases. But the Court adopted a standard for this in *Strickland v. Washington* that makes it exceedingly difficult for a defendant to establish ineffective assistance of counsel. The result is, as death penalty lawyer Stephen Bright declared: "No constitutional right is celebrated so much in the abstract and observed so little in reality as the right to counsel."[62]

Establishing justice requires adequate counsel for criminal defendants in every case. This must be a core aspect of the progressive agenda for the Constitution.

PUNISHMENT

A final component of establishing justice is reforming punishments in the criminal justice system. To begin with, there is tremendous overincarceration in the United States. In a recent article in the *Harvard Law Review*, Barack Obama wrote:

> In 1980, there were less than half a million inmates in U.S. state and federal prisons and jails. Today, that figure stands at an estimated 2.2 million, more than any other country on Earth. Many people who commit crimes deserve punishment, and many belong behind bars. But too many, especially nonviolent drug offenders, serve unnecessarily long sentences. With just 5 percent of the world's population, the United States incarcerates nearly 25 percent of the world's prisoners. We keep more people behind bars than the top thirty-five European countries combined, and our rate of incarceration dwarfs not only other western allies but also countries like Russia and Iran.[63]

The costs of this are enormous. Nationally, the country spends $81 billion a year to house its prisoners.[64] California spends more on its prisons than it does on its schools. And the human cost is far greater and much more important.

The effects of this are felt disproportionately by people of color. Professor Michelle Alexander's stunning book, *The New Jim Crow: Mass Incarceration in the Age of Colorblindness*, describes how much overincarceration especially affects racial minorities.[65] She tells how the story of Jim Crow has been transformed from one of mass segregation and disenfranchisement in the post-Reconstruction era into mass incarceration in the war on drugs and mandatory minimum sentencing era. President Obama writes: "Rates of parental incarceration are two to seven times higher for African American and Hispanic children. Over the past thirty years, the share of African American adults with a past felony conviction—and who have paid their debt to society—has more than tripled, and one in four African American men outside the correctional system now has a felony record. This number is in addition to the one in twenty African American men under correctional supervision."[66]

There is much that needs to be done about this, including lessening punishments for minor crimes, eliminating many mandatory minimum penalties, and sentencing reform. The problem, in part, stems from the Supreme Court's refusal to find draconian sentences for minor crimes to be cruel and unusual punishment. In 2003, in *Ewing v. California*, the Court, 5–4, upheld a prison sentence of twenty-five years to life for a man who stole four golf clubs worth $1,200.[67] In *Lockyer v. Andrade* (which I argued in the Supreme Court and lost), the Court, 5–4, upheld a sentence of fifty years to life for a man who stole $153 worth of videotapes from two Kmart stores.[68] Both cases involved sentences under California's three-strikes law. If these sentences are not cruel and unusual, it is hard to imagine the punishment that would be deemed so disproportionate to the crime as to be unconstitutional.[69]

Fulfilling the Preamble's commitment to justice should mean that grossly excessive sentences—like those in *Ewing* and *Andrade*—are cruel and unusual punishment in violation of the Eighth Amendment. Literally every day across the country, individuals receive enormous sentences for relatively minor crimes.

Also, the United States is the only western nation with the death penalty and only one of nine nations that continues to regularly impose capital punishment, among them countries not known for their belief in liberty: North Korea, China, Libya, Iran, and Somalia. The Court has repeatedly upheld the constitutionality of the death penalty, including most recently in 2015, holding that the burden is on a condemned person who is challenging the method of execution to demonstrate that there is a more humane way of carrying out the death penalty.[70] It is absurd that a person facing execution must convince a court that there is a better way to kill him or her when the government is using a method of capital punishment that will inflict great pain and suffering.

Justice Breyer wrote a dissent in this case in which he powerfully argued that the death penalty is unconstitutional as cruel and unusual punishment.[71] Justice Ginsburg joined the dissent. I believe that if there were a fifth vote, Justices Sotomayor and Kagan would be part of such a majority opinion. I am convinced that if Hillary Clinton had been elected as president there would have come to be five justices on the Court to finally declare the death penalty unconstitutional. Justice Breyer is not the first Supreme Court justice to come to this conclusion. Near the end of his time on the Court, Harry Blackmun famously declared: "From this day forward, I no longer shall tinker with the machinery of death."[72] Justice Blackmun came to believe that it was impossible to devise a system for administering the death penalty that was sufficiently fair, sufficiently reliable in protecting the innocent, and sufficiently humane to be constitutional. After that declaration, in every case, Justice Blackmun voted to overturn the death penalty, as Justices William Brennan and Thurgood Marshall had done before him.

It is not going to happen soon, but Justice Breyer's opinion thoroughly detailed the reasons why executing people is inherently cruel and unusual punishment. He wrote:

> Almost forty years of studies, surveys, and experience strongly indicate, however, that this effort has failed.

> Today's administration of the death penalty involves three fundamental constitutional defects: (1) serious unreliability, (2) arbitrariness in application, and (3) unconscionably long delays that undermine the death penalty's penological purpose. Perhaps as a result, (4) most places within the United States have abandoned its use. . . . For it is those changes, taken together with my own 20 years of experience on this Court, that lead me to believe that the death penalty, in and of itself, now likely constitutes a legally prohibited "cruel and unusual punishment."[73]

Justice Breyer, like many other scholars, has documented each of these reasons. He describes, for example, the inevitability that some innocent people will be convicted and sentenced to death, including giving examples of when this has occurred.[74] He explains the arbitrariness with which the death penalty is imposed, again with race playing a key factor. He documents the long delays inherent to ensuring due process but that make the death penalty particularly arbitrary and rob it of any penological benefit. He explained: "The upshot is that lengthy delays both aggravate the cruelty of the death penalty and undermine its jurisprudential rationale. And this Court has said that, if the death penalty does not fulfill the goals of deterrence or retribution, 'it is nothing more than the purposeless and needless imposition of pain and suffering and hence an unconstitutional punishment.'"[75]

A federal district court judge in California found that the imposition of the death penalty in that state was so arbitrary as to be unconstitutional. Judge Cormac Carney's decision was carefully reasoned and meticulously documented. "Since 1978, when the current death penalty system was adopted by California voters, over 900 people have been sentenced to death for their crimes. Of them, only 13 have been executed. For the rest, the dysfunctional administration of California's death penalty system has resulted, and will continue to result, in an inordinate and unpredictable period of delay preceding their actual execution. Indeed, for most, systemic delay has made their execution so unlikely that the death sentence carefully and deliberately imposed by the jury has been quietly transformed into one no rational jury or legislature could ever impose: *life in prison, with the remote possibility of death.* As for the random few for whom execution does become a reality, they will have languished for so long on Death Row that their execution will serve no retributive or deterrent purpose and will be arbitrary."[76] He concluded that such an arbitrary punishment violates the Eighth Amendment's prohibition of cruel and unusual punishment.

Judge Carney's facts are unassailable. Countless factors—the process of direct review by the California Supreme Court, the lack of qualified attorneys to handle death penalty cases, the need for multiple levels of review—contribute to long delays and unpredictability in carrying out death sentences. The average delay between sentencing and execution in California is twenty-five years. In the case before Judge Carney, the defendant was sentenced to death in 1995, and there are still appellate proceedings in his federal case.

Nor is there any fix for this. Short-circuiting appeals or proceeding without competent counsel increases the risk of executing innocent people or imposing the death penalty when there has been a serious constitutional violation. The Supreme Court long has recognized that arbitrary punishments violate the Eighth Amendment, and Judge Carney's opinion shows, as many judges and law professors have concluded, that the California death penalty system is irreparably broken. Unfortunately, the U.S. Court of Appeals for the Ninth Circuit reversed Judge

Carney's decision on procedural grounds and the death penalty remains in California.[77]

I believe that someday the United States will join with every Western nation and the vast majority of countries and declare the death penalty unconstitutional. Doing so is integral to "establishing justice."

7

SECURING LIBERTY

The Preamble says that the Constitution exists to "secure the Blessings of Liberty to ourselves and to our Posterity." The Constitution thus protects basic aspects of personal freedom. Some of these are mentioned in the Constitution, such as freedom of speech and free exercise of religion. Others are not mentioned in the text but are no less important. The Ninth Amendment says: "The enumeration in the Constitution, of certain rights, shall not be construed to deny or disparage others retained by the people." For instance, freedom of travel is a fundamental right that long has been protected by the courts even though it is never mentioned anywhere in the Constitution.[1]

I predict that two aspects of liberty will be especially important in the years ahead: privacy and religious freedom. What should be the progressive vision for each? In focusing on these areas, I realize, of course, that I am not covering other important aspects of liberty.

Most notably, I am omitting detailed consideration of freedom of speech.[2] At this point, there is more agreement between conservatives and liberals on free speech than in many other areas of constitutional law. It is why many of the recent cases have been unanimous in favor of free speech.[3] The two major disagreements at this point between conservatives and liberals regarding speech concern campaign finance regulation and restrictions of speech that serve the institutional interests of the government.

As to the former, in many cases, in 5–4 decisions, the Roberts Court has struck down campaign finance regulations, most famously in *Citizens United v. Federal Election Commission*, which held that corporations can spend unlimited amounts of money in election campaigns.[4] I believe that progressives should continue to challenge the desirability of these decisions, including disagreeing with the premise that spending money in campaigns is speech. Also, they must continue to criticize the failure to recognize the compelling interests served by campaign finance regulation in preventing corruption and the appearance of corruption, lessening disproportionate influence in the election process, and ensuring public confidence in the election system.[5]

As to the latter, although the Roberts Court generally has been protective of free speech, that has not been so when the institutional interests of the government are involved; the Court then gives great deference to the government and little protection to speech. For example, in *Garcetti v. Ceballos* (2006), the Roberts Court held, 5–4, that the First Amendment provides *no* protection for the speech of government employees on the job in the scope of their duties.[6] In other words, a government employee who reports misconduct—as Richard Ceballos did—can be disciplined or even fired and is entirely without recourse under the Constitution. In *Morse v. Frederick* (2007), the Court ruled that a student could be punished by a school for displaying, on a public sidewalk at a school event, a banner saying, "Bong Hits for Jesus."[7] The Court denied First Amendment protection even though the speech was not disruptive of school activities and unlikely to have any effect. In these decisions and other cases involving the interests of the government, the Court has given far too much deference to the government and not nearly enough protection to speech.

Another major constitutional right is the Second Amendment, which is discussed in chapter 1. The Roberts Court has provided unprecedented protection for the rights of gun owners under the Second Amendment. From 1787 until 2008, the Court said that the Second Amendment protects only a right to have firearms for militia service. But in *District of Columbia v. Heller*, the Court struck down a thirty-two-year-old District of Columbia ordinance prohibiting private ownership or possession of handguns.[8] The Court said that the Second Amendment protects a right of people to have guns in their homes for the sake of security. In *McDonald v. City of Chicago*, the Court ruled that this right is incorporated into the Fourteenth Amendment and applies to state and local governments.[9]

Progressives need to continue to argue, as the four dissenting justices concluded in these two cases, that the Second Amendment means what it says: it is a right to have guns for purposes of military service. Moreover, the progressive position must be that even if there is an individual right to have guns, it can be regulated by the government to protect public safety. In fact, the Court in *District of Columbia v. Heller* made clear that the government can regulate who owns a gun, what types of guns can be owned, and where those guns can be located in order to protect public safety. For example, Justice Scalia—also in the 2008 majority decision—used laws prohibiting the carrying of concealed weapons as an example of the type of regulations that are permissible under the Second Amendment. He further noted that "nothing in our [Supreme Court] opinion should be taken to cast doubt on longstanding prohibitions on the possession of firearms by felons and the mentally ill, or laws forbidding the carrying of firearms in sensitive places such as schools and government buildings, or laws imposing conditions and qualifications on the commercial sale of arms."[10]

Progressives need to champion gun control and its constitutionality because of the continued carnage from firearms. Study after study shows that crime has decreased in foreign countries that have adopted strict gun control laws.[11] Sensible gun regulations won't stop all the killing, but it will have a dramatic effect. The fact that people get illegal drugs, or even that people commit murders, despite the criminal prohibitions on those crimes is not an argument against the laws. Nor is the possibility of illegal possession of guns a reason to give up and fail to make it more difficult for dangerous individuals to get firearms.

PRIVACY

The word "privacy" is used to describe at least three distinct rights: freedom from government intrusion, control over information, and autonomy for crucial decisions.[12] Each of these will be very important in the years ahead.

First, privacy is about freedom from government intrusion into an individual's home or onto an individual's person. This, of course, is the focus of the Fourth Amendment, and the Supreme Court has frequently spoken of that provision as protecting a reasonable expectation of privacy.[13] This focus of the Fourth Amendment can be tied to a dissenting opinion by Justice Louis Brandeis. In *Olmstead v. United States*, in 1928, the Supreme Court held that the Fourth Amendment does not apply to wiretapping if there was no physical intrusion into a person's home.[14] Justice Brandeis, though, made an eloquent argument that the Fourth Amendment should apply because people have a reasonable expectation of privacy for their conversations. He wrote:

> The makers of our Constitution undertook to secure conditions favorable to the pursuit of happiness. They recognized the significance of man's spiritual nature, of his feelings and of his intellect. They knew that only a part of the pain, pleasure and satisfactions of life are to be found in material things. They sought to protect Americans in their beliefs, their thoughts, their emotions and their sensations. They conferred, as against the government, the right to be let alone—the most comprehensive of rights and the right most valued by civilized men. To protect that right, every unjustifiable intrusion by the government upon the privacy of the individual, whatever the means employed, must be deemed a violation of the Fourth Amendment.[15]

Brandeis also offered a reminder about governmental abuse of power that has special salience today:

> Experience should teach us to be most on our guard to protect liberty when the government's purposes are beneficent. Men born to freedom are naturally alert to repel invasion of their liberty by evil-minded rulers. The greatest dangers to liberty lurk in insidious encroachment by men of zeal, well-meaning but without understanding.[16]

It took almost forty years, but in *Katz v. United States* (1967), the Supreme Court adopted Brandeis's approach and held that the Fourth Amendment applies when there is a reasonable expectation of privacy.[17] The Supreme Court held that the government needed a warrant under the Fourth Amendment to listen to a person's conversations from a telephone booth. The Court stressed that the individual had a reasonable expectation of privacy.

The challenge ahead is bringing the Fourth Amendment into the twenty-first century and applying it to the new technology that can be used to gain information about people. So far the Court has quite a mixed record in doing so. For example, *Maryland v. King* (2013) is a very troubling decision that fails to recognize a serious threat to privacy from new technology.[18] In *Maryland v. King*, the Court held, 5–4, that the government may take DNA samples from those arrested for serious crimes to see if they are linked to crimes for which they are not suspects. This is a significant expansion of the ability of law enforcement to gather information about individuals for crimes where they are not a suspect and it fails to recognize the potential enormous loss of privacy from the government possessing a DNA database.

Alonzo Jay King, Jr., was arrested in Maryland for first- and second-degree assault. A sample of King's DNA was then taken by putting a cotton swab inside his cheek (a "buccal swab"). This was done pursuant to the Maryland DNA Collection Act (1994), which requires the collection of DNA from those arrested for serious crimes. The DNA was not collected to link King to the assaults for which he was arrested; King was arrested for pointing a gun at some individuals, and there was no dispute as to his identity: DNA was not relevant to that prosecution. The DNA was collected entirely for the purpose of potentially linking King to other crimes.

King's DNA was then matched to a profile of forensic evidence from a sexual assault. Under Maryland law, the DNA match cannot be used as evidence at trial, but it does provide probable cause for arresting an individual for the other crime and for taking another DNA sample. Based on the DNA taken from him after his arrest for sexual assault, King was charged with rape and ultimately convicted of that crime and sentenced to life in prison.

Federal law and the law in all fifty states provides that DNA will be collected from individuals convicted of felonies. The issue presented in *Maryland v. King* was whether DNA can be taken and analyzed from a person arrested for a crime, who has not yet been convicted, and for the sole purpose of investigating other crimes. The Maryland Court of Appeals found that this violated the Fourth Amendment and emphasized that the taking of DNA was a search done without any individualized suspicion. The court observed that "DNA samples contain a massive amount of deeply personal information."[19] The court stressed the importance of the distinction between convicted individuals and those who have only been arrested.

The Supreme Court reversed, with Justice Kennedy writing for the Court, joined by Chief Justice Roberts and Justices Thomas, Breyer, and Alito. Justice Scalia wrote a powerful dissent joined by Justices Ginsburg, Sotomayor, and Kagan. Justice Kennedy's majority opinion stressed that reasonableness is the key to Fourth Amendment analysis, with the Court needing to balance the law enforcement justification for taking DNA samples against the intrusion into privacy from the search. The Court said that there were significant benefits to law enforcement in gathering DNA from those arrested, especially in terms of the ability to solve cold cases and unsolved crimes.

At the same time, the Court said that the intrusion of privacy would be minimal. A swab inside a person's mouth was regarded as a minimal intrusion. The Court accepted the government's argument that this was no more intrusive than taking a suspect's picture or fingerprints, things that are routinely done when people are arrested.

The problem with this balancing is that it can leave

little left of the Fourth Amendment. Of course, the police benefit by having DNA samples. Justice Kennedy's opinion does not provide any basis for limiting the taking of DNA to those arrested for serious crimes; under his reasoning, police seemingly can take DNA from anyone arrested for any crime. And if the focus is on the benefit to law enforcement, why can't government take DNA from literally everyone? That would help law enforcement tremendously. Indeed, law enforcement would gain enormously if it could search anyone's person or property at any time.

The Fourth Amendment was meant to stop exactly that type of law enforcement action; it says that a person can be searched only for offenses where there is probable cause. *Maryland v. King* is troubling because it is about searching people to gather evidence for crimes where they are not suspects. The Court surely would not allow the police to automatically search the homes of those arrested. Why, then, allow their DNA to be taken and used against them?

The Court's answer was that the taking of DNA is minimally intrusive; a cotton swab inside the cheek was seen as no different from taking fingerprints. But there is a great difference: a tremendous amount can be learned about an individual from his or her DNA, and the amount that can be known is increasing exponentially. Fingerprints are taken to help identify the person; DNA is not used for that purpose because it takes too long to get the results from the tests. The DNA is stored in a database, which means the government has information permanently that can be used to learn deeply private things about the person. The majority opinion in *Maryland v. King* was striking in its failure to recognize that taking DNA from a person is an especially intrusive search and that there is a potentially huge threat to privacy in the government having DNA databases. The Court left great doubts as to whether it is ready to deal with the Fourth Amendment issues of the twenty-first century.

A much more hopeful sign in this regard was the Court's decision in *Riley v. California* (2014), where the Supreme Court held that absent a warrant or emergency circumstances, police cannot examine the contents of a person's cell phone as part of a search incident to an arrest.[20] Chief Justice Roberts, writing for a unanimous Court, stressed the great privacy interests people have in the contents of their cell phones. He noted that cell phones store millions of pages of text and thousands of photographs, including all aspects of the "privacies of life." He pointed out that cell phones contain material from a long period of time and can give access to Cloud or Web services where even more information can be found. The Court had previously held that police can search a person incident to an arrest to protect the safety of the officers and prevent destruction of evidence. The Court explained that neither of these interests justify looking at the contents of a cell phone.

The decision is significant in recognizing the importance of informational privacy, especially with regard to new technology. It will limit the ability of police to look at the contents of a person's laptop or tablet or phone absent a warrant or exigent circumstances. It was a stunning, unanimous victory for privacy.

But there are countless other ways in which technology poses a new threat to privacy where the Fourth Amendment has not yet caught up: police use of drones for surveillance,[21] using cellular technology to monitor a person's movements,[22] cellular companies turning over metadata to the government (information about what numbers a person called or received calls from and the duration of calls).[23]

Another positive development in the law is in the Supreme Court's recent decision in *Carpenter v. United*

States, in June 2018. The issue in *Carpenter* was whether police need to get a warrant before accessing information from cell phone companies that can be used to tell a person's location and track a person's movements. Timothy Carpenter was suspected of committing a series of armed robberies. The FBI went to his cell phone company and got the cell phone tower records that revealed his location and his movements for 127 days. The FBI received this information without a warrant from a judge. The cell tower information was crucial evidence used to convict him and sentence him to 119 years in prison.

Every time we use our cell phone—to send and receive calls or texts or emails or access the internet—it connects to cell towers. The records—generated hundreds and sometimes thousands of times per day—include the precise GPS coordinates of each tower as well as the day and time the phone tried to connect to it. It is possible to determine our location at almost any point and track our movements through this information. The police constantly use this technology: in 2016, Verizon and AT&T alone received about 125,000 requests for cellular information from law enforcement agencies.

The issue in *Carpenter v. United States* is whether the Fourth Amendment, which prohibits unreasonable searches and arrests, requires that the police obtain a warrant in order to access this information.[24] The Fourth Amendment, and its warrant requirement, is an essential protection of our privacy. It demands that the police show a judge that there is probable cause—good reason to believe that evidence of a crime will be obtained—before there is a search.

It is frightening to realize that the government can track virtually all of us and our movements any time it wants just by asking for our cell phone records. A great deal can be learned about a person from this information. As one court explained, "A person who knows all of another's travels can deduce whether he is a weekly church goer, a heavy drinker, a regular at the gym, an unfaithful husband, an outpatient receiving medical treatment, an associate of particular individuals or political groups—and not just one such fact about a person, but all such facts."[25]

The Supreme Court, in a 5–4 decision, with Chief Justice Roberts writing the majority and joined by Justices Ginsburg, Breyer, Sotomayor, and Kagan, concluded that the police must obtain a warrant before obtaining such cellular location information. This is an important victory for privacy rights.

The progressive vision for the Constitution must be to insist that the Fourth Amendment and the law of privacy provide protections for such technological intrusions.

A second distinct way in which privacy is used in constitutional law is to safeguard the ability of a person to restrict dissemination of personal information. This, of course, is a common use of the word "privacy." Alan Westin, in a seminal book on the right to privacy, focused on the information in each of our lives.[26] He analogized it to a series of circles within circles. The innermost circle contains the things we tell no one about ourselves. The next innermost circle contains the things about us that are known only by those with whom we are most intimate. The circles continue until one reaches the information that is known by all.

Statutes dealing with privacy, such as the Privacy Act of 1974, are about informational privacy. The Privacy Act concerns information obtained by the executive branch of the federal government and generally prohibits "nonconsensual disclosure of any information that has been retrieved from a protected record."[27] More specifically, the Privacy Act applies to information that is "about an individual" and that is stored in a system of records "under the control of any agency from which information is retrieved by the name of the individual or by some identifying number, symbol, or other identifying particular assigned to the individual."[28]

In tort law, there is the ability to sue for "public disclosure of private facts"; this focuses on informational privacy. Under this, there can be a suit for invasion of privacy if there is the publication of nonpublic information that is "not of legitimate concern to the public" and that the reasonable person would find offensive to have published.[29] A fairly recent example of this was Hulk Hogan successfully suing *Gawker* and obtaining a judgment for $140 million for posting, without his consent, a tape of his engaging in sexual activity. Unlike defamation, where the information is false and a retraction conceivably could lessen the harm to reputation, the tort of public disclosure of private facts involves the publication of true information and the harm that is done once publication occurs.

But to this point, there has not been constitutional protection for informational privacy. The Supreme Court has considered informational privacy in a couple of cases and refused to recognize a constitutional right, though it left that possibility open. *Whalen v. Roe* (1977) involved a New York law that required physicians to provide reports identifying patients receiving prescription drugs that have a potential for abuse.[30] The state maintained a centralized computer file that listed the names and addresses of the patients, as well as the identity of the prescribing doctors. Challengers argued that this database infringed the right to privacy because individuals have a right to avoid disclosure of personal matters.

The Court, however, rejected this privacy argument. The Court noted that the law created liability for Health Department employees who failed, either deliberately or negligently, to maintain proper security. The Court said that the state has an important interest in monitoring the use of prescription drugs that might be abused. The Court did not reject the possibility that the right to privacy might be recognized in the future to include a right to control information. Justice Stevens concluded the majority opinion by declaring: "We are not unaware of the threat to privacy implicit in the accumulation of vast amounts of personal information in computerized data banks or other massive government files. The collection of taxes, the distribution of welfare and social security benefits, the supervision of public health, the direction of our Armed Forces, and the enforcement of the criminal laws all require the orderly preservation of great quantities of information, much of which is personal in character and potentially embarrassing or harmful if disclosed."[31] Justice Stevens said, however, that the New York law did not pose such an issue.

The Court subsequently again refused to find a right to informational privacy in *National Aeronautics and Space Administration v. Nelson* (2011).[32] After 9/11, the government adopted new rules for those who worked in nonsensitive positions at the NASA Jet Propulsion Laboratory. They were required to disclose whether they have "used, possessed, supplied, or manufactured illegal drugs" in the last year. If so, the employee must provide details, including information about "treatment or counseling received." The employee must also sign a release authorizing the government to obtain personal information from schools, employers, and others during its investigation.

Employees brought a challenge to this on the grounds that it violated their "right to informational privacy."[33] The Court unanimously rejected this claim and concluded: "In light of the protection provided by the Privacy Act's nondisclosure requirement, and because the challenged portions of the forms consist of reasonable inquiries in an employment background check, we conclude that the Government's inquiries do not violate a constitutional right to informational privacy."[34] Justice Scalia wrote a separate opinion, joined by Justice Thomas, in which he declared: "A federal constitutional right to 'informational privacy' does not exist."[35]

Thus, although there is a strong argument that the Constitution should be interpreted to protect a right to control information, there has been little support for such a right from the Supreme Court or the lower courts. In fact, the U.S. Court of Appeals for the District of Columbia Circuit has gone so far as to express "grave doubts as to the existence of a constitutional right of privacy in the nondisclosure of personal information."[36]

I believe that the Supreme Court needs to recognize a fundamental right to informational privacy under the due process clauses of the Fifth and Fourteenth Amendments. The government's ability to gather, store, and collate information constantly increases, indeed grows exponentially. There is unprecedented ability to learn the most intimate and personal things about individuals. For example, the Human Genome Project offers the prospect of genetic analysis that can discover a wide array of information about individuals, including propensity for diseases, addictions, and personal characteristics. DNA databases are held by governments and constantly growing. The law simply does not provide adequate protection in this or other areas of informational privacy. As with all constitutional rights, this is not absolute; but it says that the government should be able to collect, store, or collate information only if it has an adequate justification for doing so and with adequate procedural safeguards. Progressives need to fight—through legislation and in the courts—for protection for informational privacy.

Third, and finally, privacy is also used in constitutional law to protect aspects of autonomy. The right of a person to make certain crucial personal decisions is described as privacy. It is this use of privacy that has been used to protect rights, such as reproductive autonomy, and it is an area where I have great concerns for the future. I believe that there are four votes on the current Court—Roberts, Thomas, Alito, and Gorsuch—who would vote to overrule *Roe v. Wade*, or at the very least allow virtually every government regulation of abortion to eliminate meaningful access to abortion for women in many states. Justice Kennedy's departure almost surely means that this position now has a fifth vote.

Progressives must defend constitutional protection for crucial aspects of autonomy, including the right to abortion. Constitutional protection for autonomy under the "liberty" of the due process clause has gone on for almost a century. In *Meyer v. Nebraska*, in 1923, the Supreme Court declared unconstitutional a state law that prohibited the teaching in school of any language except English.[37] The Court broadly defined the term "liberty" in the due process clause to protect basic aspects of family autonomy:

> Without doubt, [liberty] denotes not merely freedom from bodily restraint, but also the right of the individual to contract, to engage in any of the common occupations of life, to acquire useful knowledge, to marry, establish a home and bring up children, to worship God according to the dictates of his own conscience, and generally to enjoy those privileges long recognized at common law as essential to the orderly pursuit of happiness by free men.[38]

Similarly, two years later, in *Pierce v. Society of Sisters* (1925), the Supreme Court held unconstitutional a state law that required children to attend public schools.[39] The Court explained that "the fundamental theory of liberty upon which all governments in this Union repose excludes any general power of the state to standardize its children by forcing them to accept instruction from public teachers only. The child is not the mere creature of the state; those who nurture him and direct his destiny have the right, coupled with the high duty, to recognize and prepare him for his additional obligations."[40]

A half century ago, the Court began using the word "privacy" to describe aspects of autonomy protected under the word "liberty" in the due process clause. In 1965, in *Griswold v. Connecticut,* the Supreme Court declared unconstitutional a state law that prohibited the sale, distribution, and use of contraceptives.[41] The Supreme Court, in an opinion by Justice Douglas, found that the right to privacy was a fundamental right that was implicit in many of the specific provisions of the Bill of Rights, such as the First, Third, Fourth, and Fifth Amendments.

What makes protecting autonomy controversial, of course, is the Court's decision in *Roe v. Wade.*[42] It is this that causes some to question whether there should be any constitutional protection for privacy under the Constitution. I believe that it is opposition to *Roe* which especially caused conservatives to develop and embrace originalism as a method of constitutional interpretation to criticize that decision. It is why conservatives, such as Justice Clarence Thomas, declare: "I can find neither in the Bill of Rights nor any other part of the Constitution a general right of privacy."[43] Even some liberal scholars have argued that the judicial protection of autonomy was misguided. For example, Professor Kermit Roosevelt declared: "The idea that judges should be deciding cases under the Due Process Clause by determining whether a right is fundamental is bad policy and bad law."[44]

I strongly disagree. I believe that the Court in *Roe v. Wade* got it exactly right: the Constitution protects basic aspects of personal autonomy and a crucial aspect of this is the right of a woman to choose whether to terminate or continue a pregnancy.[45]

The Court in *Roe* faced three questions. First, is there a right to privacy protected by the Constitution even though it is not mentioned in the document's text? Second, if so, is the right infringed by a prohibition of abortion? Third, if so, does the state have a sufficient justification for upholding laws prohibiting abortion? These same issues will confront the Supreme Court if ever it reconsiders *Roe v. Wade.* These are the three questions that all of us must ask in appraising constitutional protection for abortion rights.

The first question, is there a right to privacy protected by the Constitution, is really the place where opponents of *Roe* have focused their attack, arguing that there is no such right because it is not mentioned in the Constitution and was not intended by its drafters. The most famous critique of the decision was written by then Harvard professor John Hart Ely, who declared: "It is, nevertheless, a very bad decision. . . . It is bad because it is bad constitutional law, or rather because it is not constitutional law and gives almost no sense of an obligation to try to be."[46] Ely's objection was that abortion and privacy are not mentioned in the Constitution, and therefore no such rights exist. This, of course, is the criticism that conservatives have launched at *Roe* since it was decided.

The problem with this argument is that it fails to acknowledge that its advocates are urging a radical change in constitutional law. Before *Roe*, the Court had expressly recognized a right to privacy, including over matters of reproduction, even though there is no mention of this in the text of the Constitution. As explained above, in *Griswold v. Connecticut*, the Court declared unconstitutional as violating the right to privacy a state law prohibiting the sale, distribution, or use of contraceptives.[47]

In *Eisenstadt v. Baird*, in 1972, the Court invalidated a state law keeping unmarried individuals from having access to contraceptives and declared: "If the right of privacy means anything, it is the right of the individual, married or single, to be free from unwarranted governmental intrusion into matters so fundamentally affecting a person as the decision whether to bear or beget a child."[48]

In fact, long before these decisions, the Court safeguarded many aspects of autonomy as fundamental rights, even though they are not mentioned in the text of the Constitution and were never contemplated by its drafters. For example, the Court has expressly held that certain aspects of family autonomy are fundamental rights, and that government interference will be allowed only if the government can prove that its action is necessary to achieve a compelling purpose. As mentioned above, in the 1920s, the Supreme Court held that parents have a fundamental right to control the upbringing of their children and used this to strike down laws prohibiting the teaching of the German language and forbidding parochial school education.[49] In the 1940s, the Court ruled that the right to procreate is a fundamental right and declared unconstitutional an Oklahoma law that required the sterilization of those convicted three times of crimes involving moral turpitude.[50] In the 1960s, the Court proclaimed that there is a fundamental right to marry and invalidated a Virginia law prohibiting interracial marriage.[51] This, of course, was the foundation for the Court declaring that laws prohibiting same-sex marriage are unconstitutional as infringing the fundamental right to marry.[52] Thus, under the rubric of "privacy," the Court has safeguarded the right to marry, the right to custody of one's children, the right to keep the family together, the right of parents to control the upbringing of children, the right to procreate, the right to purchase and use contraceptives, the right to refuse medical treatment, and the right to engage in private consensual homosexual activity.

Unless the Court intends to overrule all of these decisions, it is clear—and it was clear at the time of *Roe*—that the Constitution is interpreted as protecting basic aspects of personal autonomy as fundamental rights even though they are not mentioned in the text of the document. Put another way, the Court has never adopted the position of justices like Scalia and Thomas who insist that the Constitution is limited to those rights explicitly stated or originally intended at the time of its ratification. Rejecting privacy as a right because it is not in the text of the Constitution would mean repudiating other rights not mentioned that have long been safeguarded, such as freedom of association and the right to travel.[53]

Of course, opponents of *Roe* could argue that all of these decisions were wrong and that there should be no protection of privacy or other nontextual rights. This is Justice Clarence Thomas's position.[54] But this would be a dramatic change in the law. Harvard Law professor Cass Sunstein has explained: "[The rejection of privacy rights] is a fully plausible reading of the Constitution. But it would wreak havoc with established law. It would eliminate constitutional protections where the nation has come to rely on them—by, for example, allowing states to ban use of contraceptives by married couples."[55] And this would be an undesirable change because the Constitution should be interpreted to protect basic aspects of freedom even if they are not mentioned in the text of the Constitution. That was exactly the point of the Ninth Amendment, which is a reminder that the enumeration of some rights in the Constitution does not deny the existence of others.

The second question before the Court with regard to abortion was whether laws that prohibit abortion infringe a woman's right to privacy. Interestingly, no one, not even the staunchest opponents of abortion rights, disputes this. Opponents of *Roe* argue against there being a right to privacy and/or claim that the state had a sufficiently important interest in prohibiting abortion. But understandably, there is no disagreement that a prohibition of abortion interferes with a woman's autonomy.

Obviously, forbidding abortions interferes with a woman's ability to control her reproductive autonomy and to decide for herself, in the words of *Eisenstadt v. Baird*, whether to "bear or beget a child." Also, no one can deny that forcing a woman to continue a pregnancy against her will is an enormous intrusion on her control over her body. Justice Blackmun expressed this forcefully in his majority opinion in *Roe*: "The detriment that the State would impose upon the pregnant woman by denying this choice altogether is apparent. Specific and direct harm medically diagnosable even in early pregnancy may be involved. Maternity, or additional offspring, may force upon the woman a distressful life and future. Psychological harm may be imminent. Mental and physical health may be taxed by child care. There is also the distress, for all concerned, associated with the unwanted child, and there is the problem of bringing a child into a family already unable, psychologically and otherwise, to care for it. In other cases, as in this one, the additional difficulties and continuing stigma of unwed motherhood may be involved."[56]

The third question before the Supreme Court was whether states have a compelling interest in protecting fetal life. Once it was decided that there is a fundamental right to privacy and that laws prohibiting abortion infringe it, then the question is whether laws prohibiting abortions are needed to achieve a compelling government interest. As explained earlier, this is the test the government must meet whenever it burdens or infringes a fundamental right. The key question at this stage in the analysis was whether the government has a compelling interest in protecting the fetus from the moment of conception.

The Court rejected a state interest in outlawing abortions from the moment of conception and concluded that the state has a compelling interest in prohibiting abortion only at the point of viability, the time at which the fetus can survive outside the womb. Justice Blackmun, writing for the majority, stated: "With respect to the State's important and legitimate interest in potential life, the 'compelling' point is at viability. This is so because the fetus then presumably has the capability of meaningful life outside the mother's womb."[57]

But as many commentators noted, this begs the question of why viability is deemed the point at which the state has a sufficient interest to prohibit abortion. The choice of viability as the point where there is a compelling government interest seems at odds with Justice Blackmun's earlier declaration: "We need not resolve the difficult question of when life begins. When those trained in the respective disciplines of medicine, philosophy, and theology are unable to arrive at any consensus, the judiciary, at this point in the development of man's knowledge, is not in a position to speculate as to the answer."[58]

Ultimately, the question is, who should decide whether the fetus before viability is a human person: each woman for herself or the state legislature? Harvard law professor Laurence Tribe, in an article written soon after *Roe*, put this well: "The Court was not, after all, choosing simply between the alternatives of abortion and continued pregnancy. It was instead choosing among alternative allocations of decision-making authority, for the issue it faced was whether the woman and her doctor, rather than an agency of government, should have the authority to make the abortion decision at various stages of pregnancy."[59]

Why leave the choice as to abortion to the woman rather than to the state? There was then, and is now, no consensus as to when human life begins. As Professor Tribe explains: "But the reality is that the 'general agreement' posited above simply does not exist. Some regard the fetus as merely another part of the woman's body until quite late in pregnancy or even until birth; others believe the fetus must be regarded as a helpless human child from the time of its conception. These differences of view are endemic to the historical situation in which the abortion controversy arose."[60] The choice of conception as the point at which human life begins, which underlies state laws prohibiting abortion, thus was based not on consensus or science but religious views. Professor Tribe wrote: "And, at least at this point in the history of industrialized Western civilization, that decision in turn entails not an inference or demonstration from generally shared premises, whether factual or moral, but a statement of religious faith upon which people will invariably differ widely."[61]

A state could offer a secular argument that there is at least potential human life at the moment of conception and that the state therefore has a compelling interest in prohibiting abortion from that point. The problem with this argument is that it has no stopping point. The argument is that absent abortion there is a significant likelihood that a human person will be born. But actually, the statistics are surprising in terms of how uncertain it is whether there will be a birth if there is not an abortion. About 15 to 20 percent of known pregnancies end in miscarriage, and studies have found that 30 to 50 percent of fertilized eggs are lost before a woman finds out she is pregnant.[62] In other words, there is a reasonable chance—but no more than that—that there will be a baby but for an abortion.

But the same, of course, can be said about contraception. There is the potential for life every time a couple has sex without contraception: but for contraception there is a reasonable chance that there will be a baby. Studies indicate that "when trying to conceive, a couple with no fertility problem has about a 30 percent chance of getting pregnant each month."[63]

Thus the potential life argument justifies a ban on contraception as much as it does a ban on abortion. This, of course, is the position of the Roman Catholic Church. But then the power of Professor Tribe's argument becomes even more apparent: there is not a nonreligious basis for the prohibition of contraception and abortion. Put in this way, it becomes clearer why the choice of whether to continue a pregnancy or terminate it is for the woman, not for the state, to make.

The best approach to the abortion issue is for the Court to declare that the decision whether to have an abortion is a private judgment that the state may not encourage, discourage, or prohibit. The state must be neutral and leave this choice to each woman to make as she deems appropriate. My fear is that this is a right that progressives are going to need to fight for in the years ahead in the Supreme Court, and if they lose there, in states across the country.

RELIGIOUS FREEDOM

I predict—and worry—that some of the greatest changes in constitutional law will come in the area of the religion clauses of the First Amendment. It is an area of enormous disagreement between progressives and conservatives. Progressives favor a separation of church and state; conservatives reject this and favor allowing more religious presence in government and more government aid to religion. Conservatives favor protecting free exercise of religion even when it means denying others benefits or permitting discrimination; progressives reject this. We already have seen significant changes in the law in this area. Progressives must continue to defend a separation of church and state, and continue to argue that people should not be able to inflict injuries on others in exercising their religious freedom.

Separation of Church and State

Over a decade ago, I argued a case in the Supreme Court involving the constitutionality of a Ten Commandments monument that sits directly between the Texas State Capitol and the Texas Supreme Court.[64] The monument is six feet high and three feet wide, and atop it, in large letters and words, it states, "I am the Lord, thy God."

In the days before the argument at the Supreme Court, the case received a great deal of media attention. Some of the reports mentioned that I was the attorney who would be arguing the case against the monument before the Court, and as a result, I received a large amount of what can only be described as hate mail. Some of it was shocking in its viciousness. It showed me that there are some people who care a great deal about having religious symbols on government property and having religious presence in government.

I chose to handle this case because I feel deeply that the establishment clause of the First Amendment—"Congress shall make no law respecting an establishment of religion"—should be interpreted to create a wall that separates church and state. This notion was not invented by twenty-first-century liberal law professors. Rather, it came from Thomas Jefferson in a January 1, 1802, letter addressed to the Danbury Baptist Association and published in a Massachusetts newspaper, where he said: "I contemplate with sovereign reverence that act of the whole American people which declared that their legislature should 'make no law respecting an establishment of religion, or prohibiting the free exercise thereof,' thus building a wall of separation between Church & State."[65] The phrase can actually be traced back to Roger Williams, the founder of the first Baptist church in America, who wrote in 1644, of the need for "a hedge or wall of separation between the garden of the church and the wilderness of the world."[66]

Obviously, there cannot be total separation of church and state. If government did not provide basic services, like police and fire, to religious institutions, that would raise serious issues concerning free exercise of religion. But the goal is that religion should be kept out of government and government should be kept out of religion as much as possible.

In 1947, in *Everson v. Board of Education*, when the Supreme Court held that the establishment clause applies to state and local governments, all nine justices accepted this metaphor of a wall separating church and state as reflecting the commitment of the First Amendment.[67] They also very much accepted the reasoning of James Madison, who said that it was unconscionable to tax some to support the religions of others.

For decades, the Court followed this strict separationist philosophy. In the 1960s, the Court, in *Engel v. Vitale* and *Abbington School District v. Shempp*,[68] held that prayer—even voluntary prayer—in public schools is unconstitutional. Subsequently, the Court applied this to declare unconstitutional clergy-delivered prayers at public school graduations and student-delivered prayers at high school football games.[69] The Court allowed taxpayers to sue to challenge government support for religion and greatly restricted the ability of the government to give aid to parochial schools, especially if it is a type that could be used for religious instruction.[70] The Court limited religious symbols, like nativity scenes, on government property if they could be perceived as a symbolic endorsement of religion.[71]

But conservative justices have long rejected this approach to the establishment clause and the idea of a wall separating church and state. They dissented in all of these cases. They explicitly take an accommodationist approach, believing that religion should be accommodated into government and government should be able to support religion. From their view, the government violates the establishment clause only if it literally establishes a church or coerces religious participation.[72]

Actually, Justice Clarence Thomas goes even further in limiting the application of the establishment clause. In many opinions, he has expressed the view that this provision applies only to constrain Congress and never to state and local governments.[73] He believes that the establishment clause was meant to keep Congress from creating a national church to rival state churches that existed at the time. For Justice Thomas, nothing done by a state or local government could ever violate the establishment clause.

What does a conservative majority on the Court mean with regard to the establishment clause? It will mean a Court much more willing to allow prayer at government events, including, I fear, in schools. The conservative view is reflected in the Court's most recent decision about the establishment clause, *Town of Greece v. Galloway* (2014).[74] For a decade, the town invited exclusively Christian ministers to deliver a prayer before its monthly board meetings; most were explicitly Christian prayers.

Nonetheless, the Supreme Court, in a 5–4 decision, held that this did not violate the establishment clause of the First Amendment. Justice Kennedy wrote an opinion, joined by Chief Justice Roberts and Justice Alito, which emphasized the long history of clergy-delivered prayers before legislative sessions. In a case thirty years earlier, the Court had approved legislative prayers where there was no reference to Jesus Christ,[75] but Justice Kennedy said that legislatures were not limited to such nonsectarian prayers.

Justice Thomas, writing only for himself in a concurring opinion, reiterated his view that the establishment clause should not apply to state and local government at all. In a part of the opinion joined by Justice Scalia, Justice Thomas argued that an establishment clause violation would require "actual legal coercion . . . not the 'subtle coercive pressures' allegedly felt by respondents in this case."[76] In other words, under this view, only "legal coercion"—forcing a person to participate in religious practices or face legal penalties—violates the establishment clause.

Justice Kagan wrote a powerful dissent joined by Justices Ginsburg, Breyer, and Sotomayor. She stressed that by inviting only Christian clergy and by their delivering explicitly Christian prayers, the government had impermissibly aligned itself with Christianity. That is exactly what the establishment clause forbids.

Thus far, a majority of the Court has not indicated a desire to reconsider the rulings from a half century ago prohibiting prayers in public schools. But it should be remembered that in his dissent in *Lee v. Weisman* (1992), Justice Scalia lamented that the Court was far too concerned with the interests of those who did not want prayer and there was not enough attention to those who want public prayer at government functions, including in the schools. He said, "The Court apparently thinks [prayer] to be, some purely personal avocation that can be indulged entirely in secret, like pornography, in the privacy of one's room. For most believers it is *not* that, and has never been."[77] A conservative majority on the Court certainly is likely to allow much more in the way of religion at public events and could even overrule the earlier decisions imposing strict limits.

The conservative approach to the establishment clause imposes no limits on the ability to place religious symbols—nativity scenes, Ten Commandments displays, crosses—on government property. Religious symbols do not run afoul of the conservative concern with coercion into religious participation. When I argued the Texas Ten Commandments case to the Supreme Court in 2005, Justice Kennedy (who is consistently with the conservative justices in establishment clause cases), with hostility in his voice, asked me why my client could not simply look the other way if he objects to the monument. But a constitutional violation cannot be excused by looking the other way. Besides, there would be no stopping point. A city could put a large cross atop city hall and say if you don't like it, look the other way.

The conservative majority on the Court also will allow much more government aid to parochial schools. In fact, in June 2017, the Court for the first time held that the government is constitutionally *required* to provide aid to parochial schools, at least in the form of aid for the surfaces for playgrounds, when the aid is given to secular private schools.[78] As Justice Sonia Sotomayor lamented in her dissent: "This case is about nothing less than the relationship between religious institutions and the civil government—that is, between church and state. The Court today profoundly changes that relationship by holding, for the first time, that the Constitution requires the government to provide public funds directly to a church."[79]

Progressives need to defend a very different vision of the establishment clause, the one that was followed in case after case for a half century: the separation of church and state. Such separation is desirable for several reasons.

First, ensuring a secular government is a way of ensuring that we can all feel it is "our" government, whatever our religion or lack of religion. If government becomes aligned with a particular religion or religions, those of other beliefs are made to feel like outsiders. Justice O'Connor captured this better than anyone in her writings for the Court. She said that the establishment clause is there to make sure that none of us is led to feel that we are insiders or outsiders when it comes to our government.[80] If there were a large Latin cross atop a city hall, those who were not part of religions that accept the cross as a religious symbol would feel that it was not "their" city government. Those attending the Town of Greece board meetings who were not Christian inevitably were made to feel like outsiders.

A second important reason to favor separation of church and state is that it is wrong to tax people to support the religion of others. James Madison captured this when he talked about why he believed that it was, in his words, "immoral" to tax people to support religions that they did not believe in.[81] Each of us has our own religion, or maybe we have decided that we do not have any religion, but our tax dollars should not go to advance a religion we do not believe in, let alone a religion that teaches things that we find abhorrent.

A third reason that separation of church and state is important is that it prevents the coercion that is inherent when the government becomes aligned with religion. World history, to say nothing of the history of this country, shows us that inherently people feel coerced to participate when the government becomes aligned with religion. We have seen this at public universities. Cadets at the U.S. Air Force Academy talk movingly about being forced to participate in Christian religious ceremonies, even if they are not Christians.[82] This is the danger if we do not separate church and state.

Finally, separation of church and state is important to protect religion. Roger Williams, a cofounder of Rhode Island, talked about this prior to the drafting of the establishment clause.[83] He wanted to separate church and state, not to safeguard the state from religion but to protect religion from the state. The reality is that the more the government becomes involved in religion, the more the government will regulate religion and, consequently, the greater the danger is to religion. There is also the danger of trivializing religion. When it is claimed that the nativity scene is secular, and that is why it should remain on government property, I have often thought that this trivializes a profound religious symbol. To say that a cross is just there for secular purposes ignores how important the cross is as a religious symbol.

Separation of church and state is not hostility to religion. Rather, it is based on the idea that in an enormously religiously diverse society, our government should be secular. Soon before she left the Court, Justice Sandra Day O'Connor spoke eloquently of the need for the separation of church and state when she wrote: "Those who would renegotiate the boundaries between church and state must therefore answer a difficult question: Why would we trade a system that has served us so well for one that has served others so poorly?"[84] Why indeed?

Free Exercise of Religion

I certainly favor strong protection for the ability of people to believe what they wish and to practice their religions how they choose. But I do not believe that this freedom—or any other—gives the right to inflict injury on others. As Justice Ginsburg succinctly put it: "With respect to free exercise claims no less than [other rights], '[y]our right to swing your arms ends just where the other man's nose begins.'"[85]

Increasingly, though, conservatives are violating this precept and turning to free exercise of religion to allow people to discriminate and undermine the protection of other rights. One of the first instances of this was a few years ago in *Burwell v. Hobby Lobby* (2014), which involved the contraceptive mandate under the Patient Protection and Affordable Care Act.[86] A federal law required that the Department of Health and Human Services promulgate regulations requiring that health insurance provided by employers include preventive health care coverage for women. These regulations mandate that employer-provided insurance include contraceptive coverage for women. Although religious institutions and nonprofit corporations affiliated with religious institutions could exempt themselves from this requirement, for-profit companies were required to comply.

In a 5–4 decision, the Supreme Court held that it violated the federal Religious Freedom Restoration Act (1993) to require a family-owned corporation to provide insurance coverage for contraceptives that it says violate its owners' religion. The case was about free exercise of religion, not under the First Amendment but rather under this federal statute.[87]

The decision is deeply problematic on many levels. First, this is the first time that the Supreme Court has held that a for-profit corporation can claim to have religious beliefs. A corporation, a fictional entity, is created to protect its owner from liability. So long as the corporation is run as a separate entity, the owner is liable only for what he or she invests in it.

A fictional entity cannot have a religious conscience or religious beliefs. The liabilities of the corporation are not attributed to the owners, so why should the owners be able to attribute their beliefs to the company?

This is no different for family-owned businesses than it is for any other corporations. Hobby Lobby, the corporation that challenged the contraceptive mandate, operates in dozens of states and employs thousands of people. By creating a corporation, the owners chose to get the benefits of having an entity separate from themselves; they must accept, then, the burdens of not being able to claim that the business is an extension of their religious views. Moreover, the Court's reasoning would allow all corporations to claim religious freedom; the Court just said it was unlikely that they would do so.

Second, the Court mistakenly concluded that it substantially burdens the religious freedom of the corporation to require that it provide insurance that includes contraceptive coverage. The companies, and their owners and officers and directors, are not required to use or endorse contraception; they remain free to openly express opposition to the use of contraceptives. Never before had the Supreme Court found a substantial burden on a person's religious exercise where the individual is not himself or herself required to take or forgo action that violates his or her religious beliefs, but is merely required to take action that might enable other people to do things that are at odds with the person's religious beliefs.

This holding is sure to lead to countless other challenges. Christian Scientists will claim that they do not have to provide any health insurance to their employees. In fact, why can't an employer, at least in a family-owned business, even require as a condition of employment that no money paid as salary be used to purchase contraceptives (or other things that violate the employer's religious beliefs)? If the employer does not have to have his or her money used for things deemed religiously objectionable, why would this be limited to dollars paid for employees' insurance?

Corporations are sure now to try and claim that other laws, outside the health care context, violate their religious beliefs. Justice Alito, writing for the majority, addressed this by saying, "The Government has a compelling interest in providing an equal opportunity to participate in the workforce without regard to race, and prohibitions on racial discrimination are precisely tailored to achieve that critical goal."[88] But what of employers who have a religious belief that women with children should not work outside their homes or businesses who claim a religious belief for sexual orientation discrimination. The Court's focus solely on the government's compelling interest in stopping racial discrimination likely will cause businesses to claim that this implies that there is a right to discriminate based on religion or sex.

Hobby Lobby was the first time in American history that the Supreme Court held that people, based on their religious practices, can inflict harm on others. Even if corporations can have religious beliefs, and even if they were burdened by requiring contraceptive coverage for women, there is a compelling government interest in making sure that women have access to contraceptives to exercise their fundamental right of reproductive autonomy.

It was predictable that *Hobby Lobby* would cause businesses to challenge other laws that they said infringed on their owners' religious beliefs. In 2018, the Court had before it a case about whether a business has the right to violate state law and refuse to serve gays and lesbians based on the business owner's beliefs.

Masterpiece Cakeshop Ltd. v. Colorado Civil Rights Commission (2018) involves a bakery in Colorado that refused to bake a cake for a gay couple's wedding celebration.[89] Charlie Craig and David Mullins got married in Massachusetts and wanted to celebrate their wedding where they lived in Colorado. They went to a local bakery, Masterpiece Cakeshop, and sought to purchase a wedding cake. The owner, Jack Phillips, refused to bake the cake, saying that gay marriage violated his religious beliefs.

Colorado law, like that in California and many other

states, has a public accommodations law that prohibits business establishments from discriminating based on race or sex or religion or sexual orientation. The Colorado Civil Rights Commission found that Phillips violated Colorado's statute because he would bake a cake for opposite-sex couples celebrating a wedding, but not for same-sex couples. The Colorado Court of Appeals affirmed the commission's ruling against Masterpiece Cakeshop and the Supreme Court granted review.

This should be a simple case for the Supreme Court: the government has a compelling interest in stopping discrimination. All anti-discrimination laws interfere with freedom to discriminate; there is an inherent tension between liberty and equality. But our society has made the choice for over a half century that preventing discrimination is more important than upholding the freedom to discriminate.

This was exactly the argument raised against the federal Civil Rights Act of 1964, which prohibits hotels and restaurants from discriminating based on race and forbids employers from discriminating based on race or sex or religion. The claim was that businesses should have the freedom to choose their customers and their employees. Congress and the courts rightly rejected this argument.

Under First Amendment law, Phillips's argument based on religious freedom is quite weak. Constitutional law is clear that people cannot seek an exemption from a general law on the grounds that it burdens their religion. The landmark case, *Employment Division v. Smith* (1990), involved Native Americans who sought to use peyote in their religious observances in violation of Oregon state law.[90] The Supreme Court, in an opinion by Justice Antonin Scalia, ruled against the Native Americans and held that free exercise of religion is not violated by such a general law, even when it significantly burdens religious beliefs. Under this precedent, Phillips cannot claim that he is entitled to a religious exemption from Colorado's anti-discrimination law.

Phillips's other argument has potentially dire consequences for all laws that forbid discrimination. He contends that forcing him to bake a cake is impermissible compelled speech in violation of the First Amendment. The Court has held that the First Amendment prohibits forcing someone to speak unless the government has an overriding, crucial interest that is served.

Phillips says that he is a "cake artist" and that baking a cake is inherently expressive activity.

But if the Supreme Court regards that as speech, as Justices Thomas and Gorsuch said in a concurring opinion, then any business can discriminate by claiming that forcing it to provide services is impermissible compelled speech. If baking a cake is expressive activity, then so is cooking food. Any restaurant could discriminate based on race or religion or any other grounds by claiming that forcing it to serve customers is requiring it to engage in speech. All work can be described as a form of expressive activity, and prohibiting discrimination is, then, always compelled speech.

Even accepting that baking a cake is expressive activity, there is a clear and easy answer: the government has a compelling interest in stopping discrimination. Freedom of expression is never absolute. The government's need to end discrimination, including based on sexual orientation, should be deemed to outweigh the claim of a right to discriminate.

For decades, our society has made the correct choice that it will interfere with freedom to discriminate in order to have a more just and equal society. The Supreme Court must not abandon this commitment. More generally, free exercise of religion should not be allowed to be a basis for allowing the infringement of rights or for discrimination.

The Court in *Masterpiece Cakeshop* ducked these questions. In a 7–2 decision, with the majority opinion written by Justice Anthony Kennedy, the Court found that the members of the Colorado Civil Rights Commission had expressed impermissible hostility to religion. Yet the evidence the Court pointed to of this was quite weak. One member of the Commission said that anyone doing business in the state must serve all customers, regardless of the owner's religious beliefs. That is not hostility to religion. It is Colorado law.

Another member of the Civil Rights Commission said that many terrible things have been justified in the name of religion, including the Holocaust and slavery. That is, sadly, a factually true statement.

The final piece of evidence of hostility to religion was the fact that the Colorado Civil Rights Commission found no violation of the state's civil rights law when other bakers refused to bake cakes. But in none of those instances were the other bakers discriminating based on race or sex or religion or sexual orientation—the grounds forbidden by the Colorado law.

It is stunning that such weak evidence of discrimination was seen as evidencing hostility to religion, when the Court then found no violation of the Constitution in President Trump's travel ban, notwithstanding his repeated statements of a desire for a complete ban on Muslims entering the United States.

The issue presented in *Masterpiece Cakeshop*—can a business refuse to provide service for a customer because of the owner's religious beliefs—remains unresolved. But with Justice Kennedy's departure from the Court, it is hard to see five votes for the progressive position: people should not be able to inflict injury on others—including discriminating against them—in the name of religion.

8

ACHIEVING EQUALITY

As described in chapter 3, equality is not among the values stated in the Preamble. The proclamation in the Declaration of Independence, that "all men are created equal," was not meant to include women or nonwhites or Native Americans. The Constitution, in its seven articles and the first ten amendments, never mentions equality. But equal protection should be regarded as one of the core values of the Constitution.

There is no doubt that our country has made great progress over its history with regard to equality. Yet enormous inequalities persist: 24 percent of African Americans and 21 percent of Latinos live below the poverty level, as compared with 9 percent of whites; 40 percent of African American children are born into and live in poverty, as compared with 14 percent of white children. The incarceration rate among African American men is more than 3,000 per 100,000 citizens, roughly four times the national average, and roughly six times the rate among white men.[1] An African American male born in 2001 has a 32 percent chance of serving time in prison at some point in his life, while a white male born at the same time would have a 6 percent chance of being sent to prison.[2] While the median income level of African American families has increased over the last two decades, it is still less than two-thirds that of white families.[3]

Moreover, "middle-class blacks earn seventy cents for every dollar earned by middle-class whites, but they possess only fifteen cents for every dollar of wealth held by middle-class whites."[4] The legacy of slavery, the history of race discrimination in every corner of society, and the continuing racial inequalities all make it impossible for this country to be post-racial.

A crucial part of the progressive agenda for the Constitution must be dealing with the continuing racial inequalities. This must include advocating for allowing discrimination to be proven by showing a disparate impact, for permitting continued use of affirmative action, and for recognizing a constitutional right to minimum entitlements, including education and food and shelter and medical care.

ALLOWING DISPARATE IMPACT TO PROVE RACE DISCRIMINATION

If I could make one change in constitutional law to advance equal protection, it would be to eliminate the requirement that there be proof of a discriminatory intent in order to show the existence of discrimination; proof of a racially disparate impact to a law or government policy should be sufficient. Over the last forty years, the Supreme Court has continually held that proving discrimination requires showing that the government acted with a discriminatory purpose; demonstrating a discriminatory impact is not enough to show that a government action should be treated as racial discrimination.[5] Requiring proof of discriminatory purpose in order to demonstrate an equal protection violation has dramatically lessened the ability to use the Constitution to create a more just society. These decisions are terribly misguided, and the Court has compounded the problem by adopting a standard for proving intent that is very difficult to meet.

Whether discrimination can be proven by showing a discriminatory impact to a government action is crucial in determining the reach of the equal protection clause. Undoubtedly, there are many instances where laws that do not mention race are administered in a manner that discriminates against minorities or has a disproportionate impact against them, but there is not sufficient evidence to prove that the government acted with a discriminatory purpose.[6] Current constitutional law means that the government need not offer a racially neutral explanation for these effects and, indeed, generally need do no more than show that its action is reasonable.[7] To prove the existence of a racial classification—or at least to shift the burden to the government to prove a nonrace explanation for its action—requires proving discriminatory intent.[8]

Washington v. Davis (1976) was a key case articulating this requirement.[9] Applicants for the police force in Washington, DC, were required to take a test, and statistics revealed that blacks failed the examination much more often than whites. The Supreme Court, however, held that proof of a discriminatory impact is insufficient by itself to show the existence of a racial classification. Justice Byron White, writing for the majority, said that the Court had never held that "a law or other official act, without regard to whether it reflects a racially discriminatory purpose, is unconstitutional *solely* because it has a racially disproportionate impact."[10] The Court explained that discriminatory impact, "standing alone, . . . does not trigger the rule that racial classifications are to be subjected to the strictest scrutiny and are justifiable only by the weightiest of considerations."[11]

In other words, laws that are facially neutral as to race (they don't explicitly mention race) will receive more than rational basis review—under which they are sure to be upheld—only if there is proof of a discriminatory purpose. The Court also emphasized that allowing discriminatory impact to suffice in proving a racial classification "would raise serious questions about, and perhaps invalidate, a whole range of tax, welfare, public service, regulatory, and licensing statutes that may be more burdensome to the poor and to the average black than to the more affluent white."[12]

Many times the Court has reaffirmed this principle that discriminatory impact is not sufficient to prove a racial classification. For example, in *City of Mobile v. Bolden* (1980), the Supreme Court held that an election system that had the impact of disadvantaging minorities was not to be subjected to strict scrutiny unless there was proof of a discriminatory purpose.[13] *Mobile v. Bolden* involved a challenge to Mobile, Alabama's use of an at-large election for its city council. The city was predominately white, with a sizable African American population. The long history of racially polarized voting meant that only whites were elected in the at-large system. Nonetheless, the Supreme Court found no equal protection violation because there was not sufficient evidence of a discriminatory purpose. The Court declared: "Only if there is purposeful discrimination can there be a violation of the equal protection clause. . . . This principle applies to claims of racial discrimination affecting voting just as it does to other claims of racial discrimination."[14]

Similarly, in *McCleskey v. Kemp* (1987), the Supreme Court held that proof of discrimination impact in the administration of the death penalty was insufficient to show an equal protection violation.[15] Statistics powerfully demonstrated racial inequality in the imposition of capital punishment. A study conducted by Professor David Baldus found that the death penalty was imposed in 22 percent of the cases involving black defendants and white victims; in 8 percent of the cases involving white defendants and white victims; in 1 percent of the cases involving black defendants and black victims; and in 3 percent of the cases involving white defendants and black victims.[16] Baldus found that "prosecutors sought the death penalty in 70 percent of the cases involving black defendants and white victims; 15 percent of the cases involving black defendants and black victims; and 19 percent of the cases involving white defendants and black victims."[17] After adjusting for many other variables, Baldus concluded that "defendants charged with killing white victims were 4.3 times as likely to receive a death sentence as defendants charged with killing blacks."[18]

The Supreme Court, however, said that for the defendant to demonstrate an equal protection violation, he "must prove that the decision makers in *his* case acted with discriminatory purpose."[19] Because the defendant could not prove that the prosecutor or jury in his case were biased, no equal protection violation existed. Moreover, the Court said that to challenge the law authorizing capital punishment, the defendant "would have to prove that the Georgia Legislature enacted or maintained the death penalty statute *because* of an anticipated racially discriminatory effect."[20] These are impossible burdens to meet.

Cases such as *Washington v. Davis, Mobile v. Bolden,* and *McCleskey v. Kemp* clearly establish that proof of a discriminatory impact is not sufficient by itself to prove an equal protection violation; there must also be proof of a discriminatory purpose.[21] It should be noted that civil rights statutes can, and often do, allow violations to be proved based on discriminatory impact without evidence of a discriminatory purpose. For example, Title 7 of the 1964 Civil Rights Act allows employment discrimination to be established by proof of discriminatory impact,[22] and the 1982 amendments to the Voting Rights Act of 1965 permit proof of discriminatory impact to establish a violation of that law.[23] But the Court has said that under the Constitution, proof of discriminatory impact is, by itself, insufficient to establish government discrimination based on race (or, for that matter, sex).

What is wrong with the Court's requirement for proof of discriminatory purpose? First, it misunderstands the goal of equal protection. Equal protection should be concerned with the results of government actions and not just their underlying motivations. The government should not be able to act in a manner that harms racial minorities, regardless of why it took the action.

In *Washington v. Davis*, the Court, in imposing a requirement for proof of discriminatory intent, said that the purpose of the equal protection clause "is the prevention of official conduct discriminating on the basis of race."[24] But the Court never has justified this premise that the focus should be solely on the government's motives and not the effects of its actions. Quite the contrary, equal protection should be concerned with, and measured by, outcomes as well as intentions. A crucial question should be whether the government's action is creating inequalities on the basis of race (or other protected classifications). If so, at the very least, the government should have to offer a sufficient nondiscriminatory explanation for its actions. Professor Laurence Tribe explained this well when he stated: "The goal of the equal protection clause is not to stamp out impure thoughts, but to guarantee a full measure of human dignity for all. . . . Minorities can also be injured when the government is 'only' indifferent to their suffering or 'merely' blind to how prior official discrimination contributed to it and how current official acts will perpetuate it."[25]

Second, the Court's requirement for proof of a discriminatory purpose ignores the reality of unconscious bias. Rarely will a discriminatory motivation be expressed by legislators or government officials; benign purposes can be articulated for most laws.[26] Therefore, many laws with both discriminatory purpose and effect will be upheld simply because of evidentiary problems inherent in requiring proof of such a purpose. Scholars such as Charles Lawrence argue that this is especially true because racism is often unconscious and such "unconscious racism . . . underlies much of the disproportionate impact of governmental policy."[27]

Since *Washington v. Davis*, a large body of psychological literature has documented the reality of implicit bias and explained its significance for the legal system.[28] The science of implicit bias shows that "actors do not always have conscious, intentional control over the processes of social perception, impression formation, and judgment that motivate their actions."[29] Research on this has shown that we all have biases at an unconscious level, and these biases may influence our decision-making processes in ways of which we are completely unaware.[30]

A crucial problem with requiring proof of discriminatory intent is that it focuses solely on what is expressed; it completely ignores these unconscious biases. Professor Lawrence explained: "Traditional notions of intent do not reflect the fact that decisions about racial matters are influenced in large part by factors that can be characterized as neither intentional—in the sense that certain outcomes are self-consciously sought—nor unintentional—in the sense that the outcomes are random, fortuitous, and uninfluenced by the decision maker's beliefs, desires, and wishes."[31] The requirement for a discriminatory purpose in order to prove the existence of a racial classification fails to account for the reality of implicit bias. As Christine Jolls and Cass Sunstein explain: "Ordinary antidiscrimination law will often face grave difficulties in ferreting out implicit bias even when this bias produces unequal treatment."[32]

Implicit bias research creates a basis for believing that laws with a racially disparate impact do not result from coincidence, but rather reflect unstated—and perhaps unrealized—discriminatory intentions. Put another way, in a society with a long history of discrimination, there can be a presumption that many laws with a discriminatory impact were likely motivated by a discriminatory purpose.[33]

Third, the Court has compounded the problem by adopting a definition of "intent" that makes it very difficult to prove. The Supreme Court has made it clear that showing such a discriminatory purpose requires proof that the government desired to discriminate; it is not enough to prove that the government took an action with knowledge that it would have discriminatory consequences. In *Personnel Administrator of Massachusetts v. Feeney* (1979), the Court declared: "'Discriminatory purpose,' however, implies more than intent as volition or intent as awareness of consequences. It implies that the decisionmaker . . . selected or reaffirmed a particular course of action at least in part 'because of,' not merely 'in spite of,' its adverse effects upon an identifiable group."[34]

Feeney involved a challenge to a Massachusetts law that gave preference in hiring for state jobs to veterans. At the time of the litigation, over 98 percent of the veterans in the state were male; only 1.8 percent were female.[35] The result was a substantial discriminatory effect against women in hiring for state jobs that was known when the law was adopted. Nonetheless, the Supreme Court held that there was not a gender classification because the law creating a preference for veterans was facially gender-neutral, and there was no proof that the state's purpose in adopting the law was to disadvantage women.[36]

The Court rejected the definition of intent that is followed in much of the law: that intent can be shown by demonstrating that a person acted with knowledge of foreseeable consequences. Instead the Court adopted a criminal law definition of intent, meaning having to prove the desire to cause those results. Professor Larry Simon argues that "a showing of significant disproportionate disadvantage to a racial minority group, *without more,* gives rise to an inference that the action may have been taken or at least maintained or continued with knowledge that such groups would be relatively disadvantaged. . . . It raises a possibility sufficient to oblige the government to come forward with a credible explanation showing that the action was (or would have been) taken apart from prejudice."[37] But the Supreme Court has not taken this approach and instead has required proof that the government desired the discriminatory consequences. This makes the requirement for proof of a discriminatory purpose even more onerous and difficult to meet.

In every area of law, the requirement for proof of discriminatory intent has frustrated the ability to use equal protection to remedy race discrimination. Consider a few examples.

It is well documented that sentences for crack cocaine were as much as a hundred times greater than that for powder cocaine, even though it is the same drug. This had a huge racially discriminatory impact. As the Sentencing Project explained: "Approximately 2/3 of crack users are white or Hispanic, yet the vast majority of persons convicted of possession in federal courts in 1994 were African American, according to the [U.S. Sentencing Commission]. Defendants convicted of crack possession in 1994 were 84.5 percent black, 10.3 percent white, and 5.2 percent Hispanic. Trafficking offenders were 4.1 percent white, 88.3 percent black, and 7.1 percent Hispanic. Powder cocaine offenders were more racially mixed. Defendants convicted of simple possession of cocaine powder were 58 percent white, 26.7 percent black, and 15 percent Hispanic. The powder trafficking offenders were 32 percent white, 27.4 percent black, and 39.3 percent Hispanic. The result of the combined difference in sentencing laws and racial disparity is that black men and women are serving longer prison sentences than white men and women."[38]

Consider California as an example. People of color account for over 98 percent of those sent to California state prisons for possession of crack cocaine for sale. From 2005 to 2010, blacks accounted for 77.4 percent of state prison commitments for crack possession for sale, although they made up just 6.6 percent of the state's population. Latinos account for 18.1 percent of those convicted of crack cocaine offenses, while whites are 1.8 percent of those in prison for this. By contrast, those convicted for powder cocaine offenses are overwhelmingly white.

Yet, efforts to challenge this disparity as violating equal protection failed because the courts said that there was not proof of a discriminatory intent for the sentencing disparity.[39] The law had an enormously discriminatory effect, with the consequences of many more African Americans and Hispanics being in prison for cocaine offenses, but the courts provided no remedy. As Professor David Sklansky noted, "The federal crack penalties provide a paradigmatic case of unconscious racism."[40] Congress lessened, though did not eliminate, this disparity with the Fair Sentencing Act of 2010, which reduced the statutory penalties for crack cocaine offenses to produce an 18-to-1 crack-to-powder drug quantity ratio and eliminated the mandatory minimum sentence for simple possession of crack cocaine.

Another example of the barrier created by requiring proof of discriminatory intent is in the area of the death penalty. This, of course, was the focus of *McCleskey v. Kemp*, where the Supreme Court held that proof of discrimination impact in the administration of the death penalty was insufficient to show an equal protection violation.[41] Countless studies prove racial inequality in the imposition of capital punishment.[42] As Matt Ford noted: "The national death-row population is roughly 42 percent black, while the U.S. population overall is only 13.6 percent black, according to the latest census. . . . Some individual states are worse. In Louisiana, the most carceral state in the Union, blacks are roughly one-third of the population but more than two-thirds of the state's death-row inmates."[43] Undoubtedly, these statistics reflect the biases, often unconscious, of prosecutors as to when to seek the death penalty or juries about when to impose it. But *McCleskey v. Kemp* and the requirement for proof of a discriminatory intent makes it impossible to challenge on equal protection grounds.

One more example of the barrier created by requiring proof of discriminatory purpose is in the area of school segregation. Obviously there was no difficulty in proving discrimination in states that, by law, had required separation of the races in education. But in northern school systems, where segregated schools were not the product of state laws, the issue arose as to what had to be proved in order to demonstrate an equal protection violation and justify a federal court remedy.

The Supreme Court addressed this issue in *Keyes v. School District No. 1, Denver, Colorado* (1973).[44] The Supreme Court recognized that it was not a case where schools were segregated by statute, but the Court said, "Nevertheless, where plaintiffs prove that the school authorities have carried out a systematic program of segregation affecting a substantial portion of the students, schools, teachers, and facilities within the school system, it is only common sense to conclude that there exists a predicate for a finding of the existence of a dual school system."[45] Nonetheless, the Court held that, absent laws requiring school segregation, plaintiffs must prove intentional segregative acts affecting a substantial part of the school system.

The Court drew a distinction between de jure segregation, which existed throughout the South, and de facto segregation, which existed in the North. The latter constitutes a constitutional violation only if there is proof of discriminatory purpose. This approach is consistent with the Supreme Court cases holding that when laws are facially neutral, proof of a discriminatory impact alone is not sufficient to show an equal protection violation; there also must be proof of a discriminatory purpose. But requiring proof of discriminatory purpose also created a substantial obstacle to desegregation in northern school systems where residential segregation—which was a product of a myriad of discriminatory policies—caused school segregation.

Thus, proof of racial separation in schools is not sufficient to establish an equal protection violation or provide a basis for federal court remedies. As is true in other areas of equal protection law, there must be either proof of laws that mandated segregation or evidence of intentional acts to segregate the schools.[46] This created an enormous obstacle to courts being able to deal with segregated schools in northern cities.

I choose these three examples—cocaine sentencing, the death penalty, and education—because they are areas where there are no statutes allowing recovery based on disparate impact and thus there are enormous consequences to the Supreme Court's requirement for proof of discriminatory purpose. In fact, the areas where there are statutes that allow for proof of discrimination by a showing of disparate impact—Title VII for employment discrimination (1964),[47] the Fair Housing Act (1968),[48] and the Voting Rights Act amendments of 1982[49]—demonstrate the great difference when there can be liability without proof of discriminatory intent. A crucial part of the progressive agenda must be to change this law and allow proof of discrimination on the basis of disparate impact.

My fear, especially with Justice Kennedy's departure from the Court, is that the Court may go in the opposite direction and overturn decisions that allow disparate impact liability to prove violations of federal statutes. As mentioned above, federal laws in the areas of employment, voting, and housing allow discrimination to be proven by showing disparate impact, even though the Constitution requires proof of discriminatory intent. But conservatives long have opposed this and will seek to reverse the prior decisions allowing disparate impact liability. Even worse, it is possible that with five conservative justices, the Court will hold that disparate impact liability violates the Constitution. Their argument would be that to avoid disparate impact liability, decision makers, such as employers, must consider race. This, their argument goes, is inconsistent with their belief that decisions must always be color-blind and gender-blind. If ever this position gets five votes—and it well might—it will be a devastating blow to antidiscrimination law. It is so difficult to prove discriminatory intent that disparate impact liability is essential to remedying discrimination.

AFFIRMATIVE ACTION

Because of the history of race discrimination in the United States and continuing inequalities, affirmative action programs remain essential. Every Supreme Court decision to consider the constitutionality of affirmative action in higher education has upheld it as permissible under equal protection so long as the government shows that it is necessary to achieve diversity in the student body. But the conservative agenda has long been about eliminating race-conscious admissions programs, and with future changes on the Court they may have a majority ready to do so.

In *Regents of the University of California v. Bakke,* in 1978, the Court held that colleges and universities may use race as one factor among many in admissions decisions to achieve diversity. In the pivotal opinion, Justice Lewis Powell explained that "the interest of diversity is compelling in the context of a university's admissions program."[50] Ideally, such diversity would occur through race-blind admissions and hiring policies. But where that would not be the case, and because of the legacy of discrimination it often won't occur, affirmative action is used to enhance diversity.

Twenty-five years later, in *Grutter v. Bollinger* (2003), in a 5–4 decision, with Justice O'Connor writing for the majority, the Court ruled that colleges and universities have a compelling interest in creating a diverse student body and that they may use race as one factor, among many, to benefit minorities and enhance diversity. The Court said that the "benefits [of diversity] are substantial" and diversity "promotes cross-racial understanding, helps to break down racial stereotypes, and enables students to better understand persons of different races."[51] The Court accepted the university's argument that the education of all students is enhanced with a diverse student body.

Most recently, in 2016, in *Fisher v. University of Texas, Austin,* the Court in a 4–3 decision again upheld the constitutionality of affirmative action.[52] Justice Kagan was recused from participating in the case because of having been involved when she was the solicitor general of the United States and Justice Scalia had died before the decision was announced. In 2004, the regents of the University of Texas, seeing a lack of diversity in their undergraduate population, adopted a new admissions policy. Pursuant to Texas state law, about 75 percent of each freshman class would be admitted by taking the top

10 percent from every high school in the state. Because of racial segregation in Texas, this would produce some degree of diversity, but not enough to create a "critical mass" of minority students essential for their success and for diversity.

The University of Texas policy provided that about 25 percent of each class would be admitted based on an individualized review of applications. An admissions score was calculated for each student based on two numbers. One was an Academic Index, which was the student's grades and test scores. The other was a Personal Achievement Index, which was calculated based on the assessment of two admissions essays and a consideration of seven factors, one of which was what the student would contribute to racial diversity.

The new policy worked in enhancing diversity. There was a significant increase in applications from minority students, and a 20 percent increase in African American students and a 15 percent increase in Latino students attending the University of Texas.

Under *Grutter v. Bollinger*, this was clearly constitutional; the University of Texas used race as one factor among many in its admissions decisions. But the concern was that the composition of the Court had changed since *Grutter* was decided in 2003. Most importantly, Justice Sandra Day O'Connor, the author of the majority opinion approving affirmative action, had been replaced by Justice Samuel Alito, a staunch foe of such programs.

Anthony Kennedy came on to the Supreme Court in February 1988. From then until June 23, 2016, he never once voted to uphold an affirmative action program, not in education or contracting or employment. Yet, his majority opinion in *Fisher* and his tone left no doubt that there is, at least for now, a majority to uphold affirmative action programs.

To be sure, the Court reaffirmed that the burden is

on the educational institution to prove the need for diversity and that there is no race-neutral way to achieve diversity. The Court found that the University of Texas had met this burden. Most important, the Court expressed the need for deference to educational institutions. The Court declared: "Considerable deference is owed to a university in defining those intangible characteristics, like student body diversity, that are central to its identity and educational mission. . . . In striking this sensitive balance, public universities, like the States themselves, can serve as 'laboratories for experimentation.'"[53]

So after *Fisher*, there were five votes to allow colleges and universities to continue to engage in affirmative action: Justices Kennedy, Ginsburg, Breyer, Sotomayor, and Kagan.[54] But it is equally clear that there are four justices who will end all affirmative action if they get a fifth vote. Chief Justice John Roberts and Justices Thomas, Alito, and, I am sure, Gorsuch. For example, in *Parents Involved in Community Schools v. Seattle School District No. 1* (2007),[55] Chief Justice Roberts—joined by Justices Scalia, Thomas, and Alito—proclaimed that the Constitution requires that the government be color-blind and rejected that diversity in education is a compelling interest. Chief Justice Roberts concluded his opinion by declaring: "The way to stop discrimination on the basis of race is to stop discriminating on the basis of race."[56] I think that everyone—liberals and conservatives—believe that Justice Gorsuch will be with Roberts, Thomas, and Alito on this. So it is very likely that the newest justice will be a fifth vote for this position. It is highly probable that there are now five votes to overturn those earlier decisions and hold that *all* affirmative action is unconstitutional.

Why must progressives continue to advocate for the constitutionality of affirmative action, even in the face of a change in the composition of the Court that could create a majority to find all such programs unconstitutional? First, the simple reality is that the long history of racial discrimination means it is not possible to achieve diversity in colleges and universities without it. Some states, like California, abolished affirmative action by voter initiative. Their experience powerfully demonstrates what would happen if the Supreme Court were to reverse its earlier decisions and hold affirmative action to be unconstitutional. In a brief to the Supreme Court, the president and chancellors of the University of California explained that "the abandonment of race-conscious admissions policies resulted in an immediate and precipitous decline in the rates at which underrepresented-minority students applied to, were admitted to, and enrolled at" the university.[57]

At the University of California, Los Angeles, for example, admission rates for underrepresented minorities plummeted from 52.4 percent in 1995 (before Proposition 209) to 24 percent in 1998. As a result, the percentage of underrepresented minorities fell by more than half: from 30.1 percent of the entering class in 1995 to 14.3 percent in 1998. The admissions rate for underrepresented minorities at UCLA reached a new low of 13.6 percent in 2012.[58]

The decline in minority representation at the University of California has come even as the minority population in California has increased. At UCLA, for example, the proportion of Hispanic freshmen among those enrolled declined from 23 percent in 1995 to 17 percent in 2011, even though the proportion of Hispanic college-aged persons in California increased from 41 percent to 49 percent during that same period. The proportion of black freshmen among those enrolled at UCLA declined from 8 percent in 1995 to 3 percent in 2011, even though the proportion of black college-aged persons in California increased from 8 percent to 9 percent during that same period.[59]

The long history of race discrimination means that race-neutral admissions simply will not yield racial diversity, especially in elite colleges and universities. That has been the experience in California and Michigan and in every state that has eliminated affirmative action.

Second, racial diversity in higher education matters. This is exactly why the Court in *Bakke*, *Grutter*, and *Fisher* concluded that diversity is a compelling government interest. As the president and chancellors of the University of California explained: "Powerful empirical evidence, consistent with UC's experience, shows that, when accompanied by meaningful cross-racial interactions, diversity yields substantial educational benefits."[60]

I have been a professor for thirty-eight years, and I have taught constitutional law in classes that are almost all white and those that are racially diverse. The conversation around racial profiling by the police changes when there are African Americans and Latinos in the room who can talk powerfully about being stopped for "driving while black or brown." Preparing students for the racially diverse world they will experience requires that they learn in racially diverse classrooms.

Opponents of affirmative action must show either that it is possible to achieve racial diversity without affirmative action or that diversity in the classroom does not matter. Neither is a tenable conclusion. Opponents of race-conscious admissions policies thus have shifted to other arguments against affirmative action.

Most opposition to affirmative action is based on the false premise that colleges and universities should be admitting students solely on the basis of their grades and test scores. But that has never been the sole basis for determining "merit." Colleges and universities have always valued diversity. For example, historically it has been easier for students from North Dakota or Montana to get into elite private East Coast universities than students from New York or Boston. Those with exceptional skills and talents often have been admitted with lower grades and test scores. Many colleges and universities give preference in admission to those whose relatives attended the school, something that, overall, favors whites over students of color. As the Supreme Court has rightly recognized, assessments of merit properly look at many factors in terms of how a student will enrich the school, including how the student will enhance racial diversity.

Opponents of affirmative action, including the Trump Justice Department, also say that they are acting to protect discrimination against Asian Americans. But extensive research demonstrates that affirmative action programs benefit all students, including Asian Americans. Although not every Asian American subgroup remains underrepresented, many are, including Vietnamese, Thai, Lao, Burmese, Filipino, Native Hawaiian, and Pacific Islander students. Race-conscious admissions policies give school officials the ability to take into account the unique experiences of these individuals.

Finally, there is the argument against affirmative action based on the so-called mismatch theory. This is the hypothesis that affirmative action causes minority students to attend "better" schools than those to which they otherwise would be admitted and that they then do less well there than they would have at less prestigious schools.[61]

There are countless problems with this hypothesis, most importantly that the evidence does not support it. Many have exposed the methodological flaws in studies that purport to document the mismatch theory, and many studies have shown that it is simply not true. University of Michigan law professor and social scientist Richard Lempert filed a brief in the Supreme Court focusing on the mismatch hypothesis and concluded: "The overwhelming weight of the evidence suggests that affirmative action, as currently practiced, does not harm minorities through academic mismatch, and may in fact benefit students who might appear overmatched. If there is a mismatch problem it is that minorities are more likely to be in situations of 'undermatch'—that is, attending schools that are less selective than those they could be admitted to—than in situations of overmatch."[62]

There is an easy explanation for this: grades and test scores are a very imprecise measure of performance, and those accepted through affirmative action are qualified and capable of succeeding and doing the work. In law schools, for example, the Law School Admissions Test has only a weak correlation to first-year law school grades and no correlation to upper-level law school grades, let alone to success in the profession. The mismatch hypothesis assumes that students admitted through affirmative action with lower test scores are less likely to succeed, but the evidence does not support this. Moreover, at any school, the pool of those qualified and capable of succeeding is much greater than the number who can be accepted. Affirmative action is choosing among those who have shown the ability to succeed, and hopefully excel, at the school.

The mismatch theory also fails to account for the lifelong benefits of attending a more prestigious school. I know that attending Harvard Law School gave me a very marketable diploma and made it easier for me to get hired out of law school as an attorney at the Honors Program in the Department of Justice and subsequently as a law professor. Those opportunities are available to those attending less prestigious law schools, but less so (and for legal academia, much less so). It is no coincidence that all nine of the Supreme Court justices went to Harvard or Yale for law school.

Achieving a more just and equal society requires that affirmative action programs continue to exist. Progressives must advocate for them, even though the change in the composition of the Court will place them—and racial diversity in higher education—in grave danger.

A CONSTITUTIONAL RIGHT TO MINIMUM ENTITLEMENTS

The Preamble states that a fundamental purpose of the Constitution is to provide for the "general Welfare." Nothing seems more basic to the general welfare than food, shelter, medical care, and, for children, education. These are the prerequisites to functioning in society and often to life itself. But today it seems far-fetched to argue that the Constitution should be interpreted to create a right to minimum entitlements from the government.

Yet, I believe that if the Warren Court had lasted longer, or if Hubert Humphrey rather than Richard Nixon had picked four justices between 1969 and 1971, it would have happened. In 1969, when Harvard law professor Frank Michelman wrote a famous article in the *Harvard Law Review*, "On Protecting the Poor Through the Fourteenth Amendment," such a constitutional right to minimum entitlements seemed quite plausible.[63] Other constitutional scholars, such as Charles Black and Peter Edelman, have made a persuasive case for finding a constitutional right to basic necessities from the government.[64]

Many countries in the world have constitutions that create such a right.[65] The idea of a government-provided guaranteed annual income for all Americans seems unthinkable at this time. But in 1968, five renowned economists—John Kenneth Galbraith, Harold Watts, James Tobin, Paul Samuelson, and Robert Lampman—wrote an open letter to Congress that appeared on the front page of *The New York Times*. They urged the creation of a federal guaranteed annual income and said: "The country will not have met its responsibility until everyone in the nation is assured an income no less than the officially recognized definition of poverty."[66] They said that the costs would be "substantial, but well within the nation's economic and fiscal capacity."[67]

In 1969, Richard Nixon, no liberal, was "on the verge . . . of enacting an unconditional income for all poor families. It would have been a massive step forward in the War on Poverty, guaranteeing a family of four $1,600 a year, equivalent to roughly $10,000 in 2016."[68] President Nixon later urged the creation of a guaranteed annual income through a negative income tax, something originally proposed by conservative economist Milton Friedman a number of years earlier.[69] Not surprisingly, there was support among liberals for such a plan. In 1967, Martin Luther King, Jr., said, "The solution to poverty is to abolish it directly by a now widely discussed measure: the guaranteed income."[70] In 1972, Democratic presidential candidate George McGovern advocated the guaranteed income.

It never happened. Popular attitudes have shifted to make the idea of a guaranteed annual income—or a constitutional right to basic entitlements—seem unthinkable. But progressives should not abandon this as a long-term goal. If the Constitution will ever truly provide for the general welfare, every child should be guaranteed a quality education and every person should have the food, shelter, and medical care needed for survival.

The possibility of such a constitutional right was ended by the Supreme Court's decision in 1973 in *San Antonio Board of Education v. Rodriguez*. I regard this as one of the worst, and one the most important, decisions in my lifetime. *Rodriguez* involved a challenge to the Texas system of funding public schools largely through local property taxes. Texas's financing system meant that poor areas had to tax at a high rate, but had little to spend on education; wealthier areas could tax at low rates, but still had much more to spend on education. For example, one poorer district spent $356 per pupil, while a wealthier district spent $594 per student.[71] Using property taxes as the primary source of school funding led to even larger gaps in many areas of the country.[72]

The plaintiffs challenged this system on two grounds: it violated equal protection as impermissible wealth discrimination, and it denied the fundamental right to education. The Court rejected the former argument by holding that discriminating against the poor is not a basis for declaring laws unconstitutional as violating equal protection.

Moreover, the Supreme Court expressly rejected the claim that education is a fundamental right.[73] The Court said: "It is not the province of this Court to create substantive constitutional rights in the name of guaranteeing equal protection of the laws. Thus, the key to discovering whether education is 'fundamental' is not to be found in comparisons of the relative social significance of education as opposed to subsistence or housing. . . . Rather, the answer lies in assessing whether there is a right to education explicitly or implicitly guaranteed by the Constitution."[74] Justice Powell, writing for the majority, then concluded: "Education, of course, is not among the rights afforded explicit protection under our Federal Constitution. Nor do we find any basis for saying it is implicitly so protected."[75]

Although education obviously is inextricably linked to the exercise of constitutional rights such as freedom of speech and voting, the Court nonetheless decided that education itself is not a fundamental right. The Court said: "The logical limitations on appellees' nexus theory are difficult to perceive. How, for instance, is education to be distinguished from the significant personal interests in the basics of decent food and shelter? Empirical examination might well buttress an assumption that the ill-fed, ill-clothed, and ill-housed are among the most ineffective participants in the political process, and that they derive the least enjoyment from the benefits of the First Amendment."[76]

The decision was 5–4, with the four Nixon appointees—Burger, Blackmun, Powell, and Rehnquist—in the majority, joined by Justice Potter Stewart, who had been appointed by President Dwight Eisenhower. The Court's conclusion that there is no right to education cannot be reconciled with Chief Justice Warren's earlier eloquent statement in *Brown v. Board of Education*: "Today, education is perhaps the most important function of state and local governments. Compulsory school attendance laws and the great expenditures for education both demonstrate our recognition of the importance of education to our democratic society. It is required in the performance of our most basic public responsibilities, even service in the armed forces. It is the very foundation of good citizenship. Today it is a principal instrument in awakening the child to cultural values, in preparing him for later professional training, and in helping him to adjust normally to his environment. In these days, it is doubtful that any child may reasonably be expected to succeed in life if he is denied the opportunity of an education."[77]

Education is essential for the exercise of constitutional rights, for economic opportunity, and ultimately for achieving equality. In *Plyler v. Doe*, in 1982, the Supreme Court declared unconstitutional a Texas law that provided a free public education to citizens and to children of documented immigrants but required undocumented immigrants to pay for their public education.[78] The Court ruled that the law denied equal protection and, in part, based this conclusion on the importance of education. Justice Brennan, writing for the Court, stated: "Public education is not a 'right' granted to individuals by the

Constitution. But neither is it merely some governmental 'benefit' indistinguishable from other forms of social welfare legislation. Both the importance of education in maintaining our basic institutions, and the lasting impact of its deprivation on the life of the child, mark the distinction. . . . [E]ducation provides the basic tools by which individuals might lead economically productive lives to the benefit of us all. In sum, education has a fundamental role in maintaining the fabric of our society."[79]

But *Rodriguez* remains the law today: there is no constitutional right to an education. By contrast, several state courts have found a fundamental right to education under their state constitutions and have concluded that inequities in school funding are impermissible as a matter of state constitutional law.[80]

Moreover, if there is no right to education under the Constitution, and if discriminating against the poor does not violate the Constitution, then there also is no right to food or shelter or medical care. I believe that the Constitution, as reflected in its Preamble, had a larger and grander vision of ensuring the general welfare of all Americans. It should be interpreted to find in the Constitution a right to minimum entitlements from the government, food, shelter, medical care, and quality education.

The usual response to this is to say that the Constitution is about negative liberties—prohibitions on what the government may do, not affirmative duties that the government must fulfill. Former federal court of appeals judge Richard Posner summarized this view: "The Constitution is a charter of negative liberties; it tells the state to let people alone; it does not require the federal government or the state to provide services, even so elementary a service as maintaining law and order."[81]

But it is inaccurate to depict the Constitution as solely a charter of negative liberties. Many parts of the Constitution create affirmative duties. The Fourth Amendment requires police to obtain a warrant before a search or an arrest except under relatively limited circumstances. Almost the entire Fifth Amendment imposes affirmative duties on the government, including the requirement that the government convene a grand jury to indict a person before trial in a federal court. Also, the Fifth Amendment, as interpreted in *Miranda v. Arizona* (1966), requires the police to administer warnings before interrogation. That amendment additionally requires the government to pay just compensation if it takes private property for public use. And the due process clauses in the Fifth and Fourteenth Amendments require the government to provide notice and hearing when depriving a person of life, liberty, or property. The Sixth and Seventh Amendments require the government to provide a jury trial in criminal and civil trials, respectively. The Sixth Amendment mandates the provision of counsel in cases in which there is a possible prison sentence.

Numerous parts of the body of the Constitution also create affirmative government duties. Notable examples in Article I include the requirement for Congress to keep a journal of its proceedings, to give a regular statement and account of all expenditures, and to conduct a census. Simply put, it is descriptively wrong to see the Constitution as solely negative liberties.[82]

The Constitution does create affirmative duties on the government; it is a question of what they should be deemed to include. I believe that progressives must argue that for those living in the United States to have the "life" and "liberty" promised by the due process clauses of the Constitution, there must be a right to food, shelter, medical care, and an adequate education.

Second, the argument that the Constitution provides only negative liberties is based on a questionable distinction between government action and government inaction. The due process clause, for example, prevents government from depriving a person of life, liberty, or property without due process of law. If a police officer stands by and does nothing while a severe beating occurs, the government effectively has deprived the victim of his or her liberty. The equal protection clause prevents the government from denying any person equal protection of the laws. If the government watches blatant racial discrimination and takes no action, the government has effectively denied the person equal protection. Therefore, government inaction in the face of poverty, which results in harm or even death, should be viewed as a constitutional violation. The government's maintenance of school systems that fail to provide children an education that offers minimal literacy should be deemed unconstitutional.

Finally, the argument that the Constitution is only about negative liberties confuses rights and remedies. The Constitution's rights can almost all be phrased negatively, but remedies virtually always can be stated affirmatively. For example, a classic statement of a negative right is that the Fourth Amendment generally prohibits searches and seizures without warrants based on probable cause. The remedy, which is an affirmative duty, is that police usually must seek warrants before searches or arrests. The Fifth Amendment prohibits involuntary self-incrimination, again a negative right. The Court has prescribed the affirmative duty of administering Miranda warnings as part of the solution. The Fourteenth Amendment prohibits government-imposed segregation; the courts have mandated desegregation as a remedy.

Similarly, the Court should find that the Constitution forbids the government from ignoring starvation and homelessness and inadequate education in that they constitute deprivations of life and liberty without due process. Notice that this is a negative liberty, a prohibition on what the government may do. The remedy is affirmative: assuring minimal entitlements.

In other words, those who view the Constitution as solely a charter of negative liberties focus on the rights aspect and ignore the remedies. These individuals look at minimum entitlement solely as a remedy and ignore the underlying right. If the whole picture is examined, almost all rights—including the right to be free from the harms of homelessness, lack of medical care, and lack of adequate food—can be stated in negative terms; while virtually all remedies—including minimum entitlements—can be stated in affirmative language.

Undoubtedly, critics will charge that this type of judicial action is inconsistent with democracy and usurps the prerogatives of the legislature. Opposition to judicial action virtually always makes this argument based on democracy. But I believe that progressives should make the case for there is a constitutional right to minimum entitlements, and then it follows that it is the judicial role to enforce. The late Charles Black, a Yale law professor, argued that the Ninth Amendment permits judicial protection of such rights and explained that a number of constitutional provisions can be read together to support the conclusion that "there is and of right ought to be, a constitutional justice of livelihood."[83] Black especially emphasizes the language in the Declaration of Independence, the Preamble to the Constitution, and Article I that declare the importance of the government's securing the "general Welfare."[84] Constitutional rights should not be left to the political process for their enforcement. If there is a constitutional right to food, shelter, medical care, and education, the courts should be able to enforce it.

The other aspect of considering the judicial role is more practical: Is it realistic to imagine the judiciary creating a right to basic entitlements? Would this inevitably place the Court in the role of running the welfare bureaucracy, determining the eligibility and benefit levels for a myriad of programs? What is the content of the right; what must be provided to constitute basic subsistence? This practical dimension will need to be addressed, though it should be emphasized that creating a right to minimum subsistence need not entail the Court in managing welfare programs. The Court can declare the right to minimum entitlements and leave it to the legislatures' discretion as to how to assure provision of the benefits. Legislatures might choose a guaranteed annual income, or its cousin, a negative income tax. Or legislatures can choose guaranteed employment with sufficient income, together with assistance programs for those unable to work. Another possibility would be a combination of cash programs and in-kind assistance, such as food stamps and Medicaid. However the government chooses to meet its responsibilities, the judicial role would be in ensuring that the government has acted to assure every person the basic essentials needed for life.

Professor Peter Edelman has suggested that such judicial action could spark legislative solutions. He writes: "Using the courts when the legislature is unresponsive has a value beyond the net benefit achieved in terms of limited relief initially obtained. History suggests that judicial involvement can spark legislative reverberation (and retaliation, to be sure). The Supreme Court's involvement in race cases was surely one of the cornerstones in the foundation that underlay the great civil rights legislation of the 1960s. A declaration from the Court of a right to survival income might evoke a resonating legislative response."[85]

It is easy to become demoralized when confronted with a very conservative Court that likely will remain that way throughout most of the rest of my life. The temptation is to give up on the idea of using the Constitution for social justice. But such surrender is shortsighted. Arguments that today fall on deaf ears can be the basis for future action. A constitutional right to minimum entitlements is not going to happen in the foreseeable future. But if it will happen at all, it will result from progressives developing and defending and fighting for this vision for the Constitution.

CONCLUSION

GOING FORWARD

The words in the Constitution provide us remarkably little protection against tyranny or of our rights. Consider the following constitutional language:

> Every citizen . . . has the right to submit proposals to state bodies and public organisations for improving their activity, and to criticise shortcomings in their work. . . . Persecution for criticism is prohibited. Persons guilty of such persecution shall be called to account. . . . Citizens . . . are guaranteed freedom of speech, of the press, and of assembly, meetings, street processions and demonstrations. Exercise of these political freedoms is ensured by putting public buildings, streets, and squares at the disposal of the people and their organizations, by broad dissemination of information, and by the opportunity to use the press, television, and radio. Citizens . . . are guaranteed freedom of conscience, that is, the right to profess or not to profess any religion, and to conduct religious worship, or atheistic propaganda. Incitement of hostility or hatred on religious grounds is prohibited.

This is the language of the Stalin-era Soviet constitution. Sometimes I have begun a constitutional law class by having my students read a copy of this and a copy of the United States Constitution. I also have them read descriptions of the abuses under Soviet rule, such as by Alexander Solzhenitsyn. I want my students to see from the outset of their study of constitutional law that it takes much more than the words of the document to make its commitments a reality.

For a constitution to succeed in achieving its lofty mission—and every constitution has a lofty mission—the institutions of government at all levels must be committed to it and to the values contained within it. Ultimately, the people must be committed to it. The United States Constitution has endured and largely succeeded—and in saying this I do not minimize its great failures—because of the commitment to the values within the document. These are the values found in its Preamble.

Choices constantly must be made as to the meaning of the Constitution's provisions. That has been true since its earliest days and will be so as long as it is the nation's governing document. All laws must be interpreted, but that is especially so for a Constitution written long ago for a very different world and with language that tells very little about how to resolve the disputes that arise.

In this book, I have presented my view of a progressive vision for the core values found in the Constitution as expressed and embodied in its Preamble. As I said at the beginning, I know that because of the election of November 2016, what I have argued for is not going to be followed by the current Supreme Court. I know that Justice Kennedy's retirement and a second Trump justice will push constitutional law in the opposite direction for a long time to come.

Yet, I believe that it is essential that progressives fight for these things. Sometimes the fights will need to be in the legislative process. Congress and state legislatures can accomplish many of the reforms that I have urged in this book. Sometimes the focus will need to be on state courts. For example, the litigation for marriage equality for gays and lesbians began in the state courts and only after several had found such a right was the issue taken to the federal courts and ultimately the U.S. Supreme Court. Sometimes there can be progressive victories even in a conservative Supreme Court. It was the Burger Court, in a 7–2 decision, that decided *Roe v. Wade* and found a constitutional right to abortion. Sometimes it will take a long-term litigation strategy that someday can culminate in a Supreme Court decision.

But I deeply believe that what I have argued for can and will happen someday. History has been kind to progressives. The things they championed over conservative opposition—from abolition of slavery to economic protection for workers to desegregation to marriage equality for gays and lesbians—ultimately came to fruition and to be widely accepted. I thus am convinced that what I argue for in this book will happen sometime, too.

I also believe that if ever it is to happen, we must argue for it now. Progressives cannot give up on the Constitution or constitutional law. We must criticize the regressive policies of the Trump administration and the harmful decisions of the Supreme Court. We must develop and defend an alternative vision.

How progressives talk about the Court and the Constitution now will have long-term consequences. History shows this. As I described earlier, from the late nineteenth century until 1936, a conservative Supreme Court invalidated numerous progressive laws, especially during the first years of the New Deal. The criticism of progressives was focused on questioning the legitimacy of judicial review.[1] The progressive alternative was to emphasize judicial deference to government decisions.

After 1937, progressives became a majority of the Supreme Court and then followed this agenda. From 1937 until 1954, the Court rarely invalidated government actions, at least partially in response to the tremendous pressure toward deference created by the attacks on the conservative Court of the prior era. The Roosevelt appointees to the bench likely began with a philosophy of approving government actions in response to the many invalidations that had preceded them. This had tragic results as the Roosevelt justices upheld the evacuation of Japanese Americans during World War II and convictions during the McCarthy era.[2]

We must not repeat this mistake. Progressives must continue to develop their vision of the Constitution and must fight for it. On the Monday after the November 2016 election, the students at my law school who were very upset by the outcome convened an assembly. They asked faculty to share their thoughts and feelings after the election. I was asked to speak and concluded my remarks by saying that we have only two choices: to give up or to fight harder. And that, of course, means that we have only one real choice: to fight harder and better than ever before.

The U.S. Constitution

BILL OF RIGHTS AND AMENDMENTS

THE CONSTITUTION OF THE UNITED STATES OF AMERICA

We the People of the United States, in Order to form a more perfect Union, establish Justice, insure domestic Tranquility, provide for the common defence, promote the general Welfare, and secure the Blessings of Liberty to ourselves and our Posterity, do ordain and establish this Constitution for the United States of America.

ARTICLE I

SECTION 1. All legislative Powers herein granted shall be vested in a Congress of the United States, which shall consist of a Senate and House of Representatives.

SECTION 2. The House of Representatives shall be composed of Members chosen every second Year by the People of the several States, and the Electors in each State shall have the Qualifications requisite for Electors of the most numerous Branch of the State Legislature.

No Person shall be a Representative who shall not have attained to the Age of twenty five Years, and been seven Years a Citizen of the United States, and who shall not, when elected, be an Inhabitant of that State in which he shall be chosen.

Representatives and direct Taxes shall be apportioned among the several States which may be included within this Union, according to their respective Numbers, which shall be determined by adding to the whole Number of free Persons, including those bound to Service for a Term of Years, and excluding Indians not taxed, three fifths of all other Persons. The actual Enumeration shall be made within three Years after the first Meeting of the Congress of the United States, and within every subsequent Term of ten Years, in such Manner as they shall by Law direct. The Number of Representatives shall not exceed one for every thirty Thousand, but each State shall have at Least one Representative; and until such enumeration shall be made, the State of New Hampshire shall be entitled to chuse three, Massachusetts eight, Rhode-Island and Providence Plantations one, Connecticut five, New-York six, New Jersey four, Pennsylvania eight, Delaware one, Maryland six, Virginia ten, North Carolina five, South Carolina five, and Georgia three.

When vacancies happen in the Representation from any State, the Executive Authority thereof shall issue Writs of Election to fill such Vacancies.

The House of Representatives shall chuse their Speaker and other Officers; and shall have the sole Power of Impeachment.

SECTION 3. The Senate of the United States shall be composed of two Senators from each State, chosen by the Legislature thereof, for six Years; and each Senator shall have one Vote.

Immediately after they shall be assembled in Consequence of the first Election, they shall be divided as equally as may be into three Classes. The Seats of the Senators of the first Class shall be vacated at the Expiration of the second Year, of the second Class at the Expiration of the fourth Year, and of the third Class at the Expiration of the sixth Year, so that one third may be chosen every second Year; and if Vacancies happen by Resignation, or otherwise, during the Recess of the Legislature of any State, the Executive thereof may make temporary Appointments until the next Meeting of the Legislature, which shall then fill such Vacancies.

No Person shall be a Senator who shall not have attained to the Age of thirty Years, and been nine Years a Citizen of the United States, and who shall not, when elected, be an Inhabitant of that State for which he shall be chosen.

The Vice President of the United States shall be President of the Senate, but shall have no Vote, unless they be equally divided.

The Senate shall chuse their other Officers, and also a President pro tempore, in the Absence of the Vice President, or when he shall exercise the Office of President of the United States.

The Senate shall have the sole Power to try all Impeachments. When sitting for that Purpose, they shall be on Oath or Affirmation. When the President of the United States is tried, the Chief Justice shall preside: And no Person shall be convicted without the Concurrence of two thirds of the Members present.

Judgment in Cases of Impeachment shall not extend further than to removal from Office, and disqualification to hold and enjoy any Office of honor, Trust or Profit under the United States: but the Party convicted shall nevertheless be liable and subject to Indictment, Trial, Judgment and Punishment, according to Law.

SECTION 4. The Times, Places and Manner of holding Elections for Senators and Representatives, shall be prescribed in each State by the Legislature thereof; but the Congress may at any time by Law make or alter such Regulations, except as to the Places of chusing Senators.

The Congress shall assemble at least once in every Year, and such Meeting shall be on the first Monday in December, unless they shall by Law appoint a different Day.

SECTION 5. Each House shall be the Judge of the Elections, Returns and Qualifications of its own Members, and a Majority of each shall constitute a Quorum to do Business; but a smaller Number may adjourn from day to day, and may be authorized to compel the Attendance of absent Members, in such Manner, and under such Penalties as each House may provide.

Each House may determine the Rules of its Proceedings, punish its Members for disorderly Behaviour, and, with the Concurrence of two thirds, expel a Member.

Each House shall keep a Journal of its Proceedings, and from time to time publish the same, excepting such Parts as may in their Judgment require Secrecy; and the Yeas and Nays of the Members of either House on any question shall, at the Desire of one fifth of those Present, be entered on the Journal.

Neither House, during the Session of Congress, shall, without the Consent of the other, adjourn for more than three days, nor to any other Place than that in which the two Houses shall be sitting.

SECTION 6. The Senators and Representatives shall receive a Compensation for their Services, to be ascertained by Law, and paid out of the Treasury of the United States. They shall in all Cases, except Treason, Felony and Breach of the Peace, be privileged from Arrest during their Attendance at the Session of their respective Houses, and in going to and returning from the same; and for any Speech or Debate in either House, they shall not be questioned in any other Place.

No Senator or Representative shall, during the Time for which he was elected, be appointed to any civil Office under the Authority of the United States, which shall have been created, or the Emoluments whereof shall have been encreased during such time; and no Person holding any Office under the United States, shall be a Member of either House during his Continuance in Office.

SECTION 7. All Bills for raising Revenue shall originate in the House of Representatives; but the Senate may propose or concur with Amendments as on other Bills.

Every Bill which shall have passed the House of Representatives and the Senate, shall, before it become a Law, be presented to the President of the United States; If he approve he shall sign it, but if not he shall return it, with his Objections to that House in which it shall have originated, who shall enter the Objections at large on their Journal, and proceed to reconsider it. If after such Reconsideration two thirds of that House shall agree to pass the Bill, it shall be sent, together with the Objections, to the other House, by which it shall likewise be reconsidered, and if approved by two thirds of that House, it shall become a Law. But in all such Cases the Votes of both Houses shall be determined by yeas and Nays, and the Names of the Persons voting for and against the Bill shall be entered on the Journal of each House respectively. If any Bill shall not be returned by the President within ten Days (Sundays excepted) after it shall have been presented to him, the Same shall be a Law, in like Manner as if he had signed it, unless the Congress by their Adjournment prevent its Return, in which Case it shall not be a Law.

Every Order, Resolution, or Vote to which the Concurrence of the Senate and House of Representatives may be necessary (except on a question of Adjournment) shall be presented to the President of the United States; and before the Same shall take Effect, shall be approved by him, or being disapproved by him, shall be repassed by two thirds of the Senate and House of Representatives, according to the Rules and Limitations prescribed in the Case of a Bill.

SECTION 8. The Congress shall have Power To lay and collect Taxes, Duties, Imposts and Excises, to pay the Debts and provide for the common Defence and general Welfare of the United States; but all Duties, Imposts and Excises shall be uniform throughout the United States;

To borrow Money on the credit of the United States;

To regulate Commerce with foreign Nations, and among the several States, and with the Indian Tribes;

To establish an uniform Rule of Naturalization, and uniform Laws on the subject of Bankruptcies throughout the United States;

To coin Money, regulate the Value thereof, and of foreign Coin, and fix the Standard of Weights and Measures;

To provide for the Punishment of counterfeiting the Securities and current Coin of the United States;

To establish Post Offices and post Roads;

To promote the Progress of Science and useful Arts, by securing for limited Times to Authors and Inventors the exclusive Right to their respective Writings and Discoveries;

To constitute Tribunals inferior to the supreme Court;

To define and punish Piracies and Felonies committed on the high Seas, and Offences against the Law of Nations;

To declare War, grant Letters of Marque and Reprisal, and make Rules concerning Captures on Land and Water;

To raise and support Armies, but no Appropriation of Money to that Use shall be for a longer Term than two Years;

To provide and maintain a Navy;

To make Rules for the Government and Regulation of the land and naval Forces;

To provide for calling forth the Militia to execute the Laws of the Union, suppress Insurrections and repel Invasions;

To provide for organizing, arming, and disciplining, the Militia, and for governing such Part of them as may be employed in the Service of the United States, reserving to the States respectively, the Appointment of the Officers, and the Authority of training the Militia according to the discipline prescribed by Congress;

To exercise exclusive Legislation in all Cases whatsoever, over such District (not exceeding ten Miles square) as may, by Cession of particular States, and the Acceptance of Congress, become the Seat of the Government of the United States, and to exercise like Authority over all Places purchased by the Consent of the Legislature of the State in which the Same shall be, for the Erection of Forts, Magazines, Arsenals, dock-Yards, and other needful Buildings;—And

To make all Laws which shall be necessary and proper for carrying into Execution the foregoing Powers, and all other Powers vested by this Constitution in the Government of the United States, or in any Department or Officer thereof.

SECTION 9. The Migration or Importation of such Persons as any of the States now existing shall think proper to admit, shall not be prohibited by the Congress prior to the Year one thousand eight hundred and eight, but a Tax or duty may be imposed on such Importation, not exceeding ten dollars for each Person.

The Privilege of the Writ of Habeas Corpus shall not be suspended, unless when in Cases of Rebellion or Invasion the public Safety may require it.

No Bill of Attainder or ex post facto Law shall be passed.

No Capitation, or other direct, Tax shall be laid, unless in Proportion to the Census or Enumeration herein before directed to be taken.

No Tax or Duty shall be laid on Articles exported from any State.

No Preference shall be given by any Regulation of Commerce or Revenue to the Ports of one State over those of another: nor shall Vessels bound to, or from, one State, be obliged to enter, clear, or pay Duties in another.

No Money shall be drawn from the Treasury, but in Consequence of Appropriations made by Law; and a regular Statement and Account of the Receipts and Expenditures of all public Money shall be published from time to time.

No Title of Nobility shall be granted by the United States: And no Person holding any Office of Profit or Trust under them, shall, without the Consent of the Congress, accept of any present, Emolument, Office, or Title, of any kind whatever, from any King, Prince, or foreign State.

SECTION 10. No State shall enter into any Treaty, Alliance, or Confederation; grant Letters of Marque and Reprisal; coin Money; emit Bills of Credit; make any Thing but gold and silver Coin a Tender in Payment of Debts; pass any Bill of Attainder, ex post facto Law, or Law impairing the Obligation of Contracts, or grant any Title of Nobility.

No State shall, without the Consent of the Congress, lay any Imposts or Duties on Imports or Exports, except what may be absolutely necessary for executing it's inspection Laws: and the net Produce of all Duties and Imposts, laid by any State on Imports or Exports, shall be for the Use of the Treasury of the United States; and all such Laws shall be subject to the Revision and Controul of the Congress.

No State shall, without the Consent of Congress, lay any Duty of Tonnage, keep Troops, or Ships of War in time of Peace, enter into any Agreement or Compact with another State, or with a foreign Power, or engage in War, unless actually invaded, or in such imminent Danger as will not admit of delay.

ARTICLE II

SECTION 1. The executive Power shall be vested in a President of the United States of America. He shall hold his Office during the Term of four Years, and, together with the Vice President, chosen for the same Term, be elected, as follows:

Each State shall appoint, in such Manner as the Legislature thereof may direct, a Number of Electors, equal to the whole Number of Senators and Representatives to which the State may be entitled in the Congress: but no Senator or Representative, or Person holding an Office of Trust or Profit under the United States, shall be appointed an Elector.

The Electors shall meet in their respective States, and vote by Ballot for two Persons, of whom one at least shall not be an Inhabitant of the same State with themselves. And they shall make a List of all the Persons voted for, and of the Number of Votes for each; which List they shall sign and certify, and transmit sealed to the Seat of the Government of the United States, directed to the President of the Senate. The President of the Senate shall, in the Presence of the Senate and House of Representatives, open all the Certificates, and the Votes shall then be counted. The Person having the greatest Number of Votes shall be the President, if such Number be a Majority of the whole Number of Electors appointed; and if there be more than one who have such Majority, and have an equal Number of Votes, then the House of Representatives shall immediately chuse by Ballot one of them for President; and if no Person have a Majority, then from the five highest on the List the said House shall in like Manner chuse the President. But in chusing the President, the Votes shall be taken by States, the Representation from each State having one Vote; A quorum for this Purpose shall consist of a Member or Members from two thirds of the States, and a Majority of all the States shall be necessary to a Choice. In every Case, after the Choice of the President, the Person having the greatest Number of Votes of the Electors shall be the Vice President. But if there should remain two or more who have equal Votes, the Senate shall chuse from them by Ballot the Vice President.

The Congress may determine the Time of chusing the Electors, and the Day on which they shall give their Votes; which Day shall be the same throughout the United States.

No Person except a natural born Citizen, or a Citizen of the United States, at the time of the Adoption of this Constitution, shall be eligible to the Office of President; neither shall any Person be eligible to that Office who shall not have attained to the Age of thirty five Years, and been fourteen Years a Resident within the United States.

In Case of the Removal of the President from Office, or of his Death, Resignation, or Inability to discharge the Powers and Duties of the said Office, the Same shall devolve on the Vice President, and the Congress may by Law provide for the Case of Removal, Death, Resignation or Inability, both of the President and Vice President, declaring what Officer shall then act as President, and such Officer shall act accordingly, until the Disability be removed, or a President shall be elected. The President shall, at stated Times, receive for his Services, a Compensation, which shall neither be encreased nor diminished during the Period for which he shall have been elected, and he shall not receive within that Period any other Emolument from the United States, or any of them.

Before he enter on the Execution of his Office, he shall take the following Oath or Affirmation:—"I do solemnly swear (or affirm) that I will faithfully execute the Office of President of the United States, and will to the best of my Ability, preserve, protect and defend the Constitution of the United States."

SECTION 2. The President shall be Commander in Chief of the Army and Navy of the United States, and of the Militia of the several States, when called into the actual Service of the United States; he may require the Opinion, in writing, of the principal Officer in each of the executive Departments, upon any Subject relating to the Duties of their respective Offices, and he shall have Power to grant Reprieves and Pardons for Offences against the United States, except in Cases of Impeachment.

He shall have Power, by and with the Advice and Consent of the Senate, to make Treaties, provided two thirds of the Senators present concur; and he shall nominate, and by and with the Advice and Consent of the Senate, shall appoint Ambassadors, other public Ministers and Consuls, Judges of the supreme Court, and all other Officers of the United States, whose Appointments are not herein otherwise provided for, and which shall be established by Law: but the Congress may by Law vest the Appointment of such inferior Officers, as they think proper, in the President alone, in the Courts of Law, or in the Heads of Departments.

The President shall have Power to fill up all Vacancies that may happen during the Recess of the Senate, by granting Commissions which shall expire at the End of their next Session.

SECTION 3. He shall from time to time give to the Congress Information of the State of the Union, and recommend to their Consideration such Measures as he shall judge necessary and expedient; he may, on extraordinary Occasions, convene both Houses, or either of them, and in Case of Disagreement between them, with Respect to the Time of Adjournment, he may adjourn them to such Time as he shall think proper; he shall receive Ambassadors and other public Ministers; he shall take Care that the Laws be faithfully executed, and shall Commission all the Officers of the United States.

SECTION 4. The President, Vice President and all Civil Officers of the United States, shall be removed from Office on Impeachment for, and Conviction of, Treason, Bribery, or other high Crimes and Misdemeanors.

ARTICLE III

SECTION 1. The judicial Power of the United States, shall be vested in one supreme Court, and in such inferior Courts as the Congress may from time to time ordain and establish. The Judges, both of the supreme and inferior Courts, shall hold their Offices during good Behaviour, and shall, at stated Times, receive for their Services, a Compensation, which shall not be diminished during their Continuance in Office.

SECTION 2. The judicial Power shall extend to all Cases, in Law and Equity, arising under this Constitution, the Laws of the United States, and Treaties made, or which shall be made, under their Authority;—to all Cases affecting Ambassadors, other public Ministers and Consuls;—to all Cases of admiralty and maritime Jurisdiction;—to Controversies to which the United States shall be a Party;—

to Controversies between two or more States;—between a State and Citizens of another State;—between Citizens of different States;—between Citizens of the same State claiming Lands under Grants of different States, and between a State, or the Citizens thereof, and foreign States, Citizens or Subjects.

In all Cases affecting Ambassadors, other public Ministers and Consuls, and those in which a State shall be Party, the supreme Court shall have original Jurisdiction. In all the other Cases before mentioned, the supreme Court shall have appellate Jurisdiction, both as to Law and Fact, with such Exceptions, and under such Regulations as the Congress shall make.

The Trial of all Crimes, except in Cases of Impeachment, shall be by Jury; and such Trial shall be held in the State where the said Crimes shall have been committed; but when not committed within any State, the Trial shall be at such Place or Places as the Congress may by Law have directed.

SECTION 3. Treason against the United States, shall consist only in levying War against them, or in adhering to their Enemies, giving them Aid and Comfort. No Person shall be convicted of Treason unless on the Testimony of two Witnesses to the same overt Act, or on Confession in open Court.

The Congress shall have Power to declare the Punishment of Treason, but no Attainder of Treason shall work Corruption of Blood, or Forfeiture except during the Life of the Person attainted.

ARTICLE IV

SECTION 1. Full Faith and Credit shall be given in each State to the public Acts, Records, and judicial Proceedings of every other State. And the Congress may by general Laws prescribe the Manner in which such Acts, Records and Proceedings shall be proved, and the Effect thereof.

SECTION 2. The Citizens of each State shall be entitled to all Privileges and Immunities of Citizens in the several States.

A Person charged in any State with Treason, Felony, or other Crime, who shall flee from Justice, and be found in another State, shall on Demand of the executive Authority of the State from which he fled, be delivered up, to be removed to the State having Jurisdiction of the Crime.

No Person held to Service or Labour in one State, under the Laws thereof, escaping into another, shall, in Consequence of any Law or Regulation therein, be discharged from such Service or Labour, but shall be delivered up on Claim of the Party to whom such Service or Labour may be due.

SECTION 3. New States may be admitted by the Congress into this Union; but no new State shall be formed or erected within the Jurisdiction of any other State; nor any State be formed by the Junction of two or more States, or Parts of States, without the Consent of the Legislatures of the States concerned as well as of the Congress.

The Congress shall have Power to dispose of and make all needful Rules and Regulations respecting the Territory or other Property belonging to the United States; and nothing in this Constitution shall be so construed as to Prejudice any Claims of the United States, or of any particular State.

SECTION 4. The United States shall guarantee to every State in this Union a Republican Form of Government, and shall protect each of them against Invasion; and on Application of the Legislature, or of the Executive (when the Legislature cannot be convened), against domestic Violence.

ARTICLE V

The Congress, whenever two thirds of both Houses shall deem it necessary, shall propose Amendments to this Constitution, or, on the Application of the Legislatures of two thirds of the several States, shall call a Convention for proposing Amendments, which, in either Case, shall be valid to all Intents and Purposes, as Part of this Constitution, when ratified by the Legislatures of three fourths of the several States, or by Conventions in three fourths thereof, as the one or the other Mode of Ratification may be proposed by the Congress; Provided that no Amendment which may be made prior to the Year One thousand eight hundred and eight shall in any Manner affect the first and fourth Clauses in the Ninth Section of the first Article; and that no State, without its Consent, shall be deprived of its equal Suffrage in the Senate.

ARTICLE VI

All Debts contracted and Engagements entered into, before the Adoption of this Constitution, shall be as valid against the United States under this Constitution, as under the Confederation.

This Constitution, and the Laws of the United States which shall be made in Pursuance thereof; and all Treaties made, or which shall be made, under the Authority of the United States, shall be the supreme Law of the Land; and the Judges in every State shall be bound thereby, any Thing in the Constitution or Laws of any State to the Contrary notwithstanding.

The Senators and Representatives before mentioned, and the Members of the several State Legislatures, and all executive and judicial Officers, both of the United States and of the several States, shall be bound by Oath or Affirmation, to support this Constitution; but no religious Test shall ever be required as a Qualification to any Office or public Trust under the United States.

ARTICLE VII

The Ratification of the Conventions of nine States, shall be sufficient for the Establishment of this Constitution between the States so ratifying the Same.

Articles in addition to, and Amendment of, the Constitution of the United States of America, proposed by Congress, and ratified by the Legislatures of the several States, pursuant to the fifth Article of the original Constitution.

AMENDMENT I [1791]

Congress shall make no law respecting an establishment of religion, or prohibiting the free exercise thereof; or abridging the freedom of speech, or of the press; or the right of the people peaceably to assemble, and to petition the Government for a redress of grievances.

AMENDMENT II [1791]

A well regulated Militia, being necessary to the security of a free State, the right of the people to keep and bear Arms, shall not be infringed.

AMENDMENT III [1791]

No Soldier shall, in time of peace be quartered in any house, without the consent of the Owner, nor in time of war, but in a manner to be prescribed by law.

AMENDMENT IV [1791]

The right of the people to be secure in their persons, houses, papers, and effects, against unreasonable searches and seizures, shall not be violated, and no Warrants shall issue, but upon probable cause, supported by Oath or affirmation, and particularly describing the place to be searched, and the persons or things to be seized.

AMENDMENT V [1791]

No person shall be held to answer for a capital, or otherwise infamous crime, unless on a presentment or indictment of a Grand Jury, except in cases arising in the land or naval forces, or in the Militia, when in actual service in time of War or public danger; nor shall any person be subject for the same offence to be twice put in jeopardy of life or limb; nor shall be compelled in any criminal case to be a witness against himself, nor be deprived of life, liberty, or property, without due process of law; nor shall private property be taken for public use, without just compensation.

AMENDMENT VI [1791]

In all criminal prosecutions, the accused shall enjoy the right to a speedy and public trial, by an impartial jury of the State and district wherein the crime shall have been committed, which district shall have been previously ascertained by law, and to be informed of the nature and cause of the accusation; to be confronted with the witnesses against him; to have compulsory process for obtaining witnesses in his favor, and to have the Assistance of Counsel for his defence.

AMENDMENT VII [1791]

In Suits at common law, where the value in controversy shall exceed twenty dollars, the right of trial by jury shall be preserved, and no fact tried by a jury, shall be otherwise re-examined in any Court of the United States, than according to the rules of the common law.

AMENDMENT VIII [1791]

Excessive bail shall not be required, nor excessive fines imposed, nor cruel and unusual punishments inflicted.

AMENDMENT IX [1791]

The enumeration in the Constitution, of certain rights, shall not be construed to deny or disparage others retained by the people.

AMENDMENT X [1791]

The powers not delegated to the United States by the Constitution, nor prohibited by it to the States, are reserved to the States respectively, or to the people.

AMENDMENT XI [1795]

The Judicial power of the United States shall not be construed to extend to any suit in law or equity, commenced or prosecuted against one of the United States by Citizens of another State, or by Citizens or Subjects of any Foreign State.

AMENDMENT XII [1804]

The Electors shall meet in their respective states and vote by ballot for President and Vice-President, one of whom, at least, shall not be an inhabitant of the same state with themselves; they shall name in their ballots the person voted for as President, and in distinct ballots the person voted for as Vice-President, and they shall make distinct lists of all persons voted for as President, and of all persons voted for as Vice-President, and of the number of votes for each, which lists they shall sign and certify, and transmit sealed to the seat of the government of the United States, directed to the President of the Senate;—The President of the Senate shall, in the presence of the Senate and House of Representatives, open all the certificates and the votes shall then be counted;—The person having the greatest number of votes for President, shall be the President, if such number be a majority of the whole number of Electors appointed; and if no person have such majority, then from the persons having the highest numbers not exceeding three on the list of those voted for as President, the House of Representatives shall choose immediately, by ballot, the President. But in choosing the President, the votes shall be taken by states, the representation from each state having one vote; a quorum for this purpose shall consist of a member or members from two-thirds of the states, and a majority of all the states shall be necessary to a choice. And if the House of Representatives shall not choose a President whenever the right of choice shall devolve upon them, before the fourth day of March next following, then the Vice-President shall act as President, as in the case of the death or other constitutional disability of the President.—The person having the greatest number of votes as Vice-President, shall be the Vice-President, if such number be a majority of the whole number of Electors appointed, and if no person have a majority, then from the two highest numbers on the list, the Senate shall choose the Vice-President; a quorum for the purpose shall consist of two-thirds of the whole number of Senators, and a majority of the whole number shall be necessary to a choice. But no person constitutionally ineligible to the office of President shall be eligible to that of Vice-President of the United States.

AMENDMENT XIII [1865]

SECTION 1. Neither slavery nor involuntary servitude, except as a punishment for crime whereof the party shall have been duly convicted, shall exist within the United States, or any place subject to their jurisdiction.

SECTION 2. Congress shall have power to enforce this article by appropriate legislation.

AMENDMENT XIV [1868]

SECTION 1. All persons born or naturalized in the United States, and subject to the jurisdiction thereof, are citizens of the United States and of the State wherein they reside. No State shall make or enforce any law which shall abridge the privileges or immunities of citizens of the United States; nor shall any State deprive any person of life, liberty, or property, without due process of law; nor deny to any person within its jurisdiction the equal protection of the laws.

SECTION 2. Representatives shall be apportioned among the several States according to their respective numbers, counting the whole number of persons in each State, excluding Indians not taxed. But when the right to vote at any election for the choice of electors for President and Vice-President of the United States, Representatives in Congress, the Executive and Judicial officers of a State, or the members of the Legislature thereof, is denied to any of the male inhabitants of such State, being twenty-one years of age, and citizens of the United States, or in any way abridged, except for participation in rebellion, or other crime, the basis of representation therein shall be reduced in the proportion which the number of such male citizens shall bear to the whole number of male citizens twenty-one years of age in such State.

SECTION 3. No person shall be a Senator or Representative in Congress, or elector of President and Vice-President, or hold any office, civil or military, under the United States, or under any State, who, having previously taken an oath, as a member of Congress, or as an officer of the United States, or as a member of any State legislature, or as an executive or judicial officer of any State, to support the Constitution of the United States, shall have engaged in insurrection or rebellion against the same, or given aid or comfort to the enemies thereof. But Congress may by a vote of two-thirds of each House, remove such disability.

SECTION 4. The validity of the public debt of the United States, authorized by law, including debts incurred for payment of pensions and bounties for services in suppressing insurrection or rebellion, shall not be questioned. But neither the United States nor any State shall assume or pay any debt or obligation incurred in aid of insurrection or rebellion against the United States, or any claim for the loss of emancipation of any slave; but all such debts, obligations and claims shall be held illegal and void.

SECTION 5. The Congress shall have power to enforce, by appropriate legislation, the provisions of this article.

AMENDMENT XV [1870]

SECTION 1. The right of citizens of the United States to vote shall not be denied or abridged by the United States or by any State on account of race, color, or previous condition of servitude—

SECTION 2. The Congress shall have power to enforce this article by appropriate legislation.

AMENDMENT XVI [1913]

The Congress shall have power to lay and collect taxes on incomes, from whatever source derived, without apportionment among the several States, and without regard to any census or enumeration.

AMENDMENT XVII [1913]

The Senate of the United States shall be composed of two Senators from each State, elected by the people thereof, for six years; and each Senator shall have one vote. The electors in each State shall have the qualifications requisite for electors of the most numerous branch of the State legislatures.

When vacancies happen in the representation of any State in the Senate, the executive authority of such State shall issue writs of election to fill such vacancies: Provided, That the legislature of any State may empower the executive thereof to make temporary appointments until the people fill the vacancies by election as the legislature may direct.

This amendment shall not be so construed as to affect the election or term of any Senator chosen before it becomes valid as part of the Constitution.

AMENDMENT XVIII [1919]

SECTION 1. After one year from the ratification of this article the manufacture, sale, or transportation of intoxicating liquors within, the importation thereof into, or the exportation thereof from the United States and all territory subject to the jurisdiction thereof for beverage purposes is hereby prohibited.

SECTION 2. The Congress and the several States shall have concurrent power to enforce this article by appropriate legislation.

SECTION 3. This article shall be inoperative unless it shall have been ratified as an amendment to the Constitution by the legislatures of the several States, as provided in the Constitution, within seven years from the date of the submission hereof to the States by the Congress.

AMENDMENT XIX [1920]

The right of citizens of the United States to vote shall not be denied or abridged by the United States or by any State on account of sex.

Congress shall have power to enforce this article by appropriate legislation.

AMENDMENT XX [1933]

SECTION 1. The terms of the President and Vice President shall end at noon on the 20th day of January, and the terms of Senators and Representatives at noon on the 3d day of January, of the years in which such terms would have ended if this article had not been ratified; and the terms of their successors shall then begin.

SECTION 2. The Congress shall assemble at least once in every year, and such meeting shall begin at noon on the 3d day of January, unless they shall by law appoint a different day.

SECTION 3. If, at the time fixed for the beginning of the term of the President, the President elect shall have died, the Vice President elect shall become President. If a President shall not have been chosen before the time fixed for the beginning of his term, or if the President elect shall have failed to qualify, then the Vice President elect shall act as President until a President shall have qualified; and the Congress may by law provide for the case wherein neither a President elect nor a Vice President elect shall have qualified, declaring who shall then act as President, or the manner in which one who is to act shall be selected, and such person shall act accordingly until a President or Vice President shall have qualified.

SECTION 4. The Congress may by law provide for the case of the death of any of the persons from whom the House of Representatives may choose a President whenever the right of choice shall have devolved upon them, and for the case of the death of any of the persons from whom the Senate may choose a Vice President whenever the right of choice shall have devolved upon them.

SECTION 5. Sections 1 and 2 shall take effect on the 15th day of October following the ratification of this article.

SECTION 6. This article shall be inoperative unless it shall have been ratified as an amendment to the Constitution by the legislatures of three-fourths of the several States within seven years from the date of its submission.

AMENDMENT XXI [1933]

SECTION 1. The eighteenth article of amendment to the Constitution of the United States is hereby repealed.

SECTION 2. The transportation or importation into any State, Territory, or possession of the United States for delivery or use therein of intoxicating liquors, in violation of the laws thereof, is hereby prohibited.

SECTION 3. This article shall be inoperative unless it shall have been ratified as an amendment to the Constitution by conventions in the several States, as provided in the Constitution, within seven years from the date of the submission hereof to the States by the Congress.

AMENDMENT XXII [1951]

SECTION 1. No person shall be elected to the office of the President more than twice, and no person who has held the office of President, or acted as President, for more than two years of a term to which some other person was elected President shall be elected to the office of the President more than once. But this Article shall not apply to any person holding the office of President when this Article was proposed by the Congress, and shall not prevent any person who may be holding the office of President, or acting as President, during the term within which this Article becomes operative from holding the office of President or acting as President during the remainder of such term.

SECTION 2. This article shall be inoperative unless it shall have been ratified as an amendment to the Constitution by the legislatures of three-fourths of the several States within seven years from the date of its submission to the States by the Congress.

AMENDMENT XXIII [1961]

SECTION 1. The District constituting the seat of Government of the United States shall appoint in such manner as the Congress may direct:

A number of electors of President and Vice President equal to the whole number of Senators and Representatives in Congress to which the District would be entitled if it were a State, but in no event more than the least populous State; they shall be in addition to those appointed by the States, but they shall be considered, for the purposes of the election of President and Vice President, to be electors appointed by a State; and they shall meet in the District and perform such duties as provided by the twelfth article of amendment.

SECTION 2. The Congress shall have power to enforce this article by appropriate legislation.

AMENDMENT XXIV [1964]

SECTION 1. The right of citizens of the United States to vote in any primary or other election for President or Vice President, for electors for President or Vice President, or for Senator or Representative in Congress, shall not be denied or abridged by the United States or any State by reason of failure to pay any poll tax or other tax.

SECTION 2. The Congress shall have power to enforce this article by appropriate legislation.

AMENDMENT XXV [1967]

SECTION 1. In case of the removal of the President from office or of his death or resignation, the Vice President shall become President.

SECTION 2. Whenever there is a vacancy in the office of the Vice President, the President shall nominate a Vice President who shall take office upon confirmation by a majority vote of both Houses of Congress.

SECTION 3. Whenever the President transmits to the President pro tempore of the Senate and the Speaker of the House of Representatives his written declaration that he is unable to discharge the powers and duties of his office, and until he transmits to them a written declaration to the contrary, such powers and duties shall be discharged by the Vice President as Acting President.

SECTION 4. Whenever the Vice President and a majority of either the principal officers of the executive departments or of such other body as Congress may by law provide, transmit to the President pro tempore of the Senate and the Speaker of the House of Representatives their written declaration that the President is unable to discharge the powers and duties of his office, the Vice President shall immediately assume the powers and duties of the office as Acting President.

Thereafter, when the President transmits to the President pro tempore of the Senate and the Speaker of the House of Representatives his written declaration that no inability exists, he shall resume the powers and duties of his office unless the Vice President and a majority of either the principal officers of the executive department or of such other body as Congress may by law provide, transmit within four days to the President pro tempore of the Senate and the Speaker of the House of Representatives their written declaration that the President is unable to discharge the powers and duties of his office.

Thereupon Congress shall decide the issue, assembling within forty-eight hours for that purpose if not in session. If the Congress, within twenty-one days after receipt of the latter written declaration, or, if Congress is not in session, within twenty-one days after Congress is required to assemble, determines by two-thirds vote of both Houses that the President is unable to discharge the powers and duties of his office, the Vice President shall continue to discharge the same as Acting President; otherwise, the President shall resume the powers and duties of his office.

AMENDMENT XXVI [1971]

SECTION 1. The right of citizens of the United States, who are eighteen years of age or older, to vote shall not be denied or abridged by the United States or by any State on account of age.

SECTION 2. The Congress shall have power to enforce this article by appropriate legislation.

AMENDMENT XXVII [1992]

No law, varying the compensation for the services of the Senators and Representatives, shall take effect, until an election of Representatives shall have intervened.

ENDNOTES

PREFACE

1. *CNN*, "Exit Polls," November 23, 2016, http://www.cnn.com/election/results/exit-polls.

1. THE FUTURE OF THE SUPREME COURT AND THE CONSTITUTION

1. *National Federation of Independent Business v. Sebelius*, 132 S.Ct. 2566 (2012) (upholding the individual mandate in the Patient Protection and Affordable Care Act).

2. *Obergefell v. Hodges*, 135 S.Ct. 2584 (2015) (declaring unconstitutional state laws prohibiting same-sex marriage).

3. *Whole Woman's Health v. Hellerstedt*, 136 S.Ct. 2922 (2016) (declaring unconstitutional a Texas law that required that a doctor have admitting privileges near the facility where abortions were performed and that they have "ambulatory surgical facilities."

4. *Fisher v. University of Texas, Austin*, 136 S.Ct. 2196 (2016) (upholding University of Texas affirmative action program).

5. *District of Columbia v. Heller*, 554 U.S. 570 (2008) (declaring unconstitutional a District of Columbia ordinance prohibiting private ownership and possession of handguns).

6. *Glossip v. Gross*, 135 S.Ct. 2726 (2015) (upholding the use of a three-drug protocol for lethal injections).

7. *Citizens United v. Federal Election Commission*, 558 U.S. 310 (2010) (declaring unconstitutional key provisions of the McCain-Feingold Bipartisan Campaign Finance Reform Act).

8. *Burwell v. Hobby Lobby*, 134 S.Ct. 2751 (2004) (concluding that it violated the Religious Freedom Restoration Act to require that owners of closely held corporations provide contraceptive coverage for their employees that violates the owners' religious beliefs).

9. *Roe v. Wade,* 410 U.S. 113 (1973); *Miranda v. Arizona,* 384 U.S. 436 (1966).

10. *Planned Parenthood v. Casey,* 505 U.S. 833 (1992) (reaffirming *Roe v. Wade*; striking down some provisions and upholding others of a Pennsylvania law restricting access to abortions).

11. See, e.g., *Lee v. Weisman,* 505 U.S. 577 (1992) (declaring that clergy-delivered prayers at public school graduations violated the establishment clause of the First Amendment).

12. *District of Columbia v. Heller,* 554 U.S. 570 (2008).

13. *McDonald v. City of Chicago,* 561 U.S. 742 (2010).

14. *Abood v. Detroit Board of Education,* 431 U.S. 209 (1977) (holding that it does not violate the First Amendment to require that public employees pay the share of union dues that support the collective bargaining activities of the union).

15. *Knox v. SEIU,* 132 S.Ct. 2277 (2012); *Harris v. Quinn,* 134 S.Ct. 2618 (2014).

16. When the justices are divided 4–4, they affirm the lower court, without opinion. Here that meant that the lower court decision following *Abood* was upheld.

17. *Janus v. American Federation of State, County, and Municipal Employees, Council 31,* 138 S.Ct._(June 27, 2018).

18. I discuss this in detail in chapter 7.

19. *AT&T Mobility LLC v. Concepcion,* 563 U.S. 233 (2011).

20. *Wal-Mart Stores, Inc. v. Dukes,* 564 U.S. 339 (2011).

21. *Buckley v. Valeo,* 424 U.S. 1 (1976).

22. *Citizens United v. Federal Election Commission,* 558 U.S. 310 (2010).

23. *Marbury v. Madison,* 5 U.S. (1 Cranch) 137, 177 (1803).

24. Mark Tushnet, *Taking the Constitution Away from the Courts* (Princeton, NJ: Princeton University Press, 1999).

25. Larry Kramer, *The People Themselves: Popular Constitutionalism and Judicial Review* (Oxford: Oxford University Press, 2005).

26. James MacGregor Burns, *Packing the Court: The Rise of Judicial Power and the Coming Crisis of the Supreme Court* (New York: Penguin Press, 2009).

27. See, e.g., *Brown v. Plata,* 563 U.S. 493 (2011) (upholding a court-mandated limit on prison population to remedy cruel and unusual punishment).

28. *Gideon v. Wainwright*, 372 U.S. 335 (1963) (stating that states must provide counsel to those who cannot afford it in any criminal case where there is a possible prison sentence).

2. THE CONSERVATIVES' FALSE CLAIM OF VALUE-NEUTRAL JUDGING

1. *Brown v. Entertainment Merchants*, 564 U.S. 786 (2011).

2. Clare Kim, "Justice Scalia: Constitution Is Dead," *MSNBC*, http://www.msnbc.com/the-last-word/justice-scalia-constitution-dead.

3. Emi Kolawole, "Scalia: Constitution Does Not Protect Women from Discrimination," *Washington Post*, January 11, 2011.

4. *United States v. Jones*, 565 U.S. 400 (2012).

5. *Carpenter v. United States*, 138 S.Ct._(June 22, 2018), discussed in chapter 6.

6. Neil M. Gorsuch, "Of Lions and Bears, Judges and Legislators, and the Legacy of Justice Scalia," 66 *Case W. Res. L. Rev.* 905 (2016).

7. "New Poll: Vast Majority of Americans Want SCOTUS Nominees Who Apply Constitution as Originally Written," *Cision*, https://www.prnewswire.com/news-releases/new-poll-vast-majority-of-americans-want-scotus-nominees-who-apply-constitution-as-originally-written-300387698.html.

8. Robert Bork, "Neutral Principles and Some First Amendment Problems," 47 *Indiana L. J.* 1, 6 (1971).

9. Edwin Meese, Speech to American Bar Association on "the jurisprudence of original intention," July 9, 1985, https://www.justice.gov/sites/default/files/ag/legacy/2011/08/23/07-09-1985.pdf.

10. *Id.* at 7.

11. *Michael H. v. Gerald D.*, 491 U.S. 110, 148 n.6 (1989).

12. United States Courts, *Chief Justice Roberts Statement: Nomination Process*, http://www.uscourts.gov/educational-resources/educational-activities/chief-justice-roberts-statement-nomination-process.

13. Chuck Grassley, *The Role of Supreme Court Justices*, March 15, 2017, https://www.grassley.senate.gov/news/news-releases/role-supreme-court-justices

14. Tara Golshan, "Full Transcript: Hillary Clinton and Donald Trump's Final Presidential Debate," https://www.vox.com/policy-and-politics/2016/10/19/13336894/third-presidential-debate-live-transcript-clinton-trump.

15. *District of Columbia v. Heller,* 554 U.S. 570 (2008).

16. *United States v. Miller,* 309 U.S. 174 (1939).

17. *Citizens United v. Federal Election Commission,* 558 U.S. 310 (2010).

18. *Shelby County v. Holder,* 133 S.Ct. 2612 (2013).

19. *Id.*

20. *United States v. Windsor,* 133 S.Ct. 2655 (2013).

21. Professor Eric Segall does a superb job of examining originalism in its various forms and showing its inherent flaws; see Eric Segall, *Originalism as Faith* (Cambridge: Cambridge University Press, forthcoming).

22. *Buckley v. Valeo,* 424 U.S. 1 (1976); *Citizens United v. Federal Election Commission,* 558 U.S. 310 (2010).

23. See, e.g., *Roper v. Simmons,* 543 U.S. 551, 561 (2005); this Court has established the propriety and affirmed the necessity of referring to "the evolving standards of decency that mark the progress of a maturing society" to determine which punishments are so disproportionate as to be "cruel and unusual." See also *Trop v. Dulles,* 356 U.S. 86, 100–01 (1958).

24. See, e.g., *Atkins v. Virginia,* 536 U.S. 404 (declaring the death penalty to be cruel and unusual punishment when imposed on the intellectually disabled); *Roper v. Simmons,* 543 U.S. 551 (2005) (declaring the death penalty unconstitutional when applied for crimes committed by juveniles); *Glossip v. Gross,* 135 S.Ct. 2726 (2015) (rejecting a constitutional challenge to the method of lethal injection for imposing the death penalty).

25. *Lockyer v. Andrade,* 538 U.S. 63 (2003).

26. See Erwin Chemerinsky, *Constitutional Law: Principles and Policies,* 5th ed. (New York: Wolters Kluwer Law & Business, 2015), p. 351–52 (contrasting Hamilton's and Madison's views on inherent presidential power).

27. See *United States v. Butler,* 297 U.S. 1 (1936) (contrasting Hamilton's and Madison's views on the scope of Congress's spending power).

28. Barack Obama, *The Audacity of Hope: Thoughts on Reclaiming the American Dream* (New York: Crown 2004), p. 90.

29. William Van Alstyne, "Interpreting This Constitution: The Unhelpful Contributions of Special Theories of Constitutional Interpretation," 35 *U. Fla. L. Rev.* 209, 233 (1983).

30. R. G. Collingwood, *The Idea of History* (Eastford, CT: Martino, 1946), p. 218–19.

31. See Jack Balkin, *Living Originalism* (Cambridge, MA: Belknap, 2014); Randy Barnett, *Our Republican Constitution: Securing the Liberty and Sovereignty of We the People* (New York: Broadside, 2016); William Baude, Essay, "Is Originalism Our Law?" 115 *Colum. L. Rev.* 2349 (2015).

32. Baude, *Id.*

33. Stephen A. Siegel, "The Federal Government's Power to Enact Color-Conscious Laws: An Originalist Inquiry," 92 *NW. U. L. Rev.* 478, 499 (1998).

34. *Maryland v. King*, 465 U.S. 435 (2013).

35. See *Grutter v. Bollinger*, 509 U.S. 306 (2003); I discuss affirmative action in detail in chapter 8.

36. *Fisher v. University of Texas, Austin*, 136 S.Ct. 2198 (2013).

37. Erwin Chemerinsky, "The Vanishing Constitution," 103 *Harv. L. Rev.* (1989).

38. *McCulloch v. Maryland*, 17 U.S. (4 Wheat.) 415 (1819).

39. *Home Building & Loan v. Blaisdell*, 290 U.S. 398, 435 (1934).

40. *Brown v. Board of Education of Topeka, Kansas*, 347 U.S. 483, 492 (1954).

41. *Harper v. Virginia Board of Elections*, 383 U.S. 663 (1966).

42. *Id.* at 669.

43. *Obergefell v. Hodges*, 135 S.Ct. 2584, 2598 (2015).

44. *Id.*

3. THE VALUES OF THE CONSTITUTION

1. Joseph Story, *Commentaries on the Constitution of the United States* vol. 1, secs. 459–60, Legal Legends Series (Boston, MA: Hilliard, Gray, 1833).

2. Eric M. Axler, "The Power of the Preamble and the Ninth Amendment: The Restoration of the People's Unenumerated Rights," 24 *Seton Hall Legis. J.* 431, 432 (2000).

3. *Id.* at 471.

4. Gilbert Carrasco & Peter Rodino Jr., "'Unalienable Rights,' The Preamble, and the Ninth Amendment: The Spirit of the Constitution," 20 *Seton Hall L. Rev.* 498 (1990).

5. *Kesavananda Bharati v. State of Kerala* (1973) 4 SCC 225 (India) (Sikri, C. J.). For a discussion of different types of preambles in constitutions across the world, see Justin O. Frosini, "Constitutional Preambles: More Than Just a Narration of History," 2017 *U. Ill. L. Rev.* 603, 606 (2017).

6. Ebrahim Afsah, review of "Constitutional Preambles. At a Crossroads Between Politics and Law," by Justin O. Frosini, 11 *Int'l J. Const. L.* 831–34 (2013).

7. Brian Leiter, Carole E. Handler, & Milton Handler, "A Reconsideration of the Relevance and Materiality of the Preamble in Constitutional Interpretation," 12 *Cardozo L. Rev.* 117 (1990).

8. *Jacobson v. Massachusetts,* 197 U.S. 11 (1905).

9. Liav Orgard, "The Preamble in Constitutional Interpretation," 8 *Int. J. Const. L.* 714 (2010), https://doi.org/10.1093/icon/mor010.

10. William Crosskey, *Politics and the Constitution,* 3 vols. (Chicago, IL: U. Chi. Press 1953), pp. 363, 374–79.

11. Erwin Chemerinsky, *Constitutional Law,* 5th ed. (New York: Wolters Kluwer, 2016); Chemerinsky, *Constitutional Law: Principles and Policies.*

12. Orgard, *The Preamble in Constitutional Interpretation.*

13. *Martin v. Hunter's Lessee,* 14 U.S. 304, 324–25 (1816).

14. *McCulloch v. Maryland,* 14 U.S. 304, 324–25 (1819).

15. See Alexander Hamilton, *Federalist* No. 84, ed. Clinton Rossiter (New York: New American Library, 1961).

16. *Bolling v. Sharpe,* 347 U.S. 497 (1954).

17. Charles Black, Jr., *Structure and Relationship in Constitutional Law* (Baton Rouge: Louisiana State University Press, 1969).

18. Orgard, *The Preamble in Constitutional Interpretation.*

19. *The Records of the Federal Convention of 1787,* ed. Max Farrand, vol. 2 (New Haven, CT: Yale U. Press 1937), p. 177.

20. See Article IV, Section 2, "The Citizens of each State shall be entitled to all Privileges and Immunities of Citizens in the several States."

21. *McCulloch v. Maryland* at 403–04.

22. *Id.* at 404.

23. I discuss the Electoral College in detail in chapter 4.

24. *Supplement to Max Farrand's The Records of the Federal Convention of 1787*, ed. James H. Hutson (New Haven, CT: Yale University Press 1987), p. 183; hereinafter *Supplement to Max Farrand.*

25. *Hammer v. Dangenhart,* 247 U.S. 251 (1918).

26. *Shelby County v. Holder,* 133 S.Ct. 2612 (2013).

27. See, e.g., *New York v. United States,* 505 U.S. 144 (1992).

28. William Crosskey, *Politics and the Constitution* (Chicago, IL: U. Chi. Press, 1953), pp. 363, 374–79.

29. See John P. Kaminski, "Restoring, the Grand Security: The Debate over a Federal Bill of Rights, 1787–1792," 33 *Santa Clara L. Rev.* 887 (1993).

30. For an excellent history of the drafting and ratification of the Bill of Rights, see Burt Neuborne, *Madison's Music* (New York: The New Press, 2015), pp. 195–221.

31. *Bolling v. Sharpe,* 347 U.S. 497 (1954).

32. *Slaughterhouse Cases,* 383 U.S. (16 Wall.) 36 (1873).

33. *Id.*

34. *Minor v. Happersett,* 88 U.S. 162 (1875).

35. *Plessy v. Ferguson,* 163 U.S. 537 (1896).

36. *Id.*

37. *Id.*

38. *Cumming v. Board of Education,* 175 U.S. 528 (1899).

39. *Berea College v. Kentucky,* 211 U.S. 45 (1908).

40. *Gong Lum v. Rice,* 275 U.S. 78 (1927).

41. *Id.*

42. *Brown v. Board of Education,* 347 U.S. 483 (1954).

4. ENSURING DEMOCRATIC GOVERNMENT

1. Matthew M. Hoffman, "The Illegitimate President: Minority Vote Dilution and the Electoral College," 105 *Yale L. J.* 935, 943 (1996).

2. For a detailed description of what occurred at the Constitutional Convention, see Paul Finkelman, "The Proslavery Origins of the Electoral College," 23 *Cardozo L. Rev.* 1145, 1151 (2002).

3. Alexander Hamilton, *Federalist* No. 68, in *The Federalist Papers,* ed. Isaac Kramnick (New York: Penguin Books, 1987), p. 393.

4. *Id.*

5. Finkelman, *Proslavery Origins, supra* note 2, at 1154.

6. 2 Max Farrand, *The Records of the Federal Convention of 1787,* at 50 (rev. ed. 1966); Finkelman, *id., supra* note 2, at 1155.

7. Finkelman, *id.*

8. Farrand, *id., supra* note 5, at 32.

9. Akhil Reed Amar, *The Constitution Today: Timeless Lessons for the Issues of Our Era* 333 (New York: Basic Books, 2016); Akhil Reed Amar, "Some Thoughts on the Electoral College: Past, Present, and Future," 33 *Ohio N.U. L. Rev.* 467 (2007).

10. *Wesberry v. Sanders,* 376 U.S. 1, 8 (1964).

11. *Bush v. Gore,* 531 U.S. 98, 104 (2000).

12. This was a core insight of John Hart Ely, *Democracy and Distrust* (Cambridge, MA: Harvard U. Press, 1980).

13. *Reynolds v. Sims,* 377 U.S. 533 (1964).

14. "The Warren Court: An Editorial Preface," 67 *Mich. L. Rev.* 219, 220 (1968).

15. Note, "Rethinking the Electoral College Debate: The Framers, Federalism and One Person One Vote," 114 *Harv. L. Rev.* 2526 (2001).

16. Hoffman, *The Illegitimate President, supra* note 1, at 937.

17. "The Case for the Electoral College," *New York Times,* Dec. 19, 2000.

18. Amicus Brief of the American Jewish Committee, et al., *Gill v. Whitford,* at 3.

19. *Whitford v. Gill,* 218 F.Supp.3d 837, 854 (W.D. Wis. 2016).

20. *Id.* at 901.

21. *Id.*

22. Anne Blythe, "Why This Republican Is Challenging NC GOP Political Maps," *News & Observer,* October 16, 2017, http://www.newsobserver.com/news/politics-government/state-politics/article179194721.html.

23. Maddie Hanna & Jonathan Lai, "In Case That Could Affect 2018 Elections, Gerrymandering Suit Can Proceed, Pa. High Court Rules," *Inquirer,* November 9, 2017, http://www

.philly.com/philly/news/politics/state/gerrymandering-suit-can-proceed-pa-supreme-court-rules-20171109.html.

24. *Arizona State Legislature v. Arizona Redistricting Commission* 135 S.Ct. 2652, 2676 (2015).

25. *League of United Latin American Citizens v. Perry*, 548 U.S. 399, 440 (2006),

26. *Arizona State Legislature* at 2658.

27. James Madison, *Federalist* No. 38, in *The Federalist Papers*, ed. Clinton Rossiter (New York: New American Library, 1961), 206.

28. James Madison, *Federalist* No. 37, in *The Federalist Papers*, ed. Clinton Rossiter (New York: New American Library, 1961), 192.

29. *Vieth v. Jubelirer*, 541 U.S., at 331 (Stevens, J., dissenting) (2004).

30. *Vieth* at 292.

31. *Wesberry v. Sanders*, 376 U.S. 1, 17 (1964)

32. "Redistricting Reform Needs to Go National," *San Francisco Chronicle*, December 26, 2017.

33. *Id.*

34. *Id.*

35. *Davis v. Bandemer*, 478. U.S. 109 (1986).

36. *Id.* at 127.

37. *Vieth*, 541 U.S. 267.

38. *League of United Latin American Citizens v. Perry*, 548 U.S. 399 (2006).

39. *Whitford v. Gill*, 218 F.Supp.3d 837, 854 (W.D. Wis. 2016).

40. *Gill v. Whitford*, 138 S.Ct._(June 4, 2018).

41. Harris Poll, "Americans Across Party Lines Oppose Common Gerrymandering Practices," November 7, 2013, https://theharrispoll.com/new-york-n-y-november-7-2013-ask-a-person-on-the-street-what-they-think-of-congress-and-you-likely-know-what-sort-of-response-youll-get-the-harris-poll-did-and-the-response-was-more-dismal/.

42. Brief of Amici Historians, *Gill v. Whitford*, at 4.

43. Constitutional Rights Foundation, *Race and Voting in the Segregated South*, n.d., http://www.crf-usa.org/brown-v-board-50th-anniversary/race-and-voting.html.

44. Michael J. Pitts, "The Voting Rights Act and the Era of Maintenance," 59 *Alabama L. Rev.* 903, 909–10 (2008).

45. "Techniques of Direct Disenfranchisement, 1880–1965," http://www.umich.edu/~lawrace/disenfranchise1.htm.

46. *Id.*

47. *Id.*

48. *Id.*

49. *Id.*

50. *Id.*

51. *Shelby County,* 133 S.Ct. 2612 (2013).

52. *South Carolina v. Katzenbach,* 383 U.S. 301 (1966).

53. *Georgia v. United States,* 411 U.S. 526 (1973); *City of Rome v. United States,* 446 U.S. 156 (1980); *Lopez v. Monterey County,* 525 U.S. 266 (1999).

54. Fannie Lou Hamer, Rosa Parks, and Coretta Scott King Voting Rights Act Reauthorization and Amendments Act of 2006, 109th Cong., 2d sess., Congressional Record 152 (July 13, 2006): H 5143, https://www.congress.gov/congressional-record/2006/7/13/house-section/article/h5143-2.

55. *Denial or Abridgement of Right to Vote on Account of Race or Color Through Voting Qualifications or Prerequisites; Establishment of Violation,* 52 USC 10301, http://uscode.house.gov/view.xhtml?req=(title:52%20section:10301%20edition:prelim).

56. *Shelby County v. Holder,* 133 S.Ct. 2612, 2639 (2013) *citing to* H.R.Rep. No. 109–478, at 21.

57. *Id.* at 2643.

58. Brennan Center for Justice, *Election 2016: Restrictive Voting Laws by the Numbers,* September 28, 2016, https://www.brennancenter.org/analysis/election-2016-restrictive-voting-laws-numbers.

59. *Id.*

60. *Shelby County,* at 2631.

61. 679 F.3d 848, 901 (D.C. Cir. 2012).

62. 133 S.Ct. at 2625 (citations omitted).

63. *Id.* at 2627.

64. *Id.* at 2624.

65. *Id.* at 2623–24

66. *Id.* at 2632–33 (Ginsburg, J., dissenting).

67. *Id.* at 2649 (Ginsburg, J., dissenting). Justice Ginsburg

gave several examples of federal laws that treat some states differently from others.

68. *McCutcheon v. Federal Election Commission*, 134 S.Ct. 1434, 1440–41 (2014).

5. PROVIDING EFFECTIVE GOVERNANCE

1. See, e.g., Samuel H. Beer, *To Make a Nation: The Rediscovery of American Federalism* (Cambridge, MA: Belknap, 1993), p. 224.

2. See, e.g., *Carter v. Carter Coal Co.*, 298 U.S. 238 (1936) (invalidating federal regulation of employment, including a minimum wage; *Hammer v. Dagenhart*, 247 U.S. 251 (1918) (invalidating the federal regulation of child labor; *United States v. E. C. Knight*, 156 U.S. 1 (1895) (holding that the Sherman Antitrust Act could not be applied to businesses engaged in production).

3. See Forrest McDonald, *A Constitutional History of the United States* (Malabar, FL: Krieger, 1986), p. 193; William Manchester, *The Glory and the Dream* (Boston, MA: Little Brown, 1974), pp. 164–66.

4. Beer, supra note 1, at 19–20.

5. *Id.* at 2.

6. *National Federation of Independent Businesses v. Sebelius*, 132 S.Ct. 2566 (2012).

7. See, e.g., *Gibbons v. Ogden*, 22 U.S. (9 Wheat.) 1 (1824) (broadly defining the scope of Congress's commerce power and rejecting the existence of states as a limit upon it).

8. *Id.*

9. *Hammer v. Dagenhart*, 247 U.S. 251 (1918) (also known as the *Child Labor Case*).

10. Russell Freedman, *Kids at Work: Lewis Hine and the Crusade Against Child Labor* (New York: Clarion, 1994), pp. 1–2.

11. *Hammer*, 247 U.S. 251.

12. *Id.* at 276.

13. *Carter v. Carter Coal Co.*, 298 U.S. 238 (1936).

14. *Id.* at 303–04.

15. *Id.* at 295–96.

16. *A. L. A. Schecter Poultry Corp. v. United States*, 295 U.S. 495 (1935).

17. *Id.* at 548.

18. *Railroad Retirement Board v. Alton R. R. Co.*, 295 U.S. 330 (1935).

19. *United States v. Butler*, 297 U.S. 1 (1936).

20. See Jeff Shesol, *Supreme Power: Franklin Roosevelt vs. The Supreme Court* (New York: Norton, 2010).

21. *West Coast Hotel v. Parrish*, 300 U.S. 379 (1937); *NLRB v. Jones Laughlin Steel Corp.*, 301 US. 1 (1937).

22. *United States v. Lopez*, 514 U.S. 549 (1995).

23. *United States v. Morrison*, 529 U.S. 598 (2000).

24. *National Federation of Independent Business v. Sebelius*, 132 S.Ct. 2566 (2012).

25. *New York v. United States*, 505 U.S. 144 (2002).

26. I develop this view of federalism in my book, Erwin Chemerinsky, *Enhancing Government: Federalism for the 21st Century* (Redwood City, CA: Stanford Law Books, 2008).

27. *Nixon v. United States*, 506 U.S. 224, 235 (1993) (stating that challenges to process of impeachment are non-justiciable political questions).

28. *Youngstown Sheet & Tube Co. v. Sawyer*, 343 U.S. 579 (1952).

29. *Id.* at 635 (declaring unconstitutional President Truman's seizure of steel mills).

30. *Id.* at 635 (Jackson, J., concurring).

31. *Id.* at 637.

32. *Id.*

33. *Id.*

34. See, e.g., *State Highway Commission of Missouri v. Volpe*, 347 F. Supp. 950, 953 (W.D. Mo. 1972), aff'd, 479 F.2d 1099 (8th Cir. 1973) (finding withholding highway funds from Missouri impermissible under Federal-Aid Highway Act of 1956; *Local 2677, American Federation of Government Employees v. Phillips*, 358 F. Supp. 60, 80 (D.D.C. 1973) (finding impoundment unconstitutional; cf. *Train v. New York*, 420 U.S. 35, 43–44 (1975), rejecting argument that Federal Water Pollution Control Act authorized impoundment of federal funds).

35. 31 U.S.C. sec. 1301 (2006).

36. *United States v. U.S. District Court*, 407 U.S. 297, 324 (1972) (requiring judicial approval for surveillance).

37. Report of the Congressional Commission Investigating the Iran-Contra Affair, H. R. Rep. No. 100–433 and S. Rep. No. 100–216, 473 (1987) (minority report).

38. *Clinton v. Jones*, 520 U.S. 681 (1997) (a president can be sued for money damages for actions that allegedly occurred prior to taking office).

39. I regard the Obama executive orders on immigration—Deferred Action for Childhood Arrivals (DACA) and Deferred Action for Parents of Americans (DAPA)—differently. These were about how the executive branch of government was going to use its prosecutorial discretion as to immigration. The federal government does not have to—and does not—enforce every law. It is a federal crime to possess even a small amount of marijuana. But no one contends that the government has to punish every violation. Likewise, there are 11 million undocumented individuals in the United States and the government deports only about 400,000 a year. The president has the authority to set priorities for enforcement; that is exactly what DACA and DAPA do.

40. *Padilla v. Rumsfeld*, 352 F.3d 695, 699, 703 (2d Cir. 2003), rev'd, 124 S. Ct. 2711 (2004).

41. Brief of Respondent at 14, *Rasul v. Bush*, 542 U.S. 466 (2004) (Nos. 03-334, 03-343).

42. See *Rasul v. Bush*, 542 U.S. 466 (2004); *Boumediene v. Bush*, 553 U.S. 723 (2008).

43. See James Risen & Eric Lichtblau, "Bush Lets U.S. Spy on Callers Without Courts," *New York Times*, December 16, 2005 (based on James Risen, *State of War*).

44. See, e.g., Eric Lichtblau, "Bush Defends Spy Program and Denies Misleading Public," *New York Times*, January 2, 2006 ("[President] Bush's strong defense of the [National Security Agency] program, which he authorized in 2002 to allow some domestic eavesdropping without court warrants, came as a leading Democratic lawmaker called on the administration to make available current and former high-level officials to explain the evolution of the secret program").

45. 18 U.S.C. sec. 2511(2)(f) (2006).

46. See generally, U.S. Dep't of Justice, *Legal Authorities Supporting the Activities of the National Security Agency Described by the*

President, January 19, 2006, discussing basis for authorizing NSA's interception of international communications linked to Al Qaeda; available at http://www.usdoj.gov/opa/whitepaper onnsalegalauthorities.pdf.

47. See Memorandum from Jay S. Bybee, Assistant Attorney General, Department of Justice, to Alberto R. Gonzalez, Counsel to the President 39–46 (Aug. 1, 2002) [hereinafter Torture Memo], available at http://www.humanrightsfirst.org/us_law /etn/gonzales/memos_dir/memo_20020801_JD_%20Gonz_. pdf#search=%22jay%CCC20bybee%22.

48. *Id.*

49. *Id.* at 36–39.

50. See Memorandum from Daniel Levin, Acting Assistant Attorney Gen., Office of Legal Counsel, to James Corney, Deputy Attorney Gen. (Dec. 30, 2004), available at http://www.usdoj.gov/olc/18usc23402340a2.htm.

51. Neil Kinkopf, "The Statutory Commander in Chief," 81 *Ind. L.J.* 1169, 1171 (2006).

52. James Madison, Federalist No. 47, in *The Federalist Papers*, ed. Clinton Rossiter (New York: New American Library, 1961), p. 301.

53. See, e.g., *Printz v. United States*, 521 U.S. 898 (1997). (Justice Scalia described the theory of a "unitary executive.")

54. 28 U.S.C. secs. 591–599. The act expired in 1999 and was not renewed; 28 U.S.C. sec. 599 (pocket parts, 2001).

55. *Morrison v. Olson*, 487 U.S. 654 (1988).

56. *Id.* at 684 (Scalia, J., dissenting).

57. *Id.*

58. "This Justice Scalia Dissent Explains Why Trump Was within His Rights to Fire Sally Yates," *National Review*, January 31, 2017, http://www.nationalreview.com/article/444429 /justice-scalia-morrison-v-olson-dissent-trump-sally-yates-and-unitary-executive.

59. *Trump v. Hawaii*, 138 S.Ct._(2018).

6. ESTABLISHING JUSTICE

1. See Paul Butler, *Chokehold* (New York: The New Press, 2017). For an excellent discussion of police behavior in the

United States, *see* Barry Friedman, *Unwarranted: Policing Without Permission* (New York: Farrar, Straus and Giroux, 2017).

2. Barack Obama, "The President's Role in Criminal Justice Reform," 130 *Harv. L. Rev.* 811, 820 (2017).

3. Jon Swaine & Ciara McCarthy, "Young Black Men Again Faced Highest Race of U.S. Police Killings in 2016," *Guardian*, January 8, 2017, https://www.theguardian.com/us-news/2017/jan/08/the-counted-police-killings-2016-young-black-men. For an excellent discussion of police shootings, *see* Franklin Zimring, *When Police Kill* (Cambridge, MA: Harvard Univ. Press, 2017).

4. *Id.*

5. Sirry Alang et al., "Police Brutality and Black Health," 107 *Am. J. Public Health* 662 (2017), DOI: 10.2105/AJPH.2017.303691.

6. *Zimring, supra* note 3.

7. *United States v. Carolene Products Co.*, 304 U.S. 144 (1938).

8. *City of Los Angeles v. Lyons*, 461 U.S. 95, 101 (1983).

9. Gates said, in explaining why blacks were dying from the police chokehold at a disproportionate rate: "We may be finding that in some blacks when it is applied, the veins or arteries do not open up as fast as they do on normal people." https://www.dailybreeze.com/2014/12/04/chokeholds-have-been-banned-in-los-angeles-for-decades/.

10. If a state or local police officer allegedly violates the Constitution, he or she is sued pursuant to a federal statute, 42 U.S.C. sec. 1983. No federal statute authorizes suits against federal officers, but the Supreme Court said that federal officers can be sued for Fourth Amendment violations directly under the Constitution. *Bivens v. Six Unknown Named Agents of Federal Bureau of Narcotics*, 403 U.S. 388 (1971).

11. *Briscoe v. LaHue*, 460 U.S. 325 (1983).

12. *Imbler v. Pachtman*, 424 U.S. 409 (1976).

13. *Van de Kamp v. Goldstein*, 555 U.S. 335 (2009).

14. *Brady v. Maryland*, 373 U.S. 83 (1963).

15. *Brosseau v. Haugen*, 543 U.S. 194 (2004).

16. *Plumhoff v. Rickard*, 134 S. Ct. 2012 (2014).

17. *Monell v. Department of Social Services of City of New York*, 436 U.S. 658 (1978).

18. *Board of Commissioners of Bryan County v. Brown*, 520 U.S. 397 (1997).

19. *Connick v. Thompson*, 563 U.S. 51 (2011).

20. *Gideon v. Wainwright*, 372 U.S. at 344.

21. American Bar Association Standing Committee on Legal Aid and Indigent Defenders, *Gideon's Broken Promise: America's Continuing Quest for Equal Justice* (Chicago, IL: ABA, 2004), p. 38.

22. See Erwin Chemerinsky, "Symposium on State Court Funding: Keynote," 100 *Ky. L. Rev.* 743, 744 (2012) (describing budget cuts in court funding across the country).

23. *Haskell v. Berghuis*, 2013 WL 163965 (6th Cir. Jan. 16, 2013) (rejecting claim of ineffective assistance of counsel).

24. *Wilkinson v. Polk*, 227 Fed.Appx. 210 (4th Cir. 2007) (rejecting claim of ineffective assistance of counsel).

25. 150 Cong. Rec. S11612–13 (2004) (Statement of Senator Patrick Leahy).

26. Caroline Wolf Harlow, *Defense Counsel in Criminal Cases*, Bureau of Justice Statistics Special Report (U.S. Dept of Justice 2000), https://www.bjs.gov/content/pub/pdf/dccc.pdf.

27. *Id.* at 1.

28. Radha Iyengar, *An Analysis of the Performance of Federal Indigent Defense Counsel*, NBER Working Paper Series (2007), http://www.nber.org/papers/w13187.

29. *Id.* at 3.

30. James M. Anderson & Paul Heaton, "How Much Difference Does the Lawyer Make? The Effect of Defense Counsel on Murder Case Outcomes," 122 *Yale L.J.* 154 (2012).

31. *Id.* at 183–84.

32. *Id.*

33. James C. Beck & Robert Shumsky, "A Comparison of Retained and Appointed Counsel in Cases of Capital Murder," 21 *Law & Hum. Behav.* 525 (1997) (finding a death sentence more likely to result when the defendant was represented by appointed counsel rather than privately retained counsel); Dean J. Champion, "Private Counsels and Public Defenders: A Look at Weak Cases, Prior Records and Leniency in Plea Bargaining," 17 *J. Crim. Just.* 253 (1989) (finding that defendants represented by privately retained counsel obtained better outcomes than defendants represented by public defenders). Not

every study has found such differences. See Roger A. Hanson & Brian J. Ostrom, *Indigent Defenders Get the Job Done and Done Well* (The Center, 1992), in *The Criminal Justice System: Politics and Policies*, eds. George F. Cole, Marc G. Gertz & Amy Burger, 8th ed. (Boston, MA: Cengage Learning, 2002), p. 254 (finding small differences in performance between public defenders and appointed private counsel); Richard D. Hartley, Holly Ventura Miller & Cassia Spohn, "Do You Get What You Pay For? Type of Counsel and Its Effect on Criminal Court Outcomes," 38 *J. Crim. Just.* 1063 (2010) (finding generally that public defenders and private attorneys have no direct effect on incarceration or sentence length); Pauline Houlden & Steven Balkin, "Costs and Quality of Indigent Defense: Ad Hoc vs. Coordinated Assignment of the Private Bar Within a Mixed System," 10 *Just. Sys. J.* 159, 170 (1985) (finding that the method of assigning attorneys to cases did not affect outcomes).

34. Anderson & Heaton, supra note 30, at 188.

35. American Bar Association, *Gideon's Broken Promise,* supra note 21 at 7.

36. *Id.* at 9.

37. Walter Mondale et al., *Justice Denied: America's Continuing Neglect of Our Constitutional Right to Counsel: Report of the National Right to Counsel Committee* (Washington, D.C.: Constitution Project, 2009), pp. 6–7.

38. *Id.* at 7.

39. Anderson & Heaton, *supra* note 30, at 188–97.

40. Douglas W. Vick, "Poorhouse Justice: Underfunded Indigent Defense Services and Arbitrary Death Sentences," 43 *Buff. L. Rev.* 329, 398 (1995).

41. Mondale, *Justice Denied,* supra note 37, at 7.

42. See State Activities Map, Nat'l Center for St. Cts., http://www.ncsc.org/Information-and-Resources/Budget-Resource-Center/States-activities-map/.aspx (last visited June 7, 2012).

43. Mondale, *Justice Denied, supra* note 37, at 6 ("Wrongful convictions also have occurred as a result of inadequate representation by defense counsel.")

44. David Currie, "Positive and Negative Constitutional Rights," 53 *U. Chi. L. Rev.* 864, 873 (1986).

45. For example, in 2006, Judith Kaye, chief judge of the New York Court of Appeals, said, "New York's current fragmented system of county-operated and largely county-funded indigent defense services fails to satisfy the State's constitutional and statutory obligations to protect the rights of indigent accused"; *Commission on the Future of Indigent Defense Services: Final Report to the Chief Judge of the State of New York* (2006). See also National Legal Aid and Defender Association, *In Defense of Public Access to Justice: An Assessment of Trial-Level Indigent Defense Services in Louisiana 40 Years After* Gideon (National Association of Criminal Defense Lawyers, 2004), describing the method of funding lawyers for indigents in Louisiana.

46. Dorothy E. Roberts, "The Social and Moral Cost of Mass Incarceration in African American Communities," 56 *Stan. L. Rev.* 1271, 1272 (2004).

47. Office of the Governor, Arnold Schwarzenegger, *Comprehensive Prison Reform* (2006), https://www.cdcr.ca.gov/about_cdcr/docs/2006LegDigest.pdf.

48. *See* Michelle Alexander, *The New Jim Crow: Mass Incarceration in the Age of Colorblindness* (New York: The New Press, 2012) (describing incarceration rates especially among African Americans).

49. *Vick, Poorhouse Justice, supra* note 40, at 459.

50. *Strickland v. Washington*, 466 U.S. 668, 689 (1984).

51. *McMann v. Richardson*, 397 U.S. 759, 771 (1970).

52. *Florida v. Public Defender, Eleventh Judicial Circuit*, 12 So.3d 798 (Dist.Ct. App. 2009).

53. *Kennedy v. Carlson*, 544 N.W.2d 1 (Minn. 1996).

54. Cara H. Drinan, "The Third Generation of Indigent Defense Litigation," 33 *N.Y.U. Rev. of Law and Social Change*, 427, 431 (2009).

55. *Id.* at 467.

56. *Strickland v. Washington*, 466 U.S. 688 (1994).

57. *Id.* at 687.

58. *Id.* at 693.

59. *Id.* at 710 (Marshall, J., dissenting).

60. *Cullen v. Pinholster*, 131 S.Ct. 1388 (2011).

61. *Id.* at 1409 ("There is no reasonable probability that the

additional evidence Pinholster presented in his state habeas proceedings would have changed the jury's verdict.")

62. Stephen B. Bright, "Turning Celebrated Principles into Reality," *The Champion*, Jan.–Feb. 2003, at 6.

63. Barack Obama, "The President's Role in Criminal Justice Reform," 130 *Harv. L. Rev.* 811, 817 (2017).

64. *Id.* at 818.

65. Alexander, *The New Jim Crow.*

66. Obama, *supra* note 63, at 820.

67. *Ewing v. California*, 538 U.S. 11 (2003).

68. *Lockyer v. Andrade*, 538 U.S. 63 (2003).

69. There is only one case in which the Court has found a prison term to be so disproportionate to the crime as to violate the Eighth Amendment: *Solem v. Helm*, 463 U.S. 277 (1983). In that case, an individual was given a life sentence without parole for passing a bad check worth $100. In *Lockyer v. Andrade*, the Court distinguished *Solem v. Helm* on the ground that Andrade was potentially eligible for parole in 2046, when he would be eighty-seven years old.

70. *Glossip v. Gross*, 135 S.Ct. 2726 (2015).

71. *Id.* at 2755 (Breyer, J., dissenting).

72. *Callins v. Collins*, 510 U.S. 1127, 1130 (1994).

73. *Id.* at 2755–56.

74. *Id.* at 2756–59.

75. *Id.* at 2769–70.

76. *Jones v. Chappell*, 31 F.Supp.3d 1050 (C.D. Cal. 2014).

77. *Jones v. Davis*, 806 F.3d 538 (9th Cir. 2015).

7. SECURING LIBERTY

1. See, e.g., *Shapiro v. Thompson*, 394 U.S. 618 (1969) (describing the right to travel as a fundamental right and declaring unconstitutional a state law requiring that a person live in a state for a year in order to receive welfare benefits).

2. My views on one of the most important free speech issues—free speech on campus—are found in Erwin Chemerinsky & Howard Gillman, *Free Speech on Campus* (New Haven, CT: Yale Univ. Press, 2017).

3. See, e.g., *Matal v. Tam*, 137 S.Ct. 1744 (2017) (denying registration of a trademark to a band because the offensive name violated the First Amendment); *Packingham v. North Carolina*, 137 S.Ct. 1730 (2017) (First Amendment violated by state law keeping registered sex offenders from any use of interactive social media where minors might be present).

4. *Citizens United*, 558 U.S. 310 (2010).

5. For an excellent discussion of this, see Richard Hasen, *Plutocrats United: Campaign Money, the Supreme Court, and the Distortion of American Elections* (New Haven, CT: Yale Univ. Press, 2016).

6. *Garcetti v. Ceballos*, 547 U.S.410 (2006).

7. *Morse v. Frederick*, 551 U.S. 393 (2007).

8. *District of Columbia v. Heller*, 554 U.S. 570 (2008).

9. *McDonald v. City of Chicago*, 561 U.S. 742 (2010).

10. *District of Columbia*, 554 U.S. at 626–27.

11. Zack Beauchamp, "A Huge International Study of Gun Control Finds Strong Evidence That It Actually Works," *Vox*, November 6, 2017, https://www.vox.com/2016/2/29/11120184/gun-control-study-international-evidence.

12. Professor Solove makes a similar point, though describes the differing rights as involving information collection, information processing, information dissemination, and intrusion. Daniel J. Solove, "A Taxonomy of Privacy," 154 *U. Pa. L. Rev.* 477, 489 (2006). Professor Jerry Kang has defined privacy as involving three overlapping clusters of ideas: (1) physical space ("the extent to which an individual's territorial solitude is shielded from invasion by unwanted objects or signals"); (2) choice ("an individual's ability to make certain significant decisions without interference"); and (3) flow of personal information ("an individual's control over the processing—i.e., the acquisition, disclosure, and use—of personal information"). Jerry Kang, "Information Privacy in Cyberspace Transactions," 50 *Stan. L. Rev.* 1193, 1202–03 (1998).

13. See, e.g., *Samson v. California*, 126 S. Ct. 2193, 2196 (2006); *Georgia v. Randolph*, 126 S. Ct. 1515, 1529 (2006) (Breyer, J., concurring); *Kyllo v. United States*, 533 U.S. 27, 44 (2001).

14. *Olmstead v. United States*, 277 U.S. 438 (1928).

15. *Id.* at 478 (Brandeis, J., dissenting).

16. *Id.* at 479.

17. *Katz v. United States,* 389 U.S. 347 (1967).

18. *Maryland v. King,* 133 S.Ct. 1958 (2013).

19. *King v. State,* 425 Md. 550, 42 A.3d 549 (2012).

20. *Riley v. California,* 134 S.Ct. 2473 (2014).

21. Under current law, the use by the police of a drone or a low-flying airplane to gather information would not require a warrant. See *Florida v. Riley,* 448 U.S. 445 (1989).

22. Thus far, the lower courts have rejected the requirement for a warrant before police use cellular location technology to monitor a person's movements, but this issue is now before the Supreme Court. *United States v. Carpenter,* 819 F.3d 880 (6th Cir. 2016), *cert. granted,* 137 S.Ct. 2211 (2017) (whether the warrantless seizure and search of historical cell phone records revealing the location and movements of a cell phone user over the course of 127 days is permitted by the Fourth Amendment).

23. One of the revelations from Edward Snowden's release of data is that the government was routinely obtaining this information from cell phone companies like Verizon and AT&T. See *American Civil Liberties Union v. Clapper,* 959 F.Supp.2d 724 (S.D.N.Y. 2013) (government's collection of metadata did not violate telecommunications subscribers' Fourth Amendment rights).

24. *Carpenter v. United States,* 138 S.Ct._(June 22, 2018).

25. *United States v. Maynard,* 615 F.3d 544, 562 (D.C. Cir. 2010).

26. See Alan F. Westin, *Privacy and Freedom* (New York: Scribner, 1967), p. 33.

27. 5 U.S.C. sec. 552a(a)(4).

28. *Id.*; 5 U.S.C. sec. 552a(a)(5).

29. Restatement (Second) of Torts sec. 652D (1977).

30. *Whalen v. Roe,* 429 U.S. 589 (1977).

31. *Id.* at 605–06. For a discussion of the need to protect privacy over such information, see Grace-Marie Mowery, "A Patient's Right to Privacy in Computerized Pharmacy Records," 66 *U. Cin. L. Rev.* 697 (1998).

32. *National Aeronautics and Space Administration v. Nelson,* 562 U.S. 134 (2011).

33. *Id.* at 144.

34. *Id.* at 159.

35. *Id.* at 159 (Scalia, J., concurring in the judgment).

36. *American Federation of Government Employees v. Department of Housing & Urban Development*, 118 F.3d 786, 791 (D.C. Cir. 1997).

37. *Meyer v. Nebraska*, 262 U.S. 390 (1923).

38. *Id.* at 403.

39. *Pierce v. Society of Sisters*, 268 U.S. 510 (1925).

40. *Id.* at 535.

41. *Griswold v. Connecticut*, 381 U.S. 479 (1965).

42. *Roe v. Wade*, 410 U.S. 113 (1973).

43. *Lawrence v. Texas*, 539 U.S. 558, 605–06 (2003) (Thomas, J., dissenting).

44. Kermit Roosevelt, III, *The Myth of Judicial Activism: Making Sense of Supreme Court Decisions* (New Haven, CT: Yale Univ. Press, 2006), p. 120.

45. My discussion of abortion is drawn from (and developed more fully in) Erwin Chemerinsky & Michele Goodwin, "Abortion: A Woman's Private Choice," 95 *Texas L. Rev.* 1189 (2017).

46. John Hart Ely, "The Wages of Crying Wolf: A Comment on *Roe v. Wade*," 82 *Yale L.J.* 920, 947 (1973).

47. *Griswold*, 381 U.S. 479.

48. *Eisenstadt v. Baird*, 405 U.S. 438, 453 (1972).

49. *Meyer*, 262 U.S. 390; *Pierce*, 268 U.S. 510.

50. *Skinner v. Oklahoma*, 316 U.S. 535 (1942).

51. *Loving v. Virginia*, 338 U.S. 1 (1967).

52. *Obergefell v. Hodges*, 135 S.Ct. 2584 (2015).

53. See, e.g., *NAACP v. Alabama*, 357 U.S. 449 (1958) (protecting freedom of association as a fundamental right).

54. *Lawrence*, 539 U.S. 558 at 605–06 (Thomas, J., dissenting) ("I can find neither in the Bill of Rights nor any other part of the Constitution a general right of privacy . . .")

55. Cass Sunstein, *Radicals in Robes: Why Extreme Right-Wing Courts Are Wrong for America* (New York: Basic Books, 2015), pp. 81–82.

56. *Roe*, 410 U.S. at 153.

57. *Id.* at 163.

58. *Id.* at 159.

59. Laurence H. Tribe, "Foreword: Toward a Model of

Roles in the Due Process of Life and Law," 87 *Harv. L. Rev.* 1, 11 (1973).

60. *Id.*

61. *Id.*

62. *Understanding Miscarriage,* http:/www.babycenter.com/0_understanding-miscarriage_252.bc.

63. *What Is Infertility?* http:/www.drspock.com/article/0,1510,6262,00.html.

64. *Van Orden v. Perry,* 545 U.S. 677 (2005).

65. Library of Congress, *Jefferson's Letter to the Danbury Baptists,* January 1, 1802, https://www.loc.gov/loc/lcib/9806/danpre.html.

66. Rob Boston, "The Forgotten Founder," *Church and State Magazine* (April 2003), https://www.au.org/church-state/april-2003-church-state/featured/the-forgotten-founder.

67. *Everson v. Board of Education,* 330 U.S. 1 (1947).

68. *Engel v. Vitale,* 370 U.S. 421 (1962); *Abbington School District v. Shempp,* 374 U.S. 203 (1963).

69. *Lee v. Weisman,* 505 U.S. 577 (1992); *Doe v. Santa Fe Independent School District,* 530 U.S. 290 (2000).

70. *Flast v. Cohen,* 392 U.S. 83 (1968); *Lemon v. Kurtzman,* 403 U.S. 602 (1971).

71. *Allegheny County v. ACLU,* 492 U.S. 573 (1989).

72. *Lee v. Weisman,* 505 U.S. 557, 587 (1992) ("the Establishment Clause . . . guarantees at a minimum that a government may not coerce anyone to support or participate in religion or its exercise, or otherwise act in a way which establishes a [state] religion or religious faith, or tends to do so.")

73. See, e.g., *Elk Grove Unified School District v. Newdow,* 542 U.S. 1, 49 (2004). (Thomas, J., concurring in part and concurring in the judgment.) ("I accept that the Free Exercise Clause, which clearly protects an individual right, applies against the States through the Fourteenth Amendment. But the establishment clause is another matter. The text and history of the establishment clause strongly suggest that it is a federalism provision intended to prevent Congress from interfering with state establishments. Thus, unlike the Free Exercise Clause, which does protect an individual right, it makes little sense to incorporate the Establishment Clause.")

74. *Town of Greece v. Galloway,* 134 S.Ct. 1811 (2014).

75. *Marsh v. Chambers,* 463 U.S. 783 (1983).

76. 134 S.Ct. at 1838 (Thomas, J., concurring in part and concurring in the judgment in part).

77. 505 U.S. at 645 (Scalia, J., dissenting).

78. *Trinity Lutheran Church of Columbia, Inc. v. Comer,* 137 S. Ct. 2012 (2017). (The Free Exercise Clause prohibits a state from denying an otherwise qualified religious entity a public benefit—here, grants to help in the purchase of rubber playground surfaces made from recycled tires—solely because of its religious character.)

79. *Id.* at 2027 (Sotomayor, J., dissenting).

80. See, e.g., *Lynch v. Donnelly,* 465 U.S. 668, 688 (O'Connor, J., concurring) ("Endorsement sends a message to nonadherents that they are outsiders, and not full members of the political community, and an accompanying message to adherents that they are insiders . . .").

81. See James Madison, *Memorial and Remonstrance Against Religious Assessment* (June 20, 1785), in *The Papers of James Madison,* eds. Robert A. Rutland et al. (Chicago, IL: U. Chi. Press, 1973), pp. 295, 298–306 (urging the Commonwealth of Virginia not to enact a bill providing support to religious groups through the levy of a tax).

82. Josh White, "Intolerance Found at Air Force Academy," *Washington Post,* June 23, 2005.

83. See James P. Byrd, Jr., *The Challenges of Roger Williams* (Macon, GA: Mercer University Press, 2002), pp. 121–7 ("In the process of corrupting the church, Williams believed that Christendom had corrupted biblical exegesis by devising an interpretative method that supported the state's claim to authority over religious matters").

84. *McCreary County of Kentucky v. ACLU of Kentucky,* 545 U.S. 844, 883 (2005) (O'Connor, J., dissenting).

85. *Burwell v. Hobby Lobby,* 134 S.Ct. 2751, 2791 (2014) (Ginsburg, J., dissenting).

86. *Id.*

87. All of the justices were in agreement that the contraceptive mandate would not violate the free exercise clause because

of *Employment Division v. Smith*, 494 U.S. 872 (1990), which held that the free exercise clause cannot be used to create a religious exemption from a general law.

88. 134 S.Ct. at 2783.

89. *Masterpiece Cakeshop Ltd. v. Colorado Civil Rights Commission*, 138 S.Ct._ (June 4, 2018).

90. *Employment Division*, 494 U.S. 872.

8. ACHIEVING EQUALITY

1. E. Ann Carson & William J. Sabol, *Prisoners in 2011*, Bureau of Justice Statistics 6 (U.S. Dept. of Justice 2012), https://www.bjs.gov/content/pub/pdf/p11.pdf.

2. Thomas P. Bonczar, *Prevalence of Imprisonment in the U.S. Population, 1974–2001*, Bureau of Justice Statistics 1 (U.S. Dept. of Justice 2003), https://www.bjs.gov/content/pub/pdf/piusp01.pdf.

3. In 2008, the poverty rate was 8.6 percent for non-Hispanic whites, 24.7 percent for blacks, 11.8 percent for Asians, and 23.2 percent for Hispanics; U.S. Census Bureau, *Income, Poverty, and Health Insurance Coverage in the United States: 2008*, at 5 (2009), http://www.census.gov/prod/2009pubs/p60-236.pdf.

4. Melvin L. Oliver & Thomas M. Shapiro, *Black Wealth/White Wealth: A New Perspective on Racial Inequality*, 2d ed. (New York: Routledge, 2006), pp. 7–8.

5. See, e.g., *Washington v. Davis*, 426 U.S. 229 (1976); *City of Mobile v. Bolden*, 446 U.S. 55 (1980); *McCleskey v. Kemp* 481 U.S. 279 (1987) (all discussed below).

6. See text accompanying notes 39–40 (discussing this in the areas of crack cocaine sentencing, the death penalty, and schools).

7. As explained in chapter 2, if there is racial discrimination, the government must meet strict scrutiny and show that its action is necessary to achieve a compelling purpose. The government usually loses. But absent that, the government action only has to meet a rational basis test—being rationally related to a legitimate government purpose—and the government almost always wins.

8. The Supreme Court has said that if there is proof that a decision is "motivated in part by a racially discriminatory purpose," the burden shifts to the government to prove that "the same decision would have resulted even had the impermissible purpose not been considered." *Village of Arlington Heights v. Metropolitan Housing Development Corp.*, 429 U.S. 252, 270–71 n.21. (1977).

9. *Washington v. Davis*, 426 U.S. 229 (1976).

10. *Id.* at 239 (emphasis in original).

11. *Id.* at 242 (citation omitted).

12. *Id.* at 248.

13. *Mobile v. Bolden*, 446 U.S. 55 (1980).

14. *Id.* at 67.

15. *McCleskey v. Kemp*, 481 U.S. 279 (1987).

16. *Id.* at 286.

17. *Id.* at 287.

18. *Id.* at 287.

19. *Id.* at 292 (emphasis in original).

20. *Id.* at 298.

21. The Court also has held that proving a violation of 42 U.S.C. sec. 1982 and the Thirteenth Amendment requires proof of a discriminatory purpose. In *Memphis v. Greene*, 451 U.S. 100 (1981), the Court found no constitutional violation when a city closed down a street that was used mainly by blacks. The Court said that "the record discloses no racially discriminatory motive on the part of the City Council [and] a review of the justification for the official action challenged in this case demonstrates that its disparate impact on black citizens could not [be] fairly characterized as a badge or incident of slavery." *Id.* at 126.

22. See *Griggs v. Duke Power Co.*, 401 U.S. 424 (1971).

23. See, e.g., *Johnson v. DeGrandy*, 512 U.S. 997 (1994); *Thornburg v. Gingles*, 478 U.S. 30 (1986); see also *City of Rome v. United States*, 446 U.S. 156 (1980) (Congress has the power to allow proof of discriminatory impact to establish a violation of voting rights).

24. *Washington v. Davis*, 426 U.S. at 239.

25. Laurence H. Tribe, *American Constitutional Law*, 2d ed. (St. Paul, MN: West Academic Publishing, 1987), pp. 1516–19.

26. See Daniel R. Ortiz, "The Myth of Intent in Equal Protection," 41 *Stan. L. Rev.* 1105 (1989).

27. Charles Lawrence, "The Id, the Ego, and Equal Protection: Reckoning with Unconscious Racism," 39 *Stan. L. Rev.* 317, 355 (1987).

28. See, e.g., Anthony G. Greenwald & Linda Hamilton Krieger, "Implicit Bias: Scientific Foundations," 94 *Calif. L. Rev.* 945, 946 (2006); see also Laurie A. Rudman et al., "'Unlearning' Automatic Biases: The Malleability of Implicit Prejudice and Stereotypes," 81 *J. Personality & Soc. Psychol.* 856, 856 (2001); Annika Jones, "Implicit Bias as Social-Framework Evidence in Employment Discrimination," 165 *U. Pa. L. Rev.* 1221 (2017).

29. Greenwald & Krieger, *supra* note 28, at 846.

30. Linda Hamilton Krieger, "The Content of Our Categories: A Cognitive Bias Approach to Discrimination and Equal Employment Opportunity," 47 *Stan. L. Rev.* 1161, 1187–88 (1995) (discussing the notion that people categorize information as they receive it as part of the central premise of social cognition theory).

31. *Lawrence, supra* note 27, at 355.

32. Christine Jolls & Cass R. Sunstein, "The Law of Implicit Bias," 94 *Calif. L. Rev.* 969, 976 (2006).

33. See David Strauss, "Discriminatory Intent and the Taming of Brown," 56 *U. Chi. L. Rev.* 935 (1989).

34. *Personnel Administrator of Massachusetts v. Feeney,* 442 U.S. 256, 279 (1979) (citations omitted).

35. *Id.* at 270.

36. *Feeney* makes it clear that proving a gender classification is identical to proving a racial classification.

37. Larry G. Simon, "Racially Prejudiced Government Actions: A Motivation Theory of the Constitutional Ban Against Racial Discrimination," 15 *San Diego L. Rev.* 1041, 1111 (1978).

38. Sentencing Project, *Crack Cocaine Sentencing Policy: Unjustified and Unreasonable,* https://www.prisonpolicy.org/scans/sp/1003.pdf.

39. See, e.g., *United States v. Clary,* 34 F.3d 709 (8th Cir. 1994), *cert. denied,* 115 S. Ct. 1172 (1995) (reversing the district court's conclusion that the disparity between crack and powder

cocaine violated equal protection). See David Sklansky, "Cocaine, Race, and Equal Protection," 47 *Stanford L. Rev.* 1283, 1284 (1995) (explaining why the disparity between crack and powder cocaine sentencing could not be challenged under equal protection: "Federal appellate courts have uniformly rejected these challenges, based on a largely mechanical application of the equal protection rules developed by the Supreme Court").

40. Sklansky, *Id.* at 1384.

41. *McCleskey v. Kemp,* 481 U.S. 279 (1987).

42. U.S. General Accounting Office, *Death Penalty Sentencing: Research Indicates Pattern of Racial Disparities* (1990) (analyzing twenty-eight studies involving cases from 1972 to 1988), reprinted in 136 *Cong. Rec.* S6873, 6889 (1990); David C. Baldus et al., "Racial Discrimination and the Death Penalty in the Post-Furman Era: An Empirical and Legal Overview, with Recent Findings from Philadelphia," 83 *Cornell L. Rev.* 1638, 1738 (1998); Samuel R. Gross & Robert Mauro, "Patterns of Death: An Analysis of Racial Disparities in Capital Sentencing and Homicide Victimization," 37 *Stan. L. Rev.* 27, 108 (1984) (finding "a remarkably stable and consistent" pattern of racial discrimination in the imposition of the death penalty in Arkansas, Florida, Georgia, Illinois, Mississippi, North Carolina, Oklahoma, and Virginia); Gennaro F. Vito & Thomas J. Keil, "Capital Sentencing in Kentucky: An Analysis of the Factors Influencing Decision-Making in the Post-Gregg Period," 79 *Crim. L. & Criminology* 483 (1988) (finding that Kentucky prosecutors were more likely to seek death in white-victim cases); Leigh J. Bienen et. al, "The Reimposition of Capital Punishment in New Jersey: The Role of Prosecutorial Discretion," 41 *Rutgers L. Rev.* 27, 63 n.129 (1988) [hereinafter Reimposition] (finding pronounced race-of-victim and race-of-defendant disparities unexplained by nonracial variables).

43. Matt Ford, "Racism and the Execution Chamber," *The Atlantic,* March 24, 2014, https://www.theatlantic.com/politics/archive/2014/06/race-and-the-death-penalty/373081/.

44. *Keyes v. School District No. 1, Denver, Colorado,* 413 U.S. 189 (1973).

45. *Id.* at 201.

46. For a criticism of the Court's approach, see David Strauss, "Discriminatory Intent and the Taming of *Brown,*" 56 *U. Chi. L. Rev.* 935, 962 (1989); Owen Fiss, "Racial Imbalance in the Public Schools: The Constitutional Concepts," 78 *Harv. L. Rev.* 564 (1965).

47. See *Griggs v. Duke Power Co.*, 401 U.S. 424 (1971) (Title VII, which prohibits employment discrimination based on race, sex, or religion, allows liability based on proof of disparate impact).

48. See *Texas Department of Housing and Community Affairs v. Inclusive Communities Project, Inc.*, 135 S.Ct. 2507 (2015) (Fair Housing Act allows liability based on disparate impact).

49. These were enacted to overrule the Supreme Court's decision in *Mobile v. Bolden,* 446 U.S. 55 (1980). See *Thornburg v. Gingles,* 478 U.S. 30, 43–44 (1986) (purpose of 1982 amendments to the Voting Rights Act was to overrule *Mobile v. Bolden*).

50. *Regents of the University of California v. Bakke,* 438 U.S. at 314.

51. *Grutter v. Bollinger,* 539 U.S. at 330.

52. *Fisher v. University of Texas, Austin,* 133 S.Ct. 2198 (2016).

53. *Id.* at 2214.

54. Although Justice Kagan did not participate in *Fisher,* no one doubts that she supports the constitutionality of such programs.

55. *Parents Involved in Community Schools v. Seattle School District No. 1,* 551 U.S. 701 (2007).

56. *Id.* at 747.

57. *Brief of the President and the Chancellors of the University of California as Amicus Curiae in Support of Respondents,* Fisher v. University of Texas, Austin, at 19.

58. *Id.* at 20.

59. *Id.*

60. *Id.* at 5.

61. See, e.g., Richard H. Sander & Stuart Taylor, Jr., *Mismatch: How Affirmative Action Hurts Students It's Intended to Help, and Why Universities Won't Admit It* (New York: Basic Books, 2012).

62. *Brief Amicus Curiae Richard Lempert in Support of Respondents,* Fisher v. University of Texas, Austin, at 10.

63. Frank I. Michelman, "The Supreme Court, 1968 Term. Foreword: On Protecting the Poor Through the Fourteenth Amendment," 83 *Harv. L. Rev.* 7, 9 (1969).

64. Charles Black, "Further Reflections on the Constitutional Justice of Livelihood," 86 *Colum. L. Rev.* 1103 (1986); Peter B. Edelman, "The Next Century of Our Constitution: Rethinking Our Duty to the Poor," 39 *Hastings L.J.* 1 (1987).

65. Nadine Strossen, "Recent U.S. and International Judicial Protection of Individual Rights: A Comparative Legal Process Analysis and Proposed Synthesis," 41 *Hastings L.J.* 805 (1990).

66. Roger Bregman, "The Bizarre Tale of President Nixon and His Basic Income Tax Plan," *The Correspondent,* May 17, 2016, https://thecorrespondent.com/4503/the-bizarre-tale-of-president-nixon-and-his-basic-income-bill/173117835.

67. *Id.*

68. *Id.*

69. Noah Gordon, "The Conservative Case for a Guaranteed Income," *The Atlantic,* August 6, 2014, https://www.theatlantic.com/politics/archive/2014/08/why-arent-reformicons-pushing-a-guaranteed-basic-income/375600/.

70. *Id.*

71. *Id.* at 12–13.

72. See, e.g., John E. Coons, William H. Clune, & Stephen D. Sugarman, *Private Wealth and Public Education* (Cambridge, MA: Belknap, 1970).

73. *San Antonio Independent School District v. Rodriguez,* 411 U.S. 1 (1973).

74. *Id.* at 33.

75. *Id.* at 35.

76. *Id.* at 37.

77. *Brown,* 347 U.S. 483, 493.

78. *Plyler v. Doe,* 457 U.S. 202 (1982). *Plyler* is discussed in more detail in sec. 9.5.5.

79. *Id.* at 221 (citation omitted).

80. See, e.g., *Serrano v. Priest,* 557 P.2d 929 (Cal. 1977); *Abbott v. Burke,* 575 A.2d 359 (N.J. 1990); *Tennessee Small School System v. McWherter,* 851 S.W.2d 139 (Tenn. 1993); *McDuffy v. Secretary of Education,* 615 N.E.2d 516 (Mass. 1993); *Rose v. Council*

for Better Education, 790 S.W.2d 186 (Ky. 1989); *Edgewood Independent School District v. Kirby*, 777 S.W.2d 391 (Tex. 1989).

81. *Bowers v. DeVito*, 686 F.2d 616, 618 (7th Cir.1982).

82. Susan Bandes, "The Negative Constitution: A Critique," 88 *Mich.L.Rev.* 2271 (1990).

83. *Black, supra* note 64, at 1104.

84. *Black, supra* note 1, at 1105–6.

85. *Edelman, supra* note 64, at 54–5.

CONCLUSION

1. See, e.g., Felix Frankfurter, "The Red Terror of Judicial Reform," 40 *New Republic* 110 (1924).

2. For Japanese American internment, see *Korematsu v. United States*, 323 U.S. 214 (1944); for McCarthy era decisions, see, e.g., *Dennis v. United States*, 341 U.S. 494 (1951).

ACKNOWLEDGMENTS

I am grateful to many people who helped me tremendously in the writing and revising of this book. My wonderful literary agent, Bonnie Nadell, pushed me to write this book and helped me to sharpen its focus and thesis.

Pronoy Sarkar, my editor at Picador USA, was very enthusiastic about this project from the outset and offered excellent suggestions for how to make the manuscript better.

My terrific assistant, Whitney Mello, helped in countless ways. It is impossible to imagine doing my job without her.

My research assistant, Jamila Williams, completed the painstaking task of making sure that all of the footnotes were complete and accurate.

I benefited from comments at workshops at Drake Law School, the Berkeley Center for Law and Society, and the Berkeley Public Law Workshop.

I received great suggestions on an earlier draft of this manuscript from some very special people in my life. In the aftermath of the November 2016 election when I was feeling great despair, Burt Neuborne suggested I write a book like this. I cannot think of anyone whom I have learned more from about constitutional law than Burt. He also provided me with very insightful comments on an earlier draft.

Joan Biskupic took time from working on her own book to read the entire manuscript and offer me great suggestions. Joan's writing is a constant model for me, as is her unflagging kindness and friendship.

Finally, and most important, I am immensely grateful to my wife, Catherine Fisk. She is the smartest person I know and is the invaluable sounding board for all of my ideas, including those on every page of this book. There is no way words can thank her for this, let alone for all of the joy she brings to my life every day.

This book should be dedicated to her. But it is a book that looks to the future and it seems only appropriate to dedicate it to the future: to my grandchildren, Andrew and Sarah, in the hope that they truly will live in a world where there is liberty and justice for all.